A
Passion for Sharing

THE LIFE OF
EDITH ROSENWALD STERN

by

Gerda Weissmann Klein

Published in cooperation with the
Greater New Orleans Section, National Council of Jewish Women

CHAPPAQUA, NEW YORK

Library of Congress Cataloging in Publication Data

Klein, Gerda Weissmann, 1924–
    A passion for sharing.

    1. Stern, Edith Rosenwald, 1895-1980. 2. Women
philanthropists – United States – Biography. I. Title.
HV28.S76K43   1984   361.7'4'0924 [B]   84-17904
ISBN 0-940646-15-3

Cover and book design by Vincent Tartaro
Photographs courtesy of Longue Vue House and Gardens

No hymn we can create
is ever truly a requiem;
think of it rather as an
affirmation of life,
a beacon, a lodestar.

—*K.K.*

CONTENTS

Book One

Book Two

Preface

*I*N A 1973 VIDEO documentary taped for public television Edith Rosenwald Stern was asked, "How do you account for your family's remarkable generosity expressed through a lifetime of wonderful deeds?" After a brief pause, Mrs. Stern replied, "It's a Jewish trait. We were brought up with the philosophy of the Old Testament. You remember it states that one is permitted to glean one's field only once. Thereafter, others can partake.... One has to give a tithe."

To many of us Edith Stern epitomized the top-most tier of the Jewish ethic in her spirit and in her character. My friend Edith was known to be feisty, opinionated, occasionally temperamental, yet Ede staunchly subscribed to high principles, including enormous generosity, intense caring, thorough study, impeccable honesty, rare courage, and definitive action. She was never merely a wealthy checkwriter. On the contrary, she faced community challenges head-on, throwing her intellect and her energies into the projects to which she lent financial support.

Honesty was Ede's watchword. Since it was second nature to her, she expected it from others. Occasionally, those who sought her largesse were known for their marginal support of the cause in question. Such lethargic charity was to her a measure of dishonesty. Ede often agreed to write a check immediately for the amount requested, provided that those requesting the money agreed to match a portion of Ede's gift with an additional gift one-half or one-quarter the size. Faces blanched, knees buckled, breath shortened, but lo and behold, a dusty checkbook often appeared. Ede believed that sharing on her part called for no less on the part of the solicitor.

Edith displayed courage and steadfastness where others faltered. Among the causes she championed some were perhaps ahead of their time. Others were threatening to those who preferred to protect their personal civic or social status. But Ede proved that she cared more for a person or a cause that she supported than for what others might think of that person, that cause, or even of her.

For every request that we received, she must have received two hundred. Yet her sense of fair play kept her accessible. More often than not, she granted appointments, listened earnestly, and counseled wisely.

Truth to tell, Ede totally enjoyed the act of sharing. Yes, it was serious business to fund and personally participate in the repeated efforts to gain good government, to establish legitimate voter registration rolls free of political mischief, to seek to raise the quality of higher education for black citizens, to build and staff a preschool and a private day school, to provide maintenance for a symphony orchestra and help for a museum of art, and to endow and prepare her own home and gardens – Longue Vue – as a museum for the public. Yet such mighty challenges – even the work they required – Ede considered fun. And they were all the more fun when she could involve others to work and share with her.

Overall, Ede expended herself beyond the norm – by shoring up, initiating, reinforcing, healing, facilitating, seeding. She made positive impacts on the lives of those around her and on the organizations for which she cared. She was herself the author of many ideas and the originator of many causes.

And woven throughout the multi-patterned fabric of her life were recurring strands of whimsey and of humor. She seemed to create a magical connection to the young who delighted in her person. She could be full of fancy, concoct pranks, create original themes for parties and celebrations.

For these characteristics, among many others, a group of Orleanians, members of the New Orleans Section, National Council of Jewish Women acted to establish a Living Memorial to Edith Rosenwald Stern, following her death in the fall of 1980. Down through the years, leaders of that organization had observed and experienced the positive results that accrued whenever Edith took part in a Council effort. They noted too that substantial numbers of members tended to follow suit once Edith made a solid commitment and through her inimitable gift with words substantiated her resolve.

We were unanimous in our belief that the life of Edith Rosenwald Stern could be a positive model. To bring her story to as wide an audience as possible, we invited and encouraged another remarkable woman, Gerda Weissmann Klein, to write this biography. Gerda's complete dedication to the painstaking tasks of research and writing provide ample evidence of her special talents.

It would be impossible to acknowledge by name the many family members, friends, and colleagues who reached back into memory for rich anecdotes and experiences to share with the author, or to thank individually those who devoted months — which in some cases stretched into years — to the myriad details connected with the memorial project. Special thanks are due to the wonderful staff of Longue Vue House and Gardens. One member of the memorial project team will retain a special place in my heart. Her name: Sara Stone. Her title: Vice Chairman. A more realistic title and job description for Sara would read: Project Angel — twenty-four hour duty.

No job was unimportant, and no task too small for those of us who knew Ede, for those who came to know her through their work for the committee, and for those who know her through the many beneficences her passion for sharing bequeathed to us all. I like to believe that Ede is fully aware of the book, and that she is pleased.

Margery K. Stich
Chairman
Committee for the Edith
Rosenwald Stern Memorial
New Orleans, Louisiana
May, 1984

Acknowledgments

NEARLY THREE YEARS HAVE PASSED since Margery Stich telephoned from New Orleans on behalf of the Committee for the Edith Stern Memorial to ask if I would consider writing a biography of Edith Rosenwald Stern. I was honored and quickly accepted the challenge. Upon more sober reflection I felt it necessary to impose one restriction on my acceptance.

Although the biography was to be commissioned by an organization, I felt strongly that it should not be either authorized or subsidized. Instead, it should be submitted for publication on its merit alone. The committee acquiesced, allowing me unrestricted freedom. Then, with unceasing devotion, members of the committee engaged in the formidable task of gathering information and opening doors, enabling me to interview individuals from all over the world—the exalted and the humble—all those whose lives had been touched by Edith Stern.

I am keenly aware, in retracing the rich tapestry of Mrs. Stern's life, that certain threads may be inadvertently missing. Nevertheless, I am grateful to the members of the Stern and Rosenwald families who generously shared their memories and to Edith's friends and colleagues in the political arena, in the arts, and in the struggle for social justice—the list is endless, as is my gratitude for their contributions.

While I would wish to name each and every one individually, the list would continue for pages. With their kind permission, I must still single out a few. Special thanks are due to Margery Stich, Sara Stone, and Jane Buchsbaum; also to my publisher Seymour Rossel who, upon seeing half of the manuscript, gave me his enthusiastic endorsement; to Vincent Tartaro, for his fine sense of design; to Melvin Wolfson, for his skill as a copy editor; and to Helen Blumenthal who sifted through countless reams of correspondence and indefatigably typed the manuscript. Special gratitude goes to my husband whose patient support bolstered my spirit on more occasions than I can remember, but above all for his facile editorial pen.

Finally, I'm reminded of the spring day more than a decade ago when I visited Edith Stern quite unaware of the place she would subsequently occupy in my life. As usual, she spoke with fire and passion on matters of social justice, with warmth and pleasure on art and music, and with deep love and pride about her grandchildren. She took obvious satisfaction in my enjoyment of her garden. It is the glow of that memory which I have endeavored to preserve, hoping that its reflection might illuminate, however briefly and incompletely, a life lived nobly and fruitfully. To all who enabled me to achieve a measure of that task, my everlasting thanks.

Gerda Weissmann Klein
Kenmore, New York
August, 1984

BOOK ONE

ONE

The Store

*I*N GERMANY, the year 1853 closed on a high note. Richard Wagner had just completed his monumental tetralogy, *Der Ring des Nibelungen*. The strange and revolutionary opera, with its indefinable aural and visual power, evoked a vague, atavistic response in many a German heart. Eventually, it was to culminate in the myth of the *Übermensch*, the Superman, but even in its incipient stages, many Germans found themselves out of step with the martial climate of the times.

Young Samuel Rosenwald was determined to try his luck in a land of "limitless opportunity"–America. He arrived in 1854 and, along with so many others, made his living as a foot peddler. As business flourished, he gave thought to other matters. Sam married Augusta Hammerslough in 1857, then seized an opportunity to better himself by going to work for his brothers-in-law in Peoria, Illinois.

In the course of time he managed stores in Talladega, Alabama, and Evansville, Indiana, and, in 1861, he moved his family to Springfield, Illinois, where on August 13, 1862, his second son, Julius, was born. Sam's hard work and diligent money management paid off. A short six years later, he was able to buy out his brothers-in-law, proudly changing the store name from "Hammerslough Brothers" to "S. Rosenwald, the C.O.D. One-Price-Clothier."

In this modest but comfortable middle-American setting, Julius spent his formative years. As a boy, he watched wagons of the early pioneers traveling through Springfield on their long, arduous journey west. He would long remember the time President Ulysses S. Grant visited Springfield, and the thrill of standing in line to shake the president's hand. What impressed Julius most in this encounter were the yellow kid gloves the president wore.

After Julius had completed two years of high school in Springfield, his family felt it was time for him to broaden his horizons. He was sent to New York to work for his Hammerslough uncles. The Hammerslough brothers had become important manufacturers in the rapidly expanding men's retail clothing market. The year was 1879. When Julius started to work, he earned five dollars a week, plus an extra two dollars by working Saturday nights in the Rogers, Peet store at the corner of Broadway and Broome Street. His friends considered him well-to-do. In turn, he eagerly availed himself of the many opportunities to associate with other young men from prosperous families—among them, Henry Morgenthau, future lawyer, and Henry Goldman, banker-to-be.

These early years spent in single-minded pursuit of a career were also marked by the magical appearance of electric lights that illuminated the streets of New York for the first time in 1880.

Less than five years later, with financial help from his father, augmented by credit guarantees from his uncles—and the aid of his younger brother, Morris—Julius opened his own clothing store. It was a less than auspicious beginning. The story, now legend, tells how one day while Julius was waiting in a manufacturer's showroom to buy summer suits for the store, one of the partners betrayed his exasperation at being unable to fill the numerous summer suit orders.

Julius Rosenwald spent a fitful night thinking of how he might fill this apparent need. An idea took hold, and by dawn, he had worked out the details. It was obvious that the demand was for lightweight seersucker and alpaca suits. His father reinforced his convictions by willingly investing $2,000; and the father of a new partner, Julius' cousin Julius E. Weil, produced another $2,000 to help launch the boys' manufacturing enterprise. They set up their facility in a loft on Market Street in Chicago.

The timing was excellent. Eager buyers awaited each of the dashing suits that Rosenwald and Weil turned out in ever greater quantities. The strawboater had taken the men's fashion world by storm, as the strains of the "Gypsy Baron" floated over the Atlantic from Vienna, and smart "gents" quoted from Gilbert and Sullivan operettas, currently the rage in London. In the sweltering heat of the growing city of Chicago, these same "gents" stayed abreast of current fashion in their ready-made lightweight suits. The same was true throughout the ever-expanding American market. Julius Rosenwald and Julius Weil prospered by shrewdly finding their niche and holding their own through the years of this prevailing condition.

As a dynamic and serious young man-on-the-go, just about to turn twenty-eight, Julius felt that it was time for him to settle down and start a family. If it is true that every man subconsciously looks for a wife who possesses the virtues and qualities of his mother, Julius carried this hypothesis one step farther: he married a lovely young woman of German Jewish descent who not only incorporated many of his mother's positive traits but also bore the first name, Augusta.

The daughter of an itinerant peddler, Augusta Nusbaum was self-possessed and single-minded. She worked hard as a girl growing up among six sisters and a brother, and she was well acquainted with hardship and struggle—memories of which would serve her well in the years to come and enable her to comprehend the situations of those less fortunate. A letter in her firm and even hand, written to her husband who was in Indiana selling his latest line of suits, reveals a wholesome, warm, caring woman; a woman of considerable wit and intelligence; a woman of sound judgment.

The letter is dated Wednesday, September 24, 1891, at 10 A.M., and addressed to "My Darling Jules." Augusta described her daily chores, her joy in caring for baby Lessing, and how she had spent much time polishing the furniture to a bright luster in honor of Julius' impending return.

> Mama and Papa just started for Temple and are fretting that I would rather stay home and chat with my sweetheart husband. I am going to pick out curtains for *our home* so everything will not rush upon me at the last moment. I am wondering already whether you will think it necessary to stay home and help me move. I hope you think it necessary. It will give me so much more pleasure to have you see *me* unpack all our pretty things and put them in their places. I am just crazy to get into the house. Won't it be grand to have me await my darling, decked out in a white apron like a *regular* housekeeper? It is so hard for me to wait till I see you. I guess there is no way out but I must be patient. I did feel so much like coming to Indianapolis on an excursion ticket for $6.00 and surprising you and I would have done so, but just now, before going into housekeeping, $6.00 is an awful large amount. This will be my last letter for this time. So will send you just so much love, hugs and kisses as will last till God brings us together again. From your own devoted wife, Gussie.

This devoted young wife soon found herself with even more reason to become an equally devoted and busy mother. Lessing, the Rosenwalds' first child, had been born in February 1891, and was followed in July 1892 by a sister named Adele. It was not until May 31, 1895—in the same year that Julius Rosenwald joined Richard Warren Sears' incipient merchandising venture—that Edith Rosenwald made her entrance into the world. Two more children completed the family circle after the turn of the century: Marion, in March 1902 and William in August 1903.

Augusta's much-adored brother, the handsome Aaron Nusbaum, accumulated a sizable fortune at an early age through his cool shrewdness, and set about to invest it wisely. Among the various business enterprises in which he held an interest was the Bastedo Pneumatic Tube Company, a manufacturer of pneumatic piping for the transmittal of cash and sales slips to key points within department stores. As a salesman for the company, Aaron approached Richard Warren Sears, whose mail-order business had just burst into bloom in the most incredible fashion.

Sears was hard pressed for additional capital to cope with the rapid expansion of his business, and he was impressed by the young man. Impressed enough, in fact, to offer Aaron Nusbaum a half interest in the Sears business for the sum of $75,000. Aaron, ever cautious, was reluctant to invest so large a sum in a single undertaking, however promising, so he looked among his friends and family for someone willing to invest half the amount.

Alas, he found no takers among those he approached — people who, for the rest of their lives, were condemned to mourn this missed chance to buy into what was later termed "the greatest single investment opportunity in American business history." But Gussie's (as Augusta was known by then) husband, Julius Rosenwald, envisioned a promising future in Sears' enterprise and bought a half interest of his brother-in-law's half for $37,500. In 1895 Julius disposed of his share in the clothing business and joined Nusbaum and Sears.

Richard Warren Sears was a creative genius when it came to business. The son of a Minnesota blacksmith and wagon-maker, he was fascinated early on by the notion of mail-order selling. He would regularly send away for, and receive, all manner of goods. He rarely kept what he ordered, but found ways to exchange or sell these things to others. Once, as a young man, he took over a rejected shipment of pocket watches, which he promptly sold at a reasonable price to railroad express agents all along the railway line on which he worked. Within six months, this netted him the then enormous profit of $5,000. He left his job as stationmaster in Redwood, Minnesota, and opened the R. W. Sears Watch Company in Minneapolis.

Minneapolis soon proved too small for his imagination, so in 1887 he moved to Chicago and hired Alvah Roebuck of Indiana as a watch assembler and repairman. Into the early 1890's, he and Roebuck still specialized in watches, but already the basic building blocks of the future empire were falling into place. An 1887 catalogue featured the first version of what later became the renowned money-back guarantee. And a catalogue issued in 1892 contained more than 50 pages of testimonials from satisfied customers. And, always, the personal and emblematic style of Sears' advertising was accompanied by astoundingly low prices. The combination was electric. To keep up with the ever-expanding business, Sears worked sixteen hours a day and, nearly always, seven days a week.

The 1893 catalogue added musical instruments, shoes, sewing machines, clothing, dishes, bicycles, furniture, wagons, harnesses, and baby carriages to his watches and jewelry. It was 196 pages long, and the first to proclaim the name Sears, Roebuck & Co. By 1894 the catalogue had expanded to more than 500 pages. Roebuck was no match for the stresses and strains of keeping up with Sears. The long hours and the unrelenting weeks, coupled with Sears' habit of looking for suppliers only *after* advertising goods, damaged his health. He accepted Sears' seemingly generous offer of $25,000 and, in 1895, left the company.

The vein that the Sears, Roebuck catalogue had tapped turned out to be the mother lode. There was a palpable thirst for consumer goods in isolated areas throughout the country. Aided by the expanding network of railroad lines, Sears found that millions of people could now be reached with ease. Europe's disgorged multitudes, all in search of freedom and opportunity, did not turn deaf ears on the corollary of their new independence, possessions. Able, muscular arms freed from the yokes of age-old oppression were determined to attain dreams often no more complex than a small home, a porch to sit on in the twilight hours. It was to these masses, especially, that Sears offered the by-products of the country's prosperity. His offerings expanded their dreams to unanticipated proportions and, in the process, created new prosperity.

The genius Sears displayed in advertising brought visions of tools, furniture, Sunday suits, and finery for wives and daughters to the plain farmers. His offer of satisfaction or full refund without question gave surety to these working folk, who readily sent their hard-earned money to the store far away. In time, the partners were able to overcome all initial consumer misgivings and to establish a reputation for reliability. This was not accomplished immediately, however.

At times Sears' imaginative genius got the better of his reason, and he occasionally advertised totally nonexistent goods. As the flood of orders for these "products" came in, Nusbaum and Rosenwald were forced to find or produce the advertised goods, and swiftly. Naturally, this created problems. Julius Rosenwald's fanatical, scrupulous honesty came to the fore as he repeatedly advised Sears that the oft-repeated cliché of "honesty is the best policy" held water, and, in this case, handsome profits as well. In these confrontations his tact became proverbial and his persuasiveness allowed the partnership to prosper, as his sober attitude provided the proper equilibrium in the meteoric rise of the firm.

Nusbaum, unfortunately, possessed none of Rosenwald's tact and generosity—and few of the many virtues with which his sister was so generously endowed. He proved petty and incredibly parsimonious. Time after time, he and Sears were at loggerheads and, despite Rosenwald's intervention, it was soon acknowledged by all parties that matters could not continue thus for long. Rosenwald found himself in an agonizing bind. On the one hand, he did not wish to offend his wife's only brother, the very man who had brought him into the business. On the other, he realized the validity of Sears' grievances (despite the latter's frequent overreactions to Nusbaum's arrogance).

In 1901 matters came to a head. Sears declared his willingness to be bought out, or, together with Rosenwald, his intention to buy out Nusbaum. After much soul-searching, Rosenwald decided to throw in his lot with the original catalyst. Together with Sears, he offered Nusbaum $1,000,000 for Nusbaum's share of the enterprise. Nusbaum demanded and received $1,250,000. It was a generous and eminently fair settlement in its time. Yet Nusbaum for the rest of his life felt that he had been cheated, and his feeling only deepened as the company went from success to ever-greater success. A rift developed within the family despite Rosenwald's best efforts at generosity, honesty, and accommodation. It was never to be healed.

So the twentieth century was ushered in, entering a world that would see the most rapid and sweeping changes in all of recorded history. Following on the heels of the century of steam, this was to be the century of electricity, of untold strides in the harnessing of energy. At the Pan American Exposition in Buffalo, New York, President William McKinley tripped the switch that lit thousands of electric light bulbs. Across this new brightness, a shadow was cast in short order by the president's assassination, as he stood in a receiving line in front of the Temple of Music at the Exposition. Was it an omen, a portent for the century itself? Would this new world of brightness, of speed, of prosperity also become one of violence? Queen Victoria lay dead at Windsor. She had lent her name to an age, personified the concept of a Victorian. Now, Edward VII ascended the throne of England. But he had waited in the wings too long, pursuing the mundane but elegant pleasures that his privileged status made available to him. It was Edward who coined the concept of "détente," and his influence in men's fashion was already widespread. Soon it would affect even the humblest American farmer who ordered his clothes through the Sears catalogue.

"The Store," under Rosenwald's stewardship, still sporting the imaginative on-target advertising conceived by Sears, grew into an immense merchandising empire. The company's mail-order catalogues, which by now contained over 1,000 pages, were printed and distributed in the millions. Each reader was afforded the tantalizing promises of achieving personal aims, and the dreams proved nearly irresistible.

Legends abound concerning the fascination that the Sears catalogue held for all. A little girl, asked by her Sunday school teacher, "Who gave us the Ten Commandments?" answered without hesitation, "Sears, Roebuck." The well-known and well-respected policy of guaranteed satisfaction prompted one little boy to write in a complaint concerning his newborn sister. He carefully explained that he had really wanted a brother; if not that, then a baseball bat. Could he return her? The answer was polite, informing him that he might yet enjoy having a sister in years to come, but that in the meantime a baseball bat was on its way, free of charge.

It was just before this world of frenetic activity began that Edith was born, in 1895. Along with the other Rosenwald children, she grew up in an atmosphere of warmth and love, nurtured by her outgoing mother and her more reserved father. Indeed, Julius was renowned precisely for his reserve—as hesitant to articulate his emotions at home as he was to voice either praise or criticism at "The Store." Nonetheless, the family atmosphere was protective, and the children were shielded from the tumult of the world at large, each of them feeling loved and emotionally secure. Despite the burgeoning fortune of the Rosenwalds, Augusta was careful not to overindulge the children when it came to material possessions. And, if it was true of their mother, it was doubly true of their father.

Family intimates contend that among the five children, Edith came closest to possessing her father's attributes. She combined a soaring imagination with an astute business sense, and later developed a strong and daring social conscience. Edith was assertive, however, sometimes betraying bursts of temper that earned her the reputation of being a dormant volcano given to occasional eruption. Nonetheless, the moment her outburst was spent, the air cleared and she regained her composure without lingering emotions.

From her father, Edith also seemed to have inherited a great talent for organizational detail. Rosenwald was a genius at dealing with the minutiae of the multifaceted network that processed thousands of orders according to his system of order-taking and comprehensive record-keeping. He pioneered the mail-order field and brought to it a clocklike precision. Edith, in the years to come, would do likewise within her domain.

As to the question of heredity versus environment, it must be pointed out that here was a nearly perfect blend. In the face of ever-growing prosperity, Augusta's policy of restricting the acquisitive appetites of the children served as a restorative. To her credit Gussie understood the full extent of the harm this sudden embarrassment of riches could cause. Though the children sometimes chafed at the bit under the tight reins, they nevertheless agreed in retrospect that their parents' judgment was not only sound but instilled in them a respect for money and an understanding of the obligations of the prosperous to the needy.

Julius Rosenwald made it a point to emphasize that it was not his ability or intelligence which had catapulted him to great wealth, but rather the good fortune of being in the right place at the right time. Once, as a young man, he had confided to a friend his ambition to earn $15,000 annually in the distant future. According to his schedule, he would spend $5,000 on his family, save $5,000 for a rainy day, and have the joy of donating $5,000 to charity. The Hebrew word *tzedakah* meaning at one and the same time justice, righteousness, and sharing, seemed to have made an impression on him from early times. Characteristically, the Hebrew language has no word for "charity," only *tzedakah*, and that the Rosenwald family practiced in its truest sense.

Edith was five when the twentieth century dawned. Her earliest recollections went back to the turn of the century. Her sister Marion was born in 1902, and to her we are indebted for many of our insights into Rosenwald family life. Yet the age gap between Marion and Edith affords us glimpses of Edith mainly in her teenage years.

Reminiscing, Marion [Rosenwald] Ascoli now points to a family portrait in which the older children—Lessing, Adele, and Edith—hold the two "Benjamins"—Marion and Bill. "This is a true picture of our family and life as it was," she says. "We generally took our cues from our older siblings. They could afford to spend more time with us than our parents did and despite their youth showed a great deal of patience, when I think about it now. When we came upon the scene, our father's position as a man of prominence, both locally and on a national level, put severe restrictions on the time he could allot to family matters. And our mother was drawn into the swirl of social activities as well, and that drastically changed all our lives." Edith, in particular, was held in awe by the youngest children but the family generally thought of itself as entirely unremarkable.

Then there was "Twinnie." Today she is Mrs. Frederick Greenebaum, née Julie Friedman. But to Edith she was always known more intimately and affectionately as "Twinnie," since both girls considered themselves as close as twins. Through Twinnie's recollections, which span over seventy years, the picture of Edith Rosenwald comes into sharper focus. It is not necessarily a worshipful portrait, as some of the recollections of Edith's later friends tend to be. There is no unrestrained acceptance, born of blind devotion; no idol worship of the kind that so often arises out of the passing of one party to the relationship. Instead, Mrs. Greenebaum speaks with love and affection and respect of her lifetime friend; of the fun and the joy and the sorrow that they shared. It is likely that Julie knew Edith better, and over a greater period of time, than anyone now able to give an account. Not being related spared Julie the obligations of family loyalty. But the many scenes she paints, in the strength of her years, stem from bonds forged in a strong and intimate friendship and from a trust that was never broken.

The Rosenwald family—Lessing, Bill, Marion, Julius, Adele, Augusta, and Edith.

TWO

Twinnie

T HE SCENE IS a dull, overcast May morning. On Lake Avenue in suburban Highland Park, Illinois, stately trees and lush hedges glisten with heavy raindrops on their fresh leaves. It is a secluded and quiet street; tall front doors on elegant homes, tightly shut, protect the privacy of the inhabitants. Their life-style, their thoughts, their memories belong to them alone. It seems that only a conscious effort of will could enable one to ring the bell of a one-story gray-beige home, hear it resound within, shatter the silence, and break the spell of privacy.

A small woman appears. Her bearing is regal, her hostess gown a delightful mélange of hot pinks and bright greens that reaches down to her shoes. The green cardigan around her shoulders completes her ensemble. Smooth, beautifully wrought golden earrings gleam from under the silver-gray of her coiffure.

She opens her arms in warm welcome. After the initial amenities, she seats herself on the comfortable floral-print couch, its upholstery of dusty pinks and fading greens blending against a background of cinnamon and beige.

The large room is quiet, orderly, and discreetly elegant. No clutter, no overabundance of bric-a-brac of the kind that elderly people often accumulate. No proof seems necessary to lend substance to the past. Instead, the classic simplicity betrays tender touches: a small oval frame on a side table – and, in it, a delicate miniature. It is Edith, painted on ivory in elegant, elongated brushstrokes. Another picture portrays Julie Greenebaum's late husband, aged three or four, resplendent in a velvet Lord Fauntleroy suit, with cascading brown curls.

Next to the miniature is a larger picture, drawn with bold strokes: Frederick's mother, a handsome woman peering out with a no-nonsense glare through a pince-nez. A number of hand-tooled volumes of leatherbound books reflect a reverence of literacy. And on a masculine-looking desk near the wall stands an informal portrait of a man who looks vaguely familiar. Closer examination reveals a striking resemblance between the subject of the portrait and former President Gerald R. Ford. The man in the picture wears a casual sweater and beams a friendly smile. "My husband," Mrs. Greenebaum says, as if making an introduction. Not "My late husband," just "My husband," though death had taken him years before.

"Twinnie – that's what we called each other." Mrs. Greenebaum makes a tentative start while the rain outside resumes, falling full force before subsiding into a gentle patter. Her voice undulates with the ebb and flow of a memory that covers seventy-five years of friendship. "We were, in truth, like twins – inseparable from the moment we met in the fifth grade at the Chicago University Elementary School. 'It was love at first sight,' Edith always said. I guess it was." Julie Greenebaum speaks of Edith in the past tense most of the time, but occasionally she lapses into the present.

On the little finger of the patrician lady's left hand twirls a kinetic ring, its spiral in constant motion, revolving around some tiny invisible pole. The orb of the ring spins continuously with her gestures, as if winding unseen yarn in tune with the story unraveling. "This is Twinnie's fun ring," she says. "Edgar Jr. sent it to me after she died. He thought that his mother would have wanted me to have it." At once, Edith seems a living presence in the room. Julie's gaze is fixed on the intricately woven oriental carpet. It covers the entire room in symmetrical perfection. "I thought I would have to sell the rug when I left my previous home because it was simply too large, but Ede said," and here her voice rises as if Edith herself were speaking, "Nonsense, Twinnie, don't sell that carpet, you'll never find one like it—just cut it down. And don't let them tell you it can't be done, because it can!" Julie points to the border within the border. "I let them take this part out a couple of yards, just as Ede suggested, and you see—it fits like a glove."

When Edith came the first time to inspect the new, smaller house, she subjected every detail to the closest scrutiny. One can almost see her, still in her traveling suit, her fine gloves drawn taut over her hands, her stylish dark-red hair arranged to perfection. First, an all-encompassing look, then a smile creeping into the corner of her lips, then her voice coming clear as a bell, "I knew your home would have style!" Julie Greenebaum still smiles as she relates this memory. Edith had found the house in order, given her seal of approval.

"We would visit each other often, especially in the early days. You know, we met when we were twelve, saw each other daily. Yes, every single day, and often I would spend the night at the Rosenwald home." She brings forth an album. Its black cover and pages are somewhat worn. On the inside cover in white ink and firm backhand script, the inscription stands: Julie V. Friedman—*Her book*—1909.

One of the earliest captions reads "Spring Festival 1906." Above it, a dozen girls, among them Edith, garbed in flowing white gowns with garlands crowning their long tresses. One holds aloft an arch of flowers. Their motion is forever frozen on the flower-strewn meadow, against a background of woods. It is difficult to distinguish the faces: they all look so young, so much alike. Julie peers closer to study the photograph. "Don't we look silly?" she asks, with a chuckle. "And yet that was a wonderful part of our lives."

"Here is one of Twinnie. It's a good one, but somehow I don't remember her like that." In this picture Edith sits on a log, wearing what looks like a gray suit, the skirt reaching her ankles, the jacket way below her knees. Her round, pretty face is serious beneath a wide-brimmed straw hat. "I know why this is not like my Twinnie. She is too quiet. Twinnie was always in motion, always had something to say, to do, to plan."

She points to another picture, taken from a greater distance. It is impossible to make out the features of the girl in the long white dress sitting under a tree, sipping a drink. The caption reads, "The prettiest girl I ever saw/Was drinking lemonade through a straw."

Does Julie think her Twinnie was the prettiest girl she ever saw?

"She was, in many ways, inside and out," is the response. "Yes, very pretty. She had a certain smile that compelled you to smile back; and the merriest dark eyes and prettiest hair you can imagine. Beautiful, no. But pretty, yes. Very pretty!"

The girls walked to and from school together every day, both wearing their middies, both lugging books and swinging them in rhythmic exuberance. They quickened their steps as they approached the candy vendor. Though both mothers had admonished them not to eat unwrapped candy, neither heeded the advice. Eagerly, they spent their nickel for the caramel dippies they adored, giving little or no thought to their plumpness. They forever bubbled over with the things they needed to share; and they usually ended up at Edith's house at 4901 Ellis Avenue. (It's now a part of the University of Chicago campus, a donation of the Rosenwald family.)

Julie lived a scant two blocks away. Sometimes, she would run home to see her mother, change her good clothes for clothing less confining, and run back to the Rosenwald residence to play tennis or softball. Often she would be greeted by Twinnie with, "What took you so long?"

Vacation time was always special. Usually Lessing, Ede's big brother, would be home, back from an out-of-town school. He would tease the girls in a disarming way. Adele, the adored older sister, would tender advice to the inseparable twosome on something they should see or do. Marion and Billy, the youngest Rosenwalds, were left with Miss Luthera M. Nickerson who was hardly what might be called a "fun-and-games" governess.

In fact, Miss Nickerson came across as stiff, reserved, even sometimes hateful. All the same, Augusta Rosenwald decided that it was wasteful for Miss Nickerson to have only two charges in her care. So a class of about fifteen children (including the son of the Rosenwald chauffeur, who proudly bore the name of Renault after one of the Rosenwald cars) were gathered in the ballroom for a kindergarten class. Even so, the authoritative governess often found ways to occupy the Twinnies, as well.

Once—it must have been December, for the days were short—Miss Nickerson had Julie and Edith help with the work in the ballroom. This room was on the third floor and was immense. In it, numerous bushel baskets of candy were stored, and Miss Nickerson asked the girls to arrange baskets of confections to be distributed to orphanages and hospitals to brighten Christmas for sick and needy children. It was a task the girls performed willingly, but it took them longer than anticipated, so that it was early evening before it was all done. Julie was just going down the stairs when she met J.R. (as Julius Rosenwald was called) coming up.

He regarded her with a look of irritation, if not downright annoyance, and demanded in an unaccustomedly sharp voice, "What are you doing here so late? Don't you ever go home? Why don't you go home when it's still light outside?" Julie never forgot the jolt of his well-intentioned tirade.

But it was the only occasion, so far as Julie could remember, that she encountered temper from J.R. Normally, he was nothing if not kind to her, greeting her warmly, usually with an embrace. To Augusta Rosenwald, the very soul of the household, Julie gave unflagging devotion.

"Edith learned her thoughtfulness and her caring from her mother who was never too busy to be attuned to her children's needs and desires." For example, there was the time when both girls developed an interest in sculpture. Augusta immediately engaged a woman sculptor for Saturday morning lessons. Soon, however, the girls' interest waned. Nor did any of the fruits of their modeling survive. They did far better with French lessons, and the morning lessons were a part of the special Saturday ambience at the Rosenwald house.

On Saturday, Augusta Rosenwald herself prepared luncheon—invariably hamburger. Her special recipe was eagerly awaited, something to look forward to during the lessons, and it became a tradition fondly remembered.

Not that other meals were ordinary. Julie loved to breakfast at the Rosenwalds and was impressed that the Rosenwald home had a walk-in icebox, like the ones at the butcher shops. Julie recalls the Japanese butler, Kiku; Mrs. Voit, the housekeeper, and her son, Freddie, an occasional playmate; the gardeners, the governess, and the rest of the staff, just as she recalls the broad stairway that led to Edith's simply furnished bedroom, where together they spent so many hours of their young years.

And this was only one of the Rosenwald houses. There was also Ravinia, the magnificent summer estate, cultivated in its natural beauty and without the manicured formality of many similar estates nearby. Mrs. Rosenwald reveled in the informality of her beloved summer home. Here, she was free to surrender to the profusion of flowers growing wherever they seeded themselves, then tenderly cared for by a host of gardeners. (On Julie's wedding day, Mrs. Rosenwald sent masses of flowers from Ravinia to adorn the Friedman home. It was the kind of thoughtfulness and kindness that one expected from the lovely Augusta.) At Ravinia, there were "sleeping porches" (boys and girls duly separated), and many pleasant repasts in the airy, fragrant, outdoor dining room.

Mr. Rosenwald spent time at Ravinia reading in the shade of a tree, glancing up once in a while from his paper or book to smile at the girls or say something to them. The girls weren't aware of it at the time, but one of the books he read during that period was to change not only his life, but the lives of thousands, if not hundreds of thousands of black Americans. It was Booker T. Washington's fine work *Up from Slavery*.

Julius Rosenwald was greatly disturbed by the plight of black Americans. By his own admission, he was not certain whether to attribute this to the fact that "I belong to a people that has known persecution for centuries, or because I'm naturally inclined to sympathize with the oppressed." For one, Julius was born and raised in Springfield, Illinois, only a few short blocks from Abraham Lincoln's onetime residence. The air had always been permeated with discussions of slavery and freedom. And, too, as a patriotic American, Julius could not endure a flaw so evident in his country's character. So far as he could see, denying the inalienable rights to a minority group was denying one of the inherent principles on which the country was built.

Only in retrospect could Edith piece together the events and ideas that shaped her father's mind and ultimately led to the building of thousands of schools for black children throughout the South. Edith readily understood, however, the question that her father voiced on a tranquil evening as they walked the grounds at Ravinia. Deep in thought, he asked aloud, "Who am I to live in a park?" If it was bewildering at the time, it nonetheless left an indelible mark in her thinking and later in her actions.

"Yes, Twinnie was like that," Julie muses. "She'd devote a lot of thought to each problem as it arose, but at the same time, she could be carefree, vivacious; and was full of daring and even of mischief. Often, when her parents were out to dinner in Chicago, Edith and Julie would steal into the master bedroom and Mrs. Rosenwald's dressing room. "C'mon, Twinnie, c'mon," Edith would prompt. "Try on Mother's new fur coat and put on that velvet dress. Then I want to try it on, too." They traipsed around the room in Mrs. Rosenwald's high heels, eliciting mutual compliments. "Do I look fabulous?" Edith demanded over her shoulder, trailing her mother's chinchilla coat, as Twinnie steadied her wobbly knees to walk stiff and regal in beige lace.

These were the years of the first decade of the twentieth century. Victorian restraint was giving way to the hedonism of the Edwardian era. As the *SS Lusitania* and the *Mauritania* set new speed records across the Atlantic in 1907, and electrical wiring spread by the mile instead of the block, people wondered, what next? And, only a year later, Wilbur Wright flew a curious contraption called a biplane for a distance of thirty miles in forty minutes.

Even the astute J.R. could not quite foresee the far-reaching consequences of the changes at hand. But he and Augusta listened to news of momentous discoveries discussed in minute detail at their dinner table by a widening circle of famous personalities. And Augusta saw a particular wisdom in introducing her children to this steady stream of distinguished guests.

Out of generosity—and perhaps, to make some of the long-winded monologues delivered by these notables more palatable to the children—she allowed each of them to bring a guest to such events. Needless to say, Ede chose Julie Friedman. So, today, Mrs. Greenebaum describes Booker T. Washington and Theodore Roosevelt as she saw them from her seat below the salt as a child. As Edith observed later, "I met the world at my parents' home."

Once, Shemaryahu Levin, the noted Jewish author and Zionist leader, was the honored dinner guest. He held forth in expansive discourse, his hands underscoring the verbiage he unleashed. Edith, with her gift of mimicry, imitated the gestures and bowed in unison as the other youngsters writhed in barely suppressed mirth. At this juncture, Mr. Levin, from his place of honor at the head of the table, caught sight of Edith's gyrations. She halted in mid-air as she spied her father's icy glare. She was sent immediately to her room. She was then in her late teens.

Edith's younger sister, Marion (now Mrs. Ascoli), recalls a curious ritual that took place usually between the main course and dessert. Almost as if choreographed, Marion and Billy would rise, approach the long table from opposite sides as if enacting a *pas de deux*, and gradually make their way to their father's chair. Without a word, each would climb on one of his knees, and, without a word, he would accommodate them, embracing them both affectionately. After a short time, they would depart and return to their rightful places at the end of the table.

Marion further recalls the formal table settings, the elegant meals, the silver ice buckets, and the flawless white nappery in which the bottles were swathed. "But . . . but . . . you'd never guess—what do you suppose these great roasts and fine filets were washed down with? Grape juice! Can you imagine anything more awful! You see, father was a teetotaler—no liquor allowed in the house at all. We never questioned what seemed to us a puritanical attitude, but we did manage to tease him about it unmercifully."

Marion's earliest memories reach back to about 1908—when she was six years old—the time when the Rosenwald fortune grew to astounding proportions and the family was catapulted into a new way of life. America has no true aristocracy, only a hierarchy of money and philanthropy, and within a very short time the Rosenwalds became peers in that realm.

Marion's son, Peter, in his middle teens, returned from a stay in New Orleans with his aunt and uncle, Edith and Edgar Stern. He said, "Aunt Ede tells the most wonderful stories about your mother. You never tell us anything. How come?" She answered "Frankly, Aunt Ede and I didn't have quite the same mother. It's true what Freud says, the early years are important. I certainly was shortchanged. My father suddenly became a very wealthy man, very prominent in Chicago, and it was only natural that my mother should be thrust into prominence with him. True enough, she came from a poor family, and she often told of her mother buying a bolt of fabric to cut out seven identical dresses for the seven daughters—never mind if the color, the pattern, or the material were not becoming, as long as the dresses were serviceable. Now, suddenly, my mother found herself among very prominent persons, and she took her responsibilities very seriously. To what extent this upset the older children, I don't know. I do know that Lessing, Adele, and Edith had a very different childhood from ours.

"Mother taught Adele and Edith to cook and sew. She would never let me into the kitchen because, by then, we had a cook, a governess, a chauffeur, and Kiku—our Japanese butler. Mother never wanted an English butler, confiding to friends that the English butlers intimidated, and she did not want to subject her friends to any humiliation." Nevertheless, Marion felt that Kiku intimidated *her* playmates, the children of professionals and academicians who constituted a large part of the students in her school.

Many of her childhood memories involve Kiku. On Sunday mornings, for example, she and Billy vied for the comic section of the newspaper. She would snatch it from Billy, or vice versa, and they would run around the ornate dining room, papers in hand, with Kiku in hot pursuit in his morning coat and high collar. Nearly out of breath, Kiku would implore frantically, "Mr. William, now Mr. William, please stop!"

Not just the youngest, but all the Rosenwalds, loved Kiku, and he loved the family. So much so, in fact, that he named his own son Julius Rosenwald Yohamino.

Within the family, Marion came to bear many nicknames. Ede dubbed her "Immer," after the durable comic-strip goat. Immer could be relied upon to fetch and lug for her older sisters an endless supply of objects, nearly always from the remotest corners of the house. Immer was ever willing to be of service, as the name implies in German. Lessing, her oldest brother, called her "Mike," a wistful reminder perhaps that he had been hoping for a brother when she was born. To this day her younger brother calls her Fatima, a glorified derivative of "Fatty," an accurate, though uncomplimentary, description of her in her preteen years. "We were all fat in those days," Marion remembers. But in due time all three sisters were slender, each bearing a striking resemblance to the others. Indeed, in New Orleans, Marion was often mistaken for Edith.

The sisters lost their baby fat, but never their youthfulness. Even at age eighty, Marion Ascoli today is readily mistaken for a much younger woman, in looks and in attitude. And what is true of her, was true of all three. Their youthful, exuberant streak made for the fun the trio enjoyed together. Adele was the gentle, quiet force. Edith, the undisputed leader among the girls, also possessed the most agile and creative mind, kinetic and imaginative. "We all had our fantasies," Marion said, "but Edith would turn her fantasies into realities." The three girls, preceded and followed by a brother, lent an equilibrium to the sibling crew. The boys often betrayed traces of jealousy (as did the husbands of the three, later on) in the face of the special relationship the sisters enjoyed among themselves.

And the girls were the undisputed favorites of their father, who tended to be much more indulgent toward them than toward his sons. Of the girls, he was most amused and delighted by Edith, with her irrepressibly high spirits and her gift of mimicry, which, within the family circle, became a source of endless amusement. They teased their parents unmercifully, but it was always accepted in a spirit of fun, and there were decided boundaries that none of the children dared cross. For the times, however, the family—especially Mrs. Rosenwald—was very permissive.

They teased Augusta for her absentmindedness. She was so absentminded about names, in fact, that she sometimes recited all five of their names before she called one of the children by the right one. Then, there was the matter of excessive thrift: When, for instance, she lost a pair of scissors, the whole household might engage in the search for days. It never occurred to Augusta to simply buy another pair. "Edith, Adele, and I put all of our mother's idiosyncracies into our 'famous' family skits; and, needless to say, Edith came up with the best and most original writing."

The skits played an important role in making family life more cohesive. The children's best efforts were reserved for special occasions, such as Augusta's birthdays each December 27. Then, the entire family would gather together, and, in later years, when all had offspring of their own, would converge upon Chicago for a huge celebration. The three sisters would closet themselves in one of their girlhood bedrooms whence gales of laughter and general merriment issued while their mother complained good-naturedly that she hoped they had come to *visit* her, not just to make fun of her.

If they had, by general consensus, "a ball," Edith would usually be the belle. None of them found these Christmas/birthday celebrations replete with trees in the least incongruous, nor did they consider them as detracting in any way from their Judaism. Marion Ascoli recalls a revealing vignette in this regard. It is a story set in pre-World War I Germany, when a Jewish boy and his father stroll through an affluent section of Berlin seeing most homes adorned with Christmas trees. The boy turns to his father and asks ingenuously, "Papa, do the gentiles have Christmas trees, too?"

This was part of a special brand of Judaism the Rosenwalds practiced. Marion recalled, "I would not say that our household was overly Jewish-oriented, but it certainly was a Jewish household. My father always went to Temple on Rosh Hashanah, on Yom Kippur, and on most Sundays—the day the Reform prayer service was held. We girls did not. But we were imbued with the feeling that Jewish families are known for their closeness, for respecting each other, and for family loyalty."

Though the lion's share of Julius Rosenwald's philanthropic largesse went to ameliorate the appalling conditions under which blacks lived in this country, in his own estimation he gave the most meaningful—and sacrificial—gift of his career in behalf of the Jews of Russia. He would speak nostalgically of one evening in Chicago, when he was still a manufacturer of men's suits and not earning much. He attended a Jewish gathering and heard of the suffering being visited upon Jews in the anti-Jewish riots in Russia called pogroms. So moved was he by the terror inflicted on those faraway coreligionists that he pledged the sum of $2,500.

It was more than he would earn that year! Afterward, he grew rather worried about his emotional response and deeply concerned as to how he could meet his commitment. On the way back from the meeting, he could think of nothing but the staggering responsibility he had just assumed. At home, he confided his concern to Gussie. She promptly reassured him that he had done what was right and they would manage somehow.

All of the Rosenwalds were sensitive to criticism of Jews and acutely aware that a preponderance of non-Jews derived their views of Judaism and things Jewish from scant encounters with one or at most a handful of Jews. In the true spirit of *noblesse oblige,* and in awareness of their responsibility as members of what might be termed the American Jewish aristocracy, they attempted to comport themselves in the most exemplary manner consistent with the ideals of their religion. In the spirit of their parents, they all came to possess that innate sense of the rightness of giving that had its roots deep in the Jewish tradition.

THREE

The Children

*E*DITH'S BIRTHDAY had a dimension absent from the birthdays of the rest of the children. The Rosenwalds developed a tradition of decorating the birthday child's chair with garlands, transforming it into a throne from which the occupant ruled as King- or Queen-for-a-Day. Birthday cakes were elaborately, lovingly decorated. After the morning greetings and breakfast in the birthday chair, with all kinds of favorite foods (little emphasis was placed on gifts) served to the birthday child, Mrs. Rosenwald would decree that the day was set apart, a special treat.

This birthday celebration made a deep and lasting impression on Edith. Later, she extended it not only to her immediate family but to her servants as well. Each of her maids, her cook, all who served the household, came to count on their "day": the birthday cakes, the decorations, and Mr. Stern's caring inquiry, "Now, whose birthday is it today?"

But Edith's own birthday fell on Memorial Day and the ever-practical Augusta Rosenwald combined the celebration of Edith's day with the Memorial Day parade. Good friends, the

Seltzers, lived on 16th Street and Michigan Avenue in Chicago. From their spacious front porch, the children saw the smartly uniformed marching bands coming down Michigan Avenue, light glinting from the shiny trombones and the air reverberating with the drums as the brightly colored bunting swung in the May breeze. Afterward, all adjourned for cake and ice cream transported from the Rosenwald home. And, of course, Twinnie would be there to share Edith's birthday—a birthday that all Chicago seemed turned out to enjoy.

The Twinnies were inseparable friends. Then, when Edith turned fifteen, the Rosenwalds dropped a bombshell. Her parents announced that Edith would go to finishing school in Europe for a year. "That will finish me, all right!" Edith protested. How could she leave Chicago, her home, her family, and—of course—Twinnie? European travel was not strange to Edith; indeed, the family regularly went abroad most summers. But to stay in Europe an entire year! Edith loathed the thought, and Julie was heartbroken at the prospect of being separated from her alter ego for what seemed to them a lifetime. They tearfully pledged to write constantly.

The advice on which Ede was to be sent to Dresden came from the Goodkind family, Minnesota friends, whose daughter, Edith, had just completed her first year there. Edith Goodkind, in due course, would become Ede's sister-in-law when she married Lessing. Already, in her teens, she was a lovely girl and a renowned beauty. Within the confines of the strictly run, Prussian-style boarding school in Dresden, Edith Goodkind had formed many friendships. Ede saw no such happiness in store for herself.

From the moment her parents deposited her in the Dresden school on their summer vacation to Europe, Ede felt like a butterfly in a blacksmith's shop. She loathed the drab environment, the regimentation, and the unbending, unsmiling teachers in their stiff clothes. She even found the meals monotonous and unimaginative. She began to look forward to one thing alone: returning home. In long letters to Julie she unburdened her heart completely, detailing everything. The letters, no doubt, revealed much of what it was like to be a *backfisch*, as German adolescent girls are called.

Edith having been settled in Dresden, the rest of the family spent some time in Munich. These vacations were designed as a time devoted to the family. Dutifully, J.R. would allow the children to choose their own entertainments. Marion and Bill were allowed alternate days. On one, Marion might choose a popular puppet show, or an exploration of Munich's famous park, the *Englischer Garten*, or, perhaps, a visit to a doll collection. Whatever it was, their father willingly trotted them off, a reluctant Billy firmly in tow.

On days when Billy's will reigned supreme, there was little guesswork, or so it seemed to Marion. Billy consistently wished to explore the length and breadth of the Deutsches Museum, unquestionably the most advanced museum of technology in the world and one that opened new horizons for its visitors at the touch of a button. Obediently, the yawning Marion trailed behind her brother and father.

Characteristically, J.R. spent his time thinking about the museum itself. What was it about this presentation that so fascinated and held the interest of an eight-year-old, causing him to want to return again and again? And whatever magnetism there was, wouldn't Billy, and boys like him at home in Chicago, benefit from a similar institution?

The idea took hold. It rarely left his consciousness, as he struggled to refine every detail and to consider the best and most expeditious means to transform it into reality. On his return home, he had a fairly clear notion of exactly what he wanted done, and a plan for providing several millions of dollars in funds to enable his program.

Indeed, it was this ability to see beyond the mundane and to implement vision that set J.R. apart. Many creative people, even when possessed of desire and vision, lack the funds or the willpower to realize their objects. Julius had all of these resources, and he had the moral strength to use them for the benefit of others. It was thus that he established the Museum of Science and Industry in Chicago, an institution that became the apotheosis of what a modern museum might aspire to.

Like J.R., Edith would display this same fire and energy in bringing her inspirations to reality. But in all fairness, all the children had at least one dream that he or she would live to see fulfilled. The distinction among them was one of degree: Edith was never content with just one goal and would see the fulfillment of nearly all her dreams.

Lessing, the oldest son, followed his father in the world of business and finance, and succeeded J.R. as Chairman of the Board at Sears. When the stock market crashed in 1929, Lessing showed his mettle and the moral influence of his upbringing by insisting that the company guarantee the stock purchases of every Sears employee. Julius, still alive at that nadir of American business, set up an office solely for the purpose of aiding these desperate souls. Although his personal fortune was reduced by millions of dollars, he later characterized this as one of the most inspiring times of his life.

Lessing emulated his father in another way. He scrupulously avoided the full exercise of his power and influence within the company, both on a personal and on a general level. It might be said that he carried this policy to an extreme, particularly in the matter of Jewish issues, as did his father.

Once, while Marion was attending a school run under the auspices of the University of Chicago, where J.R. was a member of the board, one of Marion's classmates stuck out a foot and tripped Marion, to the accompaniment of a furtively whispered, "Dirty Jew." When Marion complained to her father about the incident, he inquired how many students were in the class. After listening to her response, he suggested that, among so many, there must be some who liked her. She should concentrate on cultivating their friendships.

This incident, on the personal level, mirrored his actions on the corporate level. In 1928 Julius stepped up to the chairmanship of the company, allowing General Robert Elkington Wood, who had served as quartermaster for the U.S. Army in World War I, to become president. Julius intuitively felt that General Wood's capabilities would best serve the interests of the company, despite the General's reputation for harboring anti-Jewish sentiments. Wood promptly brought his sentiments into play, going to the extreme of not hiring any Jews for managerial positions within the company. Julius did nothing to intervene. Nor did he counter Wood's policy of hiring blacks mostly for menial labor. At the same time, J.R. set out to provide educational opportunities for blacks, which he hoped would enable them to elevate their status.

Lessing continued his father's policies, even heeding the call when Wood asked him to become a member of the America First movement's board of directors. When Charles Lindbergh, speaking on behalf of the America First Committee, made his scathing attack on the Jewish people, Lessing asked Wood to repudiate it. Wood, caught in a difficult situation, stalled for time. Lessing realized the futility of further pressure and resigned from the board. Thereafter, the relationship between the two continued on a strictly formal business basis.

Increasing American-Jewish faith in Zionism provided another such glimpse of the father-son continuity of action. Julius, along with many Jews of German origin, one generation removed, was anti-Zionist. Fervently patriotic, he felt that Zionism left the American Jew open to accusations of dual loyalty. Visiting Palestine in 1924, he settled handsome gifts upon private institutions there. But following World War I he was opposed to special funds for Jewish victims of the war. Instead, he made generous donations to German relief agencies, in the mistaken belief that they would help ameliorate Jew-baiting. For a man used to seeing his ideas vindicated, it must have come as a particularly severe blow when he realized how far off the mark his assessment of the German mentality had been. Only his death, in 1932, spared him the ultimate pain of seeing Hitler come to power.

Lessing carried on the Rosenwald tradition by assuming the presidency of the American Council for Judaism. This organization is firmly anti-Zionist, identifying the Jewish cause entirely with loyalty to America.

That J.R.'s character was more complex and less extreme was reflected in the contrary activities of the youngest son, William. It was William who followed his father's earlier instincts vis-à-vis the plight of the Russian Jews suffering in the anti-Jewish riots. William balanced the scale when he became signatory to the charter that established the United Jewish Appeal (U.J.A.), a Zionist-oriented charity providing a vehicle for channeling American Jewish funds to the rebuilding of the Jewish homeland. Even so, the enormous scope of William's philanthropy is not limited to Jewish causes alone.

Lessing continued to display both his generosity and his patriotism by giving his world-renowned collection of 6,500 prints and drawings, including 236 Rembrandts, to the National Gallery of Art in Washington, D.C., and donating his priceless collection of books and first editions to the Library of Congress. Lessing, after all, had been born and raised in the relatively lean years of the Rosenwald fortune, and perhaps for that reason his responses to Jewish issues were more typical of the gratitude of first-generation Americans toward their native country.

Adele, oldest of the sisters, was gentle, introspective, and compassionate. She straddled the two worlds of the middle class, in which she was raised, and the affluent, in which she was to spend most of her life. Acutely perceptive and especially moved by the suffering of children, she was inspired by visits of such notables as Jane Addams.

Miss Addams, also a native of Illinois, grew up in a privileged society. Her father was a banker and a mill owner. It was the poverty of the mill workers and the squalor and loneliness of the children playing in cheerless surroundings that influenced her thinking and set her on the road to her life's work. As a young girl she dreamed of building a big house in which she would gather all the homeless, the lonely, and the impoverished. Becoming a social worker, she founded Hull House in Chicago, accepting the presidency of both the National Conference of Charities and Corrections and the Women's International Peace Congress. She lectured tirelessly throughout the country. And when she returned to Chicago, it was often to dine in the Rosenwald home, where she found tender friendship, compassionate understanding, and generous support for her work. The adolescent girls were riveted to this fascinating visitor, listening as her tales unfolded. Adele's dark eyes often brimmed with tears. By the time Jane Addams shared the Nobel Peace Prize in 1931, many of her devoted and admiring friends already were following in her footsteps; and none with greater dedication than Adele.

Children—poor, homeless, hungry—were foremost in Adele's life. Never was more work to be done for them than in the aftermath of World War II, when the full extent of the horror of the Nazi camps was revealed. Adele was among the initial few who went to Europe to see this at first hand. Pictures of her in the camps reveal a small, slender, gentle-looking lady embracing emaciated, skeletal youngsters. "They don't laugh like normal children," she observed; "their eyes are not full of mischief. They are so terribly, painfully docile. They were talking to me, but I didn't understand their words. I do believe they could sense that I could give them something of my love." She gave that and more. Mathilda Brailove, later national chairman of the United Jewish Appeal's Women's Division, said of Adele, by way of quoting Albert Camus: "Great ideas come into the world as gentle doves. Perhaps then, if we listen attentively, we shall hear, amid the uproar of empires and nations, a faint flutter of wings, the gentle stirring of life and hope."

Adele Rosenwald Levy returned from her mission of mercy and without a moment's hesitation accepted the opportunity to become the first chairman of the U.J.A. Women's Division. It was not long before her announcement that $8.7 million had been raised for the victims of Nazism. "This is only the beginning," she stated firmly, and these words, spoken with deep conviction and quiet determination, were more than prophetic. At home, abroad, in fact all over the world, the plight of children became her all-consuming interest, laying claim to her energies as well as her means. After her untimely death at age sixty, Eleanor Roosevelt, her friend of many years, wrote of Adele in her "My Day" syndicated column, imploring family and friends not to be saddened. "So few people leave this world with a triumphant record!" said the great humanitarian lady, as she compared Adele to a leader fallen in battle for a noble cause.

It was Marion Ascoli, declaring that she knew herself unable to fill Adele's shoes, who immediately stepped in to the vacated office, heading the Citizens Committee for Children in the ensuing years with great distinction. Though she considered herself but a pale reflection of Adele's luminescence, that was far from the fact. She was outstanding in her own right, possessed of a delicious sense of humor and a quick wit that delighted many of the great who dined at her table. She held her own with such as Arthur Schlesinger, Jr., Henry Kissinger, and Daniel Patrick Moynihan, among many who partook of her hospitality and were frequent contributors to *The Reporter*, the prestigious, erudite journal founded by her husband, Max Ascoli.

Max had fled his native Italy, recognizing the dangers of Fascism in general and when directed toward Jews, in particular. *The Reporter* became a vehicle for his intellectual talents and concerns.

By contrast, Marion makes a point of not terming herself an intellectual, neatly adding that this does not mean that she has no intellect. Rather, her orientation is toward dealing directly with people. "I have to study the maps to see where the Falkland Islands are—though I seem to remember that Darwin mentioned them once in connection with the Galápagos Islands. I've met intellectuals, American and European, and they ain't me." (She emphasizes the usage by laughing conspiratorially.) "I'm a member of a secret society, though I'm the only one left. Ede and Adele were the others. We would talk to each other every day—every single day, imagine. I miss them so terribly, but what a blessing to have known them. There are few people around who knew our lives, our particular world. Of course, I still have Bill, my 'little brother.'"

William Rosenwald, now a man bearing an international reputation for his good works, was educated at Harvard, M.I.T., and the London School of Economics. He is soft-spoken, diffident, shy, and eccentric. In Jewish circles his name commands an inordinate amount of respect. It was he who, in 1946, convinced Adele, Edith, and Marion to give $250,000 each—enabling him to announce that year that the U.J.A. had committed itself to raise the astronomical figure of $100 million, of which his family would donate the first million. Family legend has it that he returned home to tell his children, "I made a speech that, in a small way, might have changed history." Though Lessing's name is conspicuously absent from this roster, and though the brothers were diametrically opposed in their public stances on the issue of funds for Palestine, it changed nothing in their personal, warm, fraternal relationship.

One story tells how Bill went to solicit a man he considered a likely prospect for a sizable donation to the U.J.A., only to find that the man had departed for warmer climes. Without hesitation, Bill followed his prospect to Florida, locating the hotel at which he was staying. Arriving at the hotel, Bill was informed that the potential benefactor had gone to the beach. Bill lost no time in tracking him down. Approaching his candidate, Bill, still attired in his winter suit and carrying his overcoat, proceeded to launch into the salient points of his "pitch." The man was unmoved. The heat was becoming more oppressive now and the man rose and walked over the hot sand, entering the cool ocean tide. Without missing a beat in his monologue, Bill followed. As the water reached both men's waists, the prospect turned to Bill and said, "Okay, you win!"

An ardent supporter of the U.J.A. and its work on behalf of Israel, Bill also supports the New York Philharmonic and Tuskegee College. If standing waist-deep in Florida waters in a winter suit is idiosyncratic, it is nonetheless proof that once he is imbued with the fervor of an important cause, Bill becomes its guardian, willing to go to any lengths to gain his goals.

And Edith? Where does Edith stand? The middle child, with sisters and brothers on either side of her, she forms the exact apex of a V that, written out fully, might spell vitality. Born in the very year her father joined Sears, Roebuck and Co., a moment that coincides with the meteoric rise of the family fortune, she drew from the source, adding an effervescent, inquisitive, driving personality of her own that reached forth to all who came within her orbit.

The year in Dresden may have given her ample time to reflect on her life, her friends, and her family. She no doubt recalled the annual visits the whole family made, usually accompanied by Ede's Twinnie, to the black college at Tuskegee, Alabama. On the long train ride, in the luxury of a private Pullman car, to the accompaniment of the excellent meals served en route, the soft berths, and the gentle chugging of the train through the warm, moonlit Southern landscape toward what seemed an alien environment where speech was soft and heat so often stifling, they would hear again the tale, almost legend to them, of Booker T. Washington, a man who had gained their father's admiration and decisively influenced his thinking and his actions.

As the train sped through the star-studded night, Julius would tell how Booker was born a slave on a plantation in Franklin County, Virginia. A slave! And little more than fifty years earlier, in 1856. As a boy he labored in the salt works and coal mines of West Virginia, attending school at night. At sixteen, he walked—"walked, mind you," Mr. Rosenwald would emphasize—five hundred miles. "Do you know how far five hundred miles is? From Chicago to. . . ." And the train sped on, clattering on silvery tracks, traversing the countryside, devouring meadows, woods, and all those miles over which Booker T. Washington had walked—to Hampton.

At the Hampton Institute—working his way through school—Booker was considered so brilliant that he was chosen to organize a similar school for blacks at Tuskegee. At that time, no schools admitted blacks; Hampton Institute was the first notable exception, and Tuskegee was the second. And Booker had turned Tuskegee into a first-rate seat of learning.

Julius would tell of visiting Tuskegee for the first time, of befriending Booker T. Washington, and of how he finally understood, standing in that special corner of the universe for the first time, the vast achievement of this singular human being. He never mentioned how many millions of Rosenwald dollars went to help the Tuskegee Institute in its work.

Nor did he mention the faith he placed in the black people for whom the Institute was so beneficial. It was a faith he exhibited in his many offers of "matching" funds for the Institute, for other institutions, especially for the building of simple schoolhouses for blacks throughout the South. These funds were raised in so-called "arousement meetings." One such was held in Boligee, Alabama, in the winter of 1916-1917. An eyewitness account survives:

> We gathered together in a little rickety building, without any heat, only from an old rusty stove with the stove pipe protruding out of the window where a pane had been removed for the flue. . . . The farmers had been hard hit that year as the boll weevil had figured very conspicuously in that community, and most of the people were tenants on large plantations. When we reached the scene where the rally was to be staged, the teacher with thirty-five or forty little children had prepared a program which consisted of plantation melodies. . . . They sang with such fervor and devotion, until one could hardly restrain from crying. . . . The patrons and friends were all rural people, and crudely dressed. The women had on homespun dresses and aprons, while the men in the main were dressed in blue overalls. Their boots and shoes were very muddy, as they had to trudge through the mud from three to four miles. . . . When the speaking was over we arranged for the silver offering, and to tell the truth I thought we would do well to collect ten dollars from the audience; but when the Master of Ceremonies, the Rev. M. D. Wallace, who had ridden a small mule across the county through the cold and through the rain, organizing the people, began to call the collection the people responded spontaneously. You would have been over-awed with emotion if you could have seen those poor people walking up to the table, emptying their pockets for a school. . . . One old man, who had seen slavery days, with all of his life's earnings in an old greasy sack, slowly drew it from his pocket, and emptied it on the table. I have never seen such a pile of nickels, pennies, dimes and dollars, etc., in my life. He put thirty-eight dollars on the table, which was his entire savings.

These were the people who would gain the greatest benefit from Julius Rosenwald's philanthropy, yet they were the ones who, in proportion to their means, gave the most.

Arriving at the school, the family disembarked from the Pullman, leaving behind that luxurious life-style to wait for them on the tracks. For the next few days they lived simply in the dormitories, eating with the students and faculty of Tuskegeee and walking beneath the broiling Alabama sun. At sunset, they sat beneath the millions of stars lighting the Southern sky, listening to the spirituals that stirred the soul with the primeval cries for freedom and hope.

The spirituals left an indelible impression on Edith. She heard their call of sadness and joy intertwined, of restlessness and tranquillity uneasily combined, and felt their demand for action. Later, she would recognize these haunting qualities again in the glorious voices of Marion Anderson and Annabelle Bernard. Little did Edith know that the South—which now reached deep into her heart—would one day become her home.

FOUR

First Marriage

NO OFFICIAL EXPLANATION can be found connecting pubescent girls with fish, nonetheless the term *backfisch*, describing a teenage girl, was a widespread usage. Free association, or inference, might lead one to the conclusion that the young "fish" is an appetizing, succulent morsel, just ready for the frying pan of marriage. For Edith Rosenwald, at school in Germany, the frying pan that seemed an ever-present reality was the school itself. She counted weeks, days, and, finally, hours anticipating her return home. If autumn seemed to linger unnaturally, and winter to be interminable, spring brought her some consolation at last and release from the inhospitable elements.

Spring meant the approach of her sixteenth birthday—and, best of all, she could permit herself to begin thinking again of home, the family, Ravinia, and Twinnie. Despite their best efforts, the straightlaced martinets on the faculty at Dresden failed to leave any permanent imprints on her personality. She managed somehow to emerge not as a *backfisch*, but as a *forelle*, the trout so lovely in its prime and so remarkable for its ability to forge its own way upstream, against the elements.

On her return to Chicago, Ede was more daring than ever, or so it seemed to Twinnie. And Twinnie could be counted on to act as a willing accomplice to any of Ede's escapades. Heretofore, the most "devilish" thing they had done together was to smoke cigarettes in the upstairs library, blowing the smoke out the window. So what if they had turned slightly green after inhaling? Undaunted, they coughed and puffed again, feeling very sophisticated.

Twinnie, from her vantage point some seventy years later, still remembered that day in May when the two girls declared their own holiday from school. The two friends took Edith's electric car—driven without the benefit of license, since none was required then—and drove to the wilderness of Midway. The camera they brought along was their only witness, but it provided a record for posterity of the audacity of their adventure.

The photo of Ede, sprawled full-length in front of her car on the fresh grass, bears the caption, "Naughty! Naughty!" in Julie Greenebaum's album. "Scandalous and immodest!" another caption exclaims, as the photos reveal the truants frolicking, clowning in that sylvan setting on the glorious tenth day of May. Clad in ankle-length, dark-colored skirts and white, long-sleeved middy blouses with jaunty ties around the necks, their hair piled on top of their heads, it is difficult to tell the two apart. Yet it is unmistakably Edith, with her skirt hiked up almost to her knees, revealing heavy black stockings, attempting to climb a tree. The caption leading to this candid shot reads ironically, "Oh yes, modest!" And, beneath the photo, Twinnie in her naïveté recorded the unknowingly prophetic sentence, "You'll get to the top if the finish is as good as the start."

Suddenly—or so it seemed—they were grown up. Young men entered their lives, claiming evenings that were not always shared as a foursome. Julie entered Sweetbriar College in Virginia, where her roommate was Dorothy Deutsch, a friend from Chicago, whose brother Armand later married Edith's sister, Adele.

Adele and Ede had always been close, but as the difference in their ages became less and less significant, they grew nearly inseparable. They called each other "Dolly," and referred to themselves as the "Dolly Sisters." Intensifying this relationship even further was a tall, attractive man who appeared to have serious intentions where Ede was concerned. She was flattered and excited by his attentions, and in need of a confidante to share her emotions. At eighteen, she was still naive enough to be awed by the fact that an "older" man was so intrigued by her. She could not quite fathom what special allure she held for him.

Her family and friends had quite a different perspective. Bluntly, they did not like Germon Sulzberger, and J.R. at least was also aware that the Sulzberger family's meat-packing business was rumored to be in deep financial trouble. He may have imputed in a darker fashion the ardor with which Germon pressed his suit for Ede.

Ede's assertiveness, her powers of persuasion, won the day. Reluctantly, her parents gave their blessings and attempted to rejoice in Ede's radiant happiness. The glow was not to last for long.

The young couple were married, rented a fashionable apartment in New York City, and furnished it splendidly before departing for their European honeymoon. From the very start, they embarked on stormy seas. Edith lay ill for days in her stateroom aboard the ship. Years later, she confided to Twinnie that her husband had failed to even inquire about her welfare.

Edith had been raised to make the best of a situation. Both parents adhered to the motto that once a commitment had been made, it was to be honored. Nor was it for lack of trying on Edith's part that the marriage did not succeed. Upon their return from Europe, Ede studied shorthand and typing in order to make herself useful as her husband's secretary. Soon it became as evident to Ede as it had been to her family and friends beforehand that the marriage was doomed. She sought her parents' advice.

Loath as they had been to approve of the marriage, the Rosenwalds were equally reluctant to see it dissolved. Various options suggested by her parents were tried, but, in the final analysis, her parents came around to Ede's thinking and began to consider the possibility of a divorce. One major obstacle remained. Julius was gravely concerned about breaking the news of Ede's impending separation to his own mother.

A close, extremely personal, bond existed between Julius and his mother. Every day, for as long as she lived, J.R. visited Augusta on his way to "The Store" in the morning and, most of the time, had his chauffeur stop so that he might pay her a visit on the way home, as well. No one was more aware than he that the matriarch of the family was of the old school. Divorce would be an unspeakable disgrace to her. And adding to his discomfiture, he was aware that Ede was her favorite grandchild.

A letter survives in Augusta Rosenwald's spidery hand, in which she addresses "My own sweet Edith." No doubt, the letter continues, Daddy told her already how much joy her lovely letter had brought to her grandmother's heart and how delighted she was to hear that dear Germon had gotten over his indisposition. She was certain that his swift recovery was due to Edith's loving care. Turning to a different subject, she remarks on the portrait of herself recently completed by the artist August Franzen, and how averse she is to see herself as others see her. Nevertheless, she is delighted to hear that this likeness has given the family such pleasure, and in turn this makes her happy. "The assurance of the love you bear your old Granny," she calls it, and adds that she is especially gratified that dear Germon also loves the portrait. The letter closes with the hope that she will see both of them soon. Evidently, in her frequent exchange of letters, Ede had never intimated that all was not well in her marriage.

Such was the dilemma facing the bearer of ill tidings. But no matter how distasteful, neither J.R. nor his daughter ever shirked a duty. So Edith and her father set out for a visit to Augusta Rosenwald's home and placed the facts before her. Julius believed that he knew his mother very well, but nothing could have quite prepared him for her reaction. She sat silent for a moment, then embraced her granddaughter and softly voiced the statement that became a *bon mot* within the family forever after: "That is the best bad news I ever heard."

The Franzen portrait graced Julius Rosenwald's home until his death. Afterward, each of the children vied for its possession and a decision was finally reached by the drawing of straws. Ede, to her great delight, won. The painting of the dowager was installed in a place of honor in Longue Vue, Ede's palatial home in New Orleans, in the formal living room, above a mantel carved as a memorial to George Washington. Illuminated by a Waterford crystal chandelier, the aged patrician woman dressed in fine black silk, her gray hair done up in a bun, smiled down at her progeny. There are accounts by friends and family of Edith standing beneath her grandmother's portrait, wistfully uttering her oft-repeated, "I wish I looked like her."

After Ede's own death, the painting found a new home on Park Avenue with Marion Ascoli. Nor has its allure faded through the years, for Marion can often be caught remarking, "Isn't she beautiful?"

But Longue Vue would hardly seem complete without that singularly treasured possession, so a copy was commissioned that today proudly looks down from above the Washington mantel.

Edith's favorite portrait of her grandmother—Augusta Rosenwald.

FIVE

Edgar

URING THE YEARS OF World War I, Edith was a constant source of support to her father, who was deeply involved in America's war effort. Offered an Army commission by Secretary of War, Newton D. Baker, Julius declined. Instead, he devoted his considerable genius for planning and organization as a member of the Advisory Commission of the Council of National Defense. At the same time he made sizable contributions from his personal fortune. He also accepted with alacrity an invitation to visit the front lines in France and to tell the servicemen how proud America was of them. Such was the reputation of Sears, Roebuck from the urban to the most remote rural regions, that the War Department felt that a visit from the head of this ubiquitous company would give the soldiers in the trenches a true touch of home. Touring American bases and front-line positions along with high-ranking officers, Julius would introduce himself, tongue-in-cheek, as General Merchandise.

Following these tours, the ravages and tragedies that the war left behind and those J.R. observed first-hand were often discussed in the Rosenwald home. The tools of war became a matter of great concern to Julius Rosenwald. When perusing the company's financial statements he noticed that Sears, Roebuck & Co. was selling between three and four million dollars' worth of pistols a year; it troubled him deeply. Personal gain had absolutely no place where the welfare of the country was concerned. He issued a terse statement to his network of stores: "Rifles and shotguns—*yes*, because we have a lot of hunters and country people who really need them. Pistols— *no*. Boys toting small arms are only hunting for trouble. It is not our business to become an accessory to crime, however indirectly." This became policy, and henceforth Sears sold no more handguns.

During this period of patriotic involvement, Augusta Rosenwald carried a full schedule, entertaining visiting dignitaries while working ceaselessly in support of the war effort through such agencies as the Red Cross. Her daughter-in-law Edith Goodkind Rosenwald remembers her fierce expressions of patriotism. She recalls that Gussie Rosenwald never left home, be it for a weekend excursion or an extended trip, without packing an American flag in her suitcase. Gussie remained a devoted Girl Scout leader, too, sponsoring numerous activities; it might well be said of her that she found more than one good deed to do each day.

As for Edith, both Lessing's and Adele's families started to grow, and she fell quite naturally into the role of ever-doting aunt. Though her own marriage was on the point of total disintegration, the final decree had not yet been formalized.

In 1917 Edith was profoundly disturbed by the news that four women had been arrested for picketing the White House on behalf of women's suffrage. Even more upsetting was the news that these women had been sentenced to six-month jail terms. Though, on the surface, she seemed to pay little attention to such events, pursuing the more frivolous entertainments of her peers in the "smart set"—such as the craze of bobbing one's hair—nonetheless, she was already absorbing the seeds of a social awareness that would germinate much later in the warm and fertile soil of Louisiana where she would become the "Patroness Saint of Voters' Registration."

New Orleans was still far off on the horizon, despite the fact that Edith's destiny even then waited in the wings. It was in New York, in the home of a friend, that Ede met Edgar Stern. Mrs. Lucille Blum, a longtime friend and contemporary, offered this account of the occasion:

> Edith was in Manhattan on the invitation of a girl friend. Expected that evening was a gentleman caller from New Orleans. Edith's hostess adjured, "Remember, he is mine. Hands off!" But Edith said that the minute Edgar Stern entered the room she fell in love with him and vowed that she would marry him. She never told me what happened to her friendship with her hostess.

Edgar's reaction must have been similar, for both delighted in telling and retelling the story of their first encounter, agreeing that something clicked from the start. They spent time together talking that evening, to the exclusion of all else, and went out on their first date the very next night and as often as possible from that time on. Henceforth, Edgar referred to Edith as "Angelle, my Creole Yankee."

Edgar Stern was thirty-four years old, his handsome face and stately head set on broad shoulders, his high forehead crowned by dark hair. His intelligent dark eyes sparkled equally with good humor and tenderness, betraying only a hint of impishness. He was what others called "a handsome devil." And he had the grace and agility of an accomplished tennis player. Nature endowed him with a blend of traits that made him as popular among men as he was irresistible to women. His disarming candor and his spontaneous gallantry—easily traceable to his Southern roots—were coupled with a demeanor and intelligence that had been refined within the halls of academe at Harvard.

Edgar's family was prestigious and outgoing, and he had assimilated the best of whatever environment he found himself in. His father, Maurice Stern, reached America from his native Bavaria in 1871, at the age of sixteen, and made his way to New Orleans. Soon thereafter, he began to attend services in the congregation of Temple Sinai where the Reverend James Koppel Gutheim delivered bilingual sermons, alternating between German and English.

The history of that temple, one of the oldest Reform congregations in the United States, is closely intertwined with the history of the Jewish community of New Orleans.

The Jews of New Orleans had lived under four flags. Theirs is also the story of Louisiana from the early days of its discovery through the Spanish and then the French regimes; its purchase by the United States; its participation in the Confederacy; and its return to the Union. It may be a story as colorful and romantic as any recorded in the annals of American history.

The noble Judah Touro lived two-thirds of his life in New Orleans, as did Judah Benjamin, who bore the nickname "the brains of the Confederacy." Other outstanding Jews from this port city were the first American actress to win the hearts of European theater lovers, Belle Menken—poet, actress, journalist, and dancer—whose beauty and achievements won her the friendship and admiration of Charles Dickens; and Louis Moreau Gottschalk, the first American pianist to win laurels and triumphs on the European continent, whose appearance in Paris was greeted by Frédéric Chopin with the words, "Donnez moi les mains, mon enfant; je vous predis que vous serez le roi des pianistes." ("Give me your hands, my child; I predict that you will be a king of pianists.") And there was Alice Heine, daughter of a first cousin of the German national poet, Heinrich Heine. She won mention in not a few histories as a New Orleans Jew who rose to the status of reigning princess of Monaco. Romantic tales flourished in this magnolia-scented atmosphere where intrigue was whispered in mysterious courtyards hidden by wrought-iron gates. And glittering balls were held in those antebellum mansions hardly more than shouting distance away from the market where slaves were sold.

To that city, Maurice Stern came as a youth. He followed the news gleaned from reading the German paper published in New Orleans and listened to Rabbi Gutheim's bilingual sermons until he understood the English as well as the German. His arrival in town, in fact, coincided with the laying of the cornerstone for the grand new Temple Sinai, an occasion on which Rabbi Gutheim delivered a moving oration before an enormous crowd. Little did Maurice imagine that he would be president of that congregation some thirty-one years later. And, in his wildest imaginings, he could not have foreseen that his son Walter would lead the festivities on the occasion of the temple's fiftieth anniversary when Walter was president of the congregation.

Young Maurice Stern, through the intervention of Benjamin Neugass, a relative, was apprenticed to the firm of Lehman, Neugass and Co., Cotton Factors. The name was altered a while later to Lehman, Abraham & Co. when Neugass left New Orleans to return to his native England. In 1883 the local papers found three formidable events on which to dwell at length: the opening of the Brooklyn Bridge in New York, the newly organized Wild West show of frontiersman W. F. Cody ("Buffalo Bill"), and the latest wonder of the growing metropolis of Chicago, the new and dizzying ten-story skyscraper. For his part, Maurice Stern created two personal momentous events by taking to wife a beautiful New Orleans belle named Hanna Bloom, and seeing that the name of his firm was changed once more, for all to note, to Lehman, Stern & Co., Ltd., Cotton Factors and Commission Merchants. No doubt, the news of the Chicago skyscraper seemed of no special personal significance at the time, for it would have taken the craft of a fortune-teller behind her crystal ball and a small miracle besides to foretell that one day the same skyline would be dominated by the tallest building in the world, the 103-story Sears, Roebuck Tower.

In 1885 Hanna and Maurice had their first son, Walter; in 1886, their second son, Edgar; and, after an interval of years, a daughter, Sarah. The year in which Edgar Stern was born also saw the dedication of the Statue of Liberty on Bedloe's Island in New York Harbor. Maurice might have taken this as a sign — certainly his son Edgar did. Born in the year this symbol of goodwill and promise was erected, Edgar was cognizant of the opportunities America offered him throughout his life. Returning from his frequent trips to Europe, he could never look at the silhouette of the Lady with the Torch on the horizon without being profoundly affected.

The children grew up in a refined cultural environment. The Stern home on St. Charles Avenue was known for its fine furnishings and alluring garden. Hanna Stern, like her husband, had strong ties to Temple Sinai, where, long before it was fashionable for women to do so, she became one of two women to serve on its board of trustees. She often expressed her opinion that "one principle should be enforced by parents: a religious education for their children. We teach our children and ourselves to obey the laws of government. Surely, we should first observe the laws of God."

Hanna Stern became a visiting matron at the Jewish Children's Home, and served with equal distinction as president of the Touro Shakespeare Almshouse Auxiliary, as board member of the Kingsley House, the black Sylvania Williams Community Center, and the Red Cross. She was an early enthusiastic supporter of the Council of Jewish Women.

In her love for good music she was not content to be merely an entertained listener, but became an active participant in a small group of public-spirited citizens convinced that New Orleans could and should have a symphony orchestra of its own. To that end, she became a charter member of the parent organization of the present Symphony Society. When Maurice died, she equipped a child-welfare station and a medical library at Tulane University in his memory.

It is hardly surprising that young Edgar, growing up in this milieu of charitable pursuits, absorbed a dedication to public service that was as much a part of his family life as were crayfish bisque and heavenly hash. He attended public school in New Orleans, then went on to Tulane University. His winning ways, coupled with his handsome good looks, made it easy to indulge him.

If, as the popular saying goes, a person is known by the company he keeps, high marks must be given to Edgar for his choice of a closest friend, Montefiore Mordecai Lemann— Monte, as he was affectionately known. This friendship endured from the days of carefree boyhood until death separated them in the eighth decade of their lives. Lemann was a formidable presence in the courts of law, respected by presidents, a giant in his profession. His name is linked with that of Felix Frankfurter and Supreme Court Justice White. The esteem in which he was held can best be understood from a letter bearing birthday greetings to him from the preeminent Judge Learned Hand, which closes in tribute: ". . . and always, my dear Monte, remember that I deem it one of the joys and achievements of my own life that you have let me into your circle of friends."

Edgar's outgoing ways evoked spontaneous responses among all he encountered at Tulane. New Orleans was his oyster; he was now ready for a greater challenge. He maintained a uniformly high grade average, which led him to consider continuing his schooling at Yale University. In a letter to Dr. Albert S. Cook of Yale, dated August 8, 1903, J. W. Pearce recorded his recommendation of Edgar, being careful to point out that the letter was initiated at his own suggestion:

> Mr. Edgar B. Stern of this city tells me that he expects to enter Yale University in September and I should like to commend him to your notice at the earliest possible moment. He studied two years with me at the Boys' High School here and afterwards took the freshman year at Tulane. I feel assured that you will find him polite and gentlemanly in his deportment, careful and attentive in his work, and fully capable of achieving excellent results in scholarship. He will, I am sure, do your great institution no discredit.

Edgar chose to enter Harvard University instead, arriving there on September 29, 1903. Pearce's confidence in him was, nevertheless, fully vindicated. Edgar's intellectual capabilities came into full play as he caught up effortlessly with his class despite having missed three full months of his sophomore year because of typhoid fever.

On arriving at Cambridge, he wrote to his family in his open, well-formed script on paper emblazoned with the emblem of the Harvard Union:

> Dear Mama, Papa, Walter & Sister:
>
> I have just been with Monte Lemann and saw the most wondrous sight I ever saw: 75 or 100 men (and college has not yet begun). Every one of them wore crimson clothes. They were practicing running and scrimmaging.

He went on to report that he spent the first night at Harvard in Monte's room, his own not having been made ready. The letter continues for more than eight pages, describing in detail what he ate, whom he recognized, and what his reactions had been. He requested that his parents keep all his missives, which would serve him in later years far better than could a diary of his college activities.

Thus began the long tradition of daily correspondence. And, while most of the letters regard the college life and his own activities, one—written on October 11 to his father—confines itself to pecuniary matters:

Dear Papa:

I have written to you all today, but address this other letter to you, because it pertains to finances only.

I do not like to make a kick already about money matters, but you told me that you would set my allowance at $1,000 for the year, and that I should see how I got along and what my expenses would be, and report to you thereon. Accordingly I have been figuring out my expenses and have found that it will be impossible to get along on $1,000, and that I cannot live on less than $1,200 at least.

I do not wish to be extravagant, on the contrary I am as economical as I can be, and I think on looking over the list below you will see only the necessaries of life.

Tuition	$150.00
Board at $5 per week	180.00
Room rent	225.00
Christmas trip home	100.00
Coal & Wood	12.00
Text Books	15.00
Washing @ 3.50 per mo.	31.50
Pressing clothes for yr.	10.00
Laundry @ .50 per wk.	18.00
Tips to Chambermaid @ $1 per month	9.00
Furnishing Room (as per enclosed bill)	185.00
Window Seat Cushion	10.00
Lounge	20.00
Laboratory Fee	10.00
Already spent	45.00
	$1,020.50

I have already spent $45 since leaving N.Y., which includes my boat trip, my dues and subscriptions for the whole year to the Harvard Union, the *Crimson, Lampoon,*

and *Advocate* (Harvard papers), the two or three times I
went to the theatre and my meals for the half week before
Memorial opened and my season ticket for football &
baseball and shades for my room, the barber shop, checking my trunk, stamps, carfare and some other expenses
which I cannot just now remember.

The letter continues. Edgar asks for $1,300 a year, hoping
his father will find it reasonable and not extravagant. He states
that he is aware of the business like tenor of his correspondence, but that he had written another letter that very day
bringing the family up to date on all the latest news.

Meanwhile, his social life had begun to flourish. He wrote
that he had submitted his choice of courses, about which
Monte had previously advised him, and that his selection was
accepted. He needed only to make a grade of "C" in all except
Physics, in which even a "D" would make him a sophomore the
following year. Elementary Physics, English Composition, and
Rhetoric were compulsory for him, as was German. He also
selected Second-Year French and Latin and desired to take an
extra course in English Literature, which he reported as one of
his best. He thought that would make him quite a *macher*,
Yiddish slang for a "somebody." In the context of the ivy-
covered walls of Harvard, his word choice no doubt lent a
certain homey touch, along with a tinge of irony. This letter was
accompanied by a sample swatch of wallpaper to give his
mother a taste of how his sitting room was done. She could be
relied upon to understand how sensitive he was to the details
of his surroundings. He apologized to her for his extravagance,
but in his inimitable, charming way managed to convey that
she should take full credit for his good taste. In fact, he was
totally enamored of Harvard, and no doubt the dominant
crimson of his decor was influenced by his love for that
venerable institution.

At Harvard, wide vistas regarding social attitudes opened
to Edgar, impressing and startling him. He remarked with obvious astonishment that the Student Union was open to *everyone*.
He might have added, "including Jews." He reported that a
student could try out for any team and apply for membership
in any club. His assumption that acceptance was automatically

assured may have been somewhat naive. Nonetheless, this was a giant step forward from the world he had known up to then.

He was likewise impressed by the entrance he could gain into the world of American "High Society." Students, he remarked, were in the habit of sending out engraved invitations to parties held in their rooms. Edgar happily joined this whirl of entertainment and mixed comfortably with his peers. In fact, he excelled in those pursuits to such an extent that his social engagement book was soon filled to overflowing. His grades stayed around "B" and "C," considered good for Harvard, but he might have done better had not his extracurricular activities claimed so much of his energies. His letters continually reflected the totally uninhibited *joie de vivre* that had been unleashed. He thought nothing of ending some of them with "Harvard! Harvard! Rah! Rah! Rah! Harvard! Harvard! Harvard!"

His letters contain numerous references to girls, who apparently were not oblivious to his considerable charm. Edgar appears to have carried on many a lighthearted romance. Sisters of his college friends, girls he was introduced to at various functions – many a passing reference alludes to them and even mention to one special girl he met at a football game. There were also girls he met on board ship during the trans-Atlantic voyages taken with his family.

Maurice Stern still maintained close ties with his relatives in Germany, and Edgar, once introduced to this world, was fascinated by it. He collected many mementos of these trips, including such minutiae as the dining-room seating arrangements on shipboard during the crossing in the summer of 1905. This chart shows the Sterns seated at the captain's table while members of the Woolworth family were relegated to less favorable placement.

Edgar carried on a spirited and voluminous correspondence with a variety of young women from nearby colleges. One can only wonder about some of his omissions in the reports to his parents.

Daily letters also arrived from New Orleans. His mother unfailingly addressed him as "My darling sweet boy." She expressed constant concern about the state of his health. In one letter, she wrote:

> When the weather is bad and cars should not be running
> and you have a distance to go, take a cab, but my dear boy,
> do not go to the theater or to any dances in this cold
> weather; you are not accustomed to it and might catch a
> cold. Don't, my dear boy, go over to Wellesley, to see Mina
> in this weather and do wear your Jaeger underwear.

Whether or not he went over to Wellesley, Edgar did
remark on the weather and the fact that he needed an additional ton of coal and some kindling wood which necessitated
an unexpected and inopportune outlay of ten dollars. In the
same letter, he reports that he had been shopping in Boston the
previous day and bought a new derby hat. He thanks his
mother for her generous offer to buy him a cane or an umbrella,
but tactfully suggests an alternative.

> I don't carry a cane and lose too many umbrellas to justify
> my possession of a good one. I would much prefer a chafing
> dish and am surprised at you being afraid to trust me with
> one. You really seem to have a very low opinion of my ability
> to take care of myself. All the fellows here have chafing
> dishes and I can assure you there is not the slightest danger.

The social whirl was reflected in his attendance at the
theater and the opera. On February 4, 1904, he wrote:

> This afternoon I went to a matinee with Moise to see Nance
> O'Neill in *Camille*. As you know, *Camille* is rather sad and
> calls for some heavy acting. The star has a big reputation but
> I was rather disappointed in her. The play which is *Traviata*
> [sic] is a very strong one but pretty immoral.

(No rejoinder came from the home front.)

In due course, Edgar turned his impressive resources to
less frivolous pursuits, buckling down to some serious studying. He must also have allotted part of his time to charitable
work, for a letter written to him in 1906 states, "I wish to thank
you for your willingness to give up one hour one evening each
week to this very deserving philanthropic work." No reference
is made to the specific nature of his concern.

The studying was rewarded more specifically. The
Harvard *Crimson*, under the headline "Phi Beta Kappa Dinner
Tonight," reported in May: "The annual dinner of the
undergraduate members of the Phi Beta Kappa Society will be
held at 7 o'clock this evening at the Hotel Lenox in Boston."
Among the names of those attending is "E. B. Stern, '07."

Another significant notice, printed in the New Orleans press beneath Edgar's name, reads in bold letters, "Wins Honors in Scholarship and Honored in Athletics."

> Edgar Bloom Stern, son of Mr. & Mrs. Maurice Stern of this city, returned from Harvard University yesterday to spend the Christmas holidays with his parents in New Orleans. Before leaving for his short vacation, Mr. Stern was honored by being appointed to a scholarship in Harvard, this being the second highest honor which he could have received and a great university distinction. Last fall, another honor was given him when he was chosen manager of the University Football Association, having served previously as assistant manager. He will graduate next June. Mr. Stern studied in the public schools of New Orleans, entering the High School from McDonough No. 7 and winning the medal given by the Patriotic Order of Sons of America for the best examination paper on American history.

Monte M. Lemann, attorney at law in New Orleans, was among the first to write an enthusiastic letter of congratulations after hearing the good news of the scholarship from Edgar's father. He also adds his pleasure at hearing that Edgar had been chosen as an alternate in the Princeton debate. He closes by inquiring whether Edgar would be returning the following October to enter the office after the summer camping trip he knew Edgar was planning. Edgar did, indeed, enter his father's business office.

The ensuing decade was as productive as it was enjoyable. Edgar cut a wide swath through the ranks of hopeful girls in New Orleans and New York. There were many trips to Europe and to Palm Beach and prolific correspondence with his ever-widening circle of male and female friends. Edgar seemed to delight in every friendship he made and every invitation he received, and often wrote enthusiastically of them to his mother. Part of his delight might have been due to the touch of shyness, which rendered him attractive but at the same time caused him disappointment when he failed to receive answers to letters he had written. There were whispers of attachments, infatuations, "more than friendship," even near-engagements.

Nothing compared, however, with the sweep of emotion that propelled Edgar into a whirlwind courtship in the hope of making Edith Rosenwald his wife at the earliest possible moment. They were motoring in the countryside near New York City on a sunny weekend and stopped to take tea in a quaint old inn named Longue Vue that overlooked the Hudson River. In this romantic setting, Edgar proposed and was joyously accepted. Appropriately, the name of the inn was memorialized as the name of their first home and later transferred to their second. They spent most of their adult lives in these two homes in New Orleans, and it was the second Longue Vue that they bequeathed as part of their legacy to the people of that city.

Edgar's proposal gave Edith the impetus she had lacked to make her divorce final. In the meantime, circumstances caused them to return to their individual homes—Edgar to New Orleans and Edith to the Rosenwald home in Chicago. She wrote to him:

> And so, my dear, here we are, both of us back to our Main Streets, with only a few rose-lined clouds, beautiful sunsets, and many happy hours tucked away, for no one else, but where we can always find them.
>
> The trip home was ghastly.... The fact that Father was not at the station at first, made the sight of him all the more welcome, and again I was glad of the impulse that made me return to them. I found a family, not bowed in grief, but greatly overcome by our loss, which was very poignant to me when I as usual went right over to Grandmother's house—this time to see her companion, who naturally is suffering from the severe strain. They always teased her that she wept whenever she saw me, but this time it was my turn to shed the tears when I found her room empty for the first time in my memory. So we are spending the near future away from outsiders, continuing our life with her, for she gave us so much to carry on, and think about.
>
> Some day I would like you to read a letter, written two years ago—at seventy-seven, which, to my mind, explains why she was a personage. There was with it a letter, also, to be opened after her death, written twenty years before, and the most striking thing to me was her mental progress and development in her old age. The first letter could not compare either in English or composition to the later one.

Her hours of meditation were indeed well spent. This afternoon I went out to the cemetery and had the gratification of paying her my last tribute and farewell, and now I am very tired, glad to be home, and frightfully thoughtful.

This is not a very cheerful message to send to you, but you have been so always considerate, and understanding, that I know you will not mind an expression of thoughts crowding themselves through my brain.

There ensued a furious exchange of letters and telegrams, regarding arrangements for the wedding:

Mrs. Edith Sulzberger
% Julius Rosenwald
Ravinia, Illinois

WILL YOU PLEASE WIRE ME AS SOON AS YOU HAVE LAWYER'S OPINION ON ILLINOIS REQUIREMENTS—YOUR LETTER TODAY OTHERWISE DELIGHTFUL

EDGAR

May 19, 1921. Telegram to Edgar:

IS IT SATISFACTORY FOR MOTHER AND ME TO ARRIVE 5/27—NOT TOO MANY PARTIES PLEASE

EDITH

Edgar's reply of the same date:

WANT YOU TO STAY AT LEAST A WEEK—NOT TOO MANY PARTIES PLANNED

And the following day:

THRILLED AT THE THOUGHT OF HEARING YOUR VOICE—ALL SORTS OF LOVE

EDGAR

And the following day, Monte Lemann, attorney, dispatched a wire to Carl Meyer, Chicago lawyer:

CAN THEY MARRY IN ILLINOIS ALTHOUGH LESS THAN ONE YEAR FOR DIVORCE INTERLOCUTORY DECREE RENDERED IN NEW YORK IN JUNE 1920—FINAL DECREE IN SEPTEMBER 1920—WANT TO MARRY IN JUNE AND GO ABROAD IN JULY

Another telegram followed on May 21, 1921, to Carl Meyer:

CAN THEY MARRY IN INDIANA AND HAVE
CHICAGO CEREMONY
                    MONTE LEMANN

A host of papers with various legal opinions on how the Sterns could get married attest to the extensive research the lawyers accomplished. Finally the green light was given, and Edgar dispatched the following wire:

JUNE 3, 1921

TO CUNARD STEAMSHIP LINES

CONFIRM ROOM AND BATH ON AQUITANIA
SAILING 7/5/21

The wedding was set for the 29th of June. On June 23, in the last letter Edith wrote to Edgar before his departure from New Orleans for the wedding, she said:

> I remember once saying what a perfect background I would make for some real man's career, and I feel now I know this real man and nothing can make me happier than to take second place and back him up with all that is in me. And it will be *moral* support this time, Edgar, dearest. I am so very proud of you, and if you could only be a woman for five minutes, you would realize that we ask no more of marriage.

This revealing message, by the child that Julius called "the lion of my flock," set a tone for Edith. In all their years together, she never failed to strive for Edgar's glory and honor, though she remained her own person chalking up impressive achievements in her own right and not averse to taking credit or honor when they were due. Her proudest title would always remain Mrs. Edgar B. Stern.

Before his departure, she sent Edgar yet another telegram:

A GOODBYE KISS ONCE MORE WITH A REAL
FOLLOW-UP TOMORROW—HURRY UP—ALL
MY LOVE
                    EDE

The Chicago papers carried the following notice:

ROSENWALD GIRL WED IN INDIANA
ON SPECIAL CAR

Mrs. Edith R. Sulzberger, the daughter of Mr. and Mrs. Julius Rosenwald, and Edgar B. Stern of New Orleans, were married in Hammond, Ind. yesterday by Dr. Emil G. Hirsch of 4606 Grand Boulevard. They went to Hammond in a special car on the Illinois Central Railroad, accompanied only by the immediate members of their families and returned to Chicago right after the ceremony.

A wedding supper, attended by a number of friends and relatives, was held last night at Mr. Rosenwald's summer home in Ravinia. Mr. & Mrs. Stern will leave today for New York.

On July 5 they will sail on the *Aquitania* for Europe where they will spend a honeymoon of several months. On their return they will take up residence in New Orleans where Mr. Stern is secretary-treasurer of Lehman, Stern & Co. and president of the Chamber of Commerce.

Mr. Stern and Mrs. Sulzberger met while they were wintering at Palm Beach late in 1920. He is 35 years old and she is 26.

Mrs. Sulzberger formerly was the wife of Germon F. Sulzberger of the Chicago family of packers, whose firm has been succeeded in business by T. E. Wilson & Co. She was married to Mr. Sulzberger in 1913 and divorced him last May.

The article (correct in its particulars, except for the scene of their meeting) failed to convey the couple's excitement at being able to wed. The wedding license had to be obtained in Crown Point, Indiana, and the marriage had to take place in Indiana because Illinois required an interval of one year after a divorce decree became final. The Pullman car was rented in the name of a Sears, Roebuck officer to forestall the inevitable glare of publicity. And Rabbi Emil G. Hirsch, a family friend, agreed to perform the wedding, "somewhere in Indiana."

At the supper party, innumerable toasts were drunk to the happiness of the newlyweds. Edgar was beaming; Edith was radiant. They joked that the profusion of flowers in the Pullman car was reminiscent of a gangland funeral. As laughter echoed through the fine old forests of Ravinia, everyone vowed never to forget the ride through Indiana.

SIX

New Orleans

*T*HEIR STATEROOM aboard the *Aquitania* filled with
newly labeled steamer trunks, flowers, beribboned baskets of
fruit and candy, and stacks of "Bon Voyage" telegrams, the
golden young couple, Mr. and Mrs. Edgar B. Stern, were off on
their honeymoon. The gleaming white ocean liner pointed her
bow eastward into the calm waters of a summer sea.

Somewhere in mid-journey, on a beautiful evening, Edgar
and Edith were dressing for dinner. Edith donned a sleek, black
evening gown, designed with low décolletage to emphasize its
austere and dramatic simplicity. She wound several strands of
shimmering pearls around her neck. Edgar stood back, admiring his lovely bride, and complimented her on her enchanting
ensemble. She studied herself in the mirror.

Then, with a totally unexpected impetuousness, she tore
the ropes of pearls from her throat, spurting out, "This is awful!
I just don't like the way I look!"

"But, darling, you look absolutely—" Edgar began, attempting to placate her. Then he froze. To his utter astonishment and
dismay, she was flinging the precious pearls through an open

porthole into the dark waters of the Atlantic. He stood by helplessly, unable to restrain her.

Observing his look of pained consternation, she collapsed into a chair, her body wracked by paroxysms of laughter. All Edgar could do was stammer, "But your priceless pearls. . . ."

Recovering sufficiently, she let out the truth.

"Hardly precious, Edgar dear—they cost exactly $3.95."

She threw herself into his arms and proceeded to confess her hitherto undisclosed weakness: "Woolworth's—I bought them at Woolworth's!" She absolutely adored those stores, she said, and it gave her great joy to acquire any number of trinkets, which she had packed for the voyage together with an impressive array of authentic jewelry. Here she proclaimed another line that later made the round of friends and family alike: "On me they look real, don't they, Edgar dear?" And, taking his arm as he led her to dinner, she wistfully remarked that she would have preferred to be an heiress within the Woolworth empire instead of the Sears, Roebuck one.

Edgar, his *savoir faire* fully restored, assured Edith that she could indeed use her Sears dividends to indulge herself at will in even the most extravagant baubles to be found at Woolworth's five-and-ten-cent stores.

The Sterns returned to New Orleans after the "dog days" of late summer, having taken a lease on the fashionable Vaira home. There was eager and predatory anticipation in certain circles regarding the young wife of the man who had been the most eligible bachelor of the city, and how she would fit into the staid mold of New Orleans' *haute société*. Lucille (Mrs. Edwin Henry) Blum remembers those days in 1921:

> Edith came to New Orleans as the bride of Edgar, and from the moment she arrived, her presence was felt. I first saw her at a reception given by mutual friends. The spacious drawing rooms were filled with guests when the newlyweds made their appearance. Edgar very proudly introduced his bride, who immediately charmed everyone by her gracious, cordial manner. She was perfectly groomed from the top of her stylish, perky hat to the fingertips of

her white kid gloves. Clearly, the handsome couple emanated an aura of happiness.

If some nasty, narrow minds were looking for a fly in the ointment, expecting to find a flashy Eastern heiress, dressed to her teeth and flaunting her wealth, they were bound to be disappointed. Edith was lively and sparkling, yes, but she also had perfect manners and an easy grace, instilled, no doubt, by her mother. She was flawlessly groomed, yet she dressed with understatement. Even those who scrutinized her very carefully had to give their grudging approval.

But would Edith, who had lived in exceptional style in Chicago and New York, find New Orleans too provincial? Would the vivacious, intelligent, sophisticated heiress soon be bored by the slow, time-honored ways of the South?

Two novels gained popular recognition during that first year of the Sterns' marriage: John Galsworthy's *A Family Man* and D. H. Lawrence's *Women in Love*. Edgar and Edith, despite their disparate backgrounds, might well have defined their relationship by these two titles. Edgar quickly became the most devoted kind of family man, reveling in his new role; Edith continued to display the same adoring affection for her husband that had caused her to fall in love with him.

At the same time, Edith set out to learn more about the city that Edgar loved so well. Inquisitive by nature, she sought out all the information she could find regarding New Orleans customs, taboos, and idiosyncrasies. The people of New Orleans could do little more than be impressed. Edith was a quick study. When it came to flowers, which she found an obsession among the natives, she had her own extraordinary way with arrangements, inherited from her mother. She could select a single bloom, strip it from a profusion of foliage, place it in just the proper vase, and set it in just the right place to allow it to speak with advantage.

(Nor was Mrs. Rosenwald's talent limited to flowers. A vivid picture of her remains etched in the mind of Lillian Feibelman, dating from a visit with Edith in her parents' home.

She had called on Mrs. Rosenwald in the afternoon and was duly ushered into her bedroom. "I found her propped up in bed, amidst a profusion of lace, fancy pillows, ribbons and sundry frou frou. She was busily stirring a meatball mixture in a large copper bowl while an impeccably uniformed maid was adding cream, drop by drop, with total concentration on her task. I suppose we had meatballs for dinner that evening.")

Edith never distinguished herself in the culinary arts, but memories of her brand of entertainment still persist. Hortense Hirsch, her friend of long standing, remembers visiting Edith shortly after Edith had come to New Orleans: "When we arrived, we were met at the station by a big brass band and immediately ushered into a whirl of unforgettable parties. But then Edith would take us on a tour of the city and show us *her* New Orleans." That included, of course, the *Vieux Carré*, the French Quarter, which spread in three directions to boundaries at Canal Street, Esplanade, and Rampart Street.

"Do you know how the city got its name?" Edith would ask. It was, to be sure, *Nouvelle-Orléans* in honor of Louis Phillipe, duc d'Orléans. But that is getting ahead of the story. In 1699 Jean Baptiste LeMoyne, Sieur de Bienville, was entrusted by the French government to find a site on the "Fleuve Saint Louis," or the Mississippi—the "Great Water," as the Indians called it. He chose an old Indian village overlooking the crescent. This site also had a bayou that connected it to beautiful Lake Pontchartrain.

Edith went on to speak of the many influences that converged there, each leaving a distinctive imprint on the city's architecture—for example, the *portes cochères*, with which the French were wont to adorn their homes and the *ollas* in which the Spanish potted their plants. "Older citizens still speak the *patois*, the unique French jargon of their ancestors," added Edith, "and the balconies are called galleries. Creole cuisine includes over 300 original recipes. You won't have time to taste them all," Edith went on, "but, we'll do our best." And the party would be on its way to Rue St. Louis.

There, Antoine's, the venerable eating establishment, first opened its doors to gourmands and gourmets of the world in 1840. Its unprepossessing facade at first glance conveys little of what can be expected of one of the world's great eating places.

Neither marble nor gilt nor velvet portieres adorn the simple wooden doorways. Instead, the door is inlaid with beveled glass, the floor is checkered in tiles of black and white, and guests are ushered to round tables to sit in simple chairs with oval backrests and cane seats. Old fluted gas lamps have been converted to electricity with no loss of charm. Edith especially loved the table in a front corner from which she could see "the world" entering Antoine's. The waiters knew Edgar well and soon deferred to Edith, too.

At times she would lunch or dine in one of the many private rooms—the "Dungeon," where slaves were kept at one time; or perhaps the famous Rex Room, named after the king of the Mardi Gras, where the decor consists of crowns and scepters and other regalia of royalty used in previous Mardi Gras processions and the royalty of the years past are captured in framed photographs. There are empty frames for royalty to come. Edith would point to these portraits with a smile, as well as to the photo depicting the Duchess of Windsor and King Edward VIII—she curtsying, he bowing to the royal heads of the Mardi Gras on his visit.

"Well, now," Edith would say, "let's have some lunch." She would peruse carefully the extensive menu printed exclusively in French, a bill of fare that has not changed in many a decade. Waiters unfailingly take orders without notes of any kind, a training that requires a minimum of ten years. And Edith displayed a thorough knowledge of the menu and of the names of the *spécialités de la maison,* and how the names originated. She had stored the vast array of knowledge that guide books try to point out. She might remark on the cellar, which stocks well over five thousand bottles, the oldest brandy bearing the date 1811. Or she might casually wonder which of the four hundred cookbooks owned by Antoine's had been used in the creation of the spectacular cuisine of the day. And, often, she would recommend the Pompano en Papillote, both because it was delicious and because of the story behind it. The fish is cooked in a uniquely designed paper bag to retain its flavor and juices, and during preparation the bag inflates like a hot-air balloon. What a perfect dish to create for the visit of a distinguished French balloonist!

Then she would escort her guests, fortified by these diverse comestibles, on a walking tour. They would amble along Conti and St. Louis Streets and on to Royal and to Jackson Square. Or they might stroll as far as Toulouse Street at Bourbon. Edith would point out the old Oliver Mansion, designed in 1837 and still considered one of the finest structures in New Orleans. And she would add that the street was named for the Comte de Toulouse, son of Louis XIV, after whom Louisiana was named.

Gesturing in the air, she would ask her guests to "Look at the light here, the color. . . ." She became an early patron of William Woodward, New Orleans' own impressionist, who managed to infuse his gentle romanticism into his dedication to realism, creating a record of New Orleans that caused critics to compare him to Maurice Utrillo, "documenter of Montmartre." In fact, New Orleans is a city just made for the canvas of the impressionist. When Degas visited, he found time to paint several of his masterpieces, among them *The Cotton Market at New Orleans*, and he wrote excitedly to his fellow artists Henri Rouart and James Tissot,

> Fair France still has a quarter of a foot in Louisiana. Villas with columns in different styles, painted white, in gardens of magnolias, orange trees, banana trees; Negroes in old clothes, rosy white children in black arms, omnibuses drawn by mules, the tall funnels of steamboats towering at the end of the main street, that is a bit of the local colour. Everything is beautiful here in this world of people. Manet would see lovely things – even more than I do.

When it came to art, Edith instinctively favored bolder strokes and primary colors. Yet her favorite flower was the modest lily-of-the-valley – not, as one might assume, the more dramatic rose or carnation – the tiny, bell-shaped blossoms that can grow in the shade of a shrub, making their presence known by their pervasive, unforgettable perfume.

New Orleans after dark was Edgar's domain. He escorted his guests on "a night in New Orleans." They would dine at Antoine's or Galatoire's, where, despite the fact that reservations were never taken, a table would always miraculously materialize for Edgar and his guests, and it could be counted on to be a good one. Again, at times, he would spirit his entourage to an unprepossessing place uptown, Pascal's Manale. As only natives knew, here one could find barbecued shrimp that rank among the best in the world. Huge bibs would be tied around the necks of the diners, and soup plates full of unpeeled shrimp in piquant sauce would appear, accompanied by freshly baked, crusty French bread.

Then they were customarily driven to the Quarter, Edith exhorting them to "walk off the shrimp." Soft laughter emanated from the wrought-iron enclosed courtyards; the ladies of the night went slinking by as sailors ogled. And the Sterns and their guests would be enthralled by a beat that nowhere in the world sounds better than Bourbon Street, the true cradle of jazz. Here the syncopations brought by the black slaves from Africa mingle with the quadrilles of the early French settlers. The brassy sound of two cornets, a trombone, a clarinet, and a banjo or guitar, a drum, a string bass or tuba carried off into the velvet sky far above the latticed balconies.

They would sometimes sit in one of these jam-packed places, laughing, listening, making small talk about a young jazz musician born in New Orleans who had learned to play the trumpet in a Waifs' Home. His name was Louis Armstrong—better known to those who frequented the Quarter as "Satchmo"—and he had just left for Chicago to join the band led by his childhood friend and early teacher Joe "King" Oliver. Edgar sagely observed that the world would hear from him, and added wryly that he had brought Edith from Chicago in exchange. The Sterns loved jazz and would seek out performances by all the greats in the days when the idiom was young and unspoiled: Coleman Hawkins, Fletcher Henderson—better known as "Smack"—and time and again, Duke Ellington. The clock would strike one and two, and slowly the group would meander toward Jackson Square, admiring the Spanish provincial church with its tall central steeple tower and the two shorter ones flanking it that had been erected in 1794.

From Jackson Square was but a short trip to the Mississippi, where boats large and small stood rocking softly in their berths. Many a night out lasted until dawn. In such a case, it was a time-honored tradition to continue to the French

Market. They might repair to the Morning Call where people in evening clothes and work clothes mingled freely and democratically at the counter. At other times, they might prefer the *Café du Monde,* which was open around the clock. On this site, from 1791, stood a Spanish structure housing a meat market. After the Spanish building was destroyed in a hurricane, it was rebuilt by the French in 1813. Since the early 1860's the cavernous interior, consisting of a colonnaded hall, has served the finest *café au lait* and *beignets* (square, French doughnut-like pastries) this side of the Atlantic. Edgar liked to partake of this limited menu sitting outdoors around wrought-iron tables beneath the green-and-white striped awning. There the company would devour the fresh, warm, feather-light *beignets* covered by a snowdrift of fragrant confectioner's sugar; drink the rich, chicory-laced coffee; and watch the dawn breaking over the river.

At dawn, the market would come to life in preparation for the new day. A fresh catch of soft-shelled crabs and crayfish and a bounty of fruits and vegetables would begin to fill the French market stalls. The company would disperse to the cries of the vendors selling their wares in the new morning light.

SEVEN

Fabric of Commitment

THE SPRING OF 1922 was particularly happy for the Sterns. Edith discovered that she was pregnant and, to her delight, that her sister Marion was also expecting in the fall. Their daily conversations dwelled largely on the imminent arrivals. Adele, recognized as an authority since she was already the mother of two sons, dispensed sisterly advice. Augusta and Julius Rosenwald were frequent visitors to both of their "ladies-in-waiting." Their excitement seemed nearly equal to that of the two women, and it was enhanced by the fact that they were particularly fond of Edgar.

For his part, Edgar had formed a deep attachment to his father-in-law, based initially on respect and appreciation. This ripened into heartfelt affection, if not worship.

Edith, delighted at the prospect of a baby, took her condition in her usual no-nonsense manner. She pursued her activities as before, attending public and private luncheons, contrary to the unspoken mores of the time. There was no withdrawal from society for her, even as the heir became all too apparent. Once, in New York, for example, she chose to take lunch with an old friend, Hortense Hirsch, who was also in the "delicate condition." It created something of a stir when both appeared at the Ritz Carlton wearing loose, ugly golf capes. They considered themselves nothing more than trend setters of the *haute monde.*

On September 1, 1922, Edgar and Edith's first child, Edgar B., Jr., was born. Three weeks later, Edith's sister Marion, then Mrs. Alfred Stern of Chicago (though Alfred Stern's family was not related to Edgar's), gave birth to her first child, also a son, who was named Alfred Robert Stern. The sisters eagerly awaited an occasion that would bring them and their infant sons together. It took place several months later in Chicago on a visit to the grandparents. Marion's baby, despite all maternal pride, was, as Marion herself recalls, little short of ugly—a gangly body with a mop of unruly, dark hair falling low across his forehead. Her sister, Adele, picked up the baby and commented, "You do look like Honest Abe." This was among the kinder pronouncements. Ede arrived, carrying Edgar who was blue-eyed, pink-cheeked, dimpled, and gurgling with pleasure. The disparity in looks between the babies notwithstanding, the celebration was hard to hold in check. Marion, recalling the time, emphasized, "My son, too, grew up to be a handsome man, indeed."

The Stern family of New Orleans continued to prosper and grow. Maurice and Hanna had every reason to be satisfied. They rejoiced in the many-faceted achievements of their children. Their eldest son, Walter, became involved in matters concerning Temple Sinai, the same concerns to which his parents had given so much of their loving care. He served as president from 1918 to 1921, during which time the temple celebrated its fiftieth Jubilee Year. The rabbi was the distinguished Max Heller, who generously dedicated the Souvenir Book to the memory of his predecessor, Rabbi James

Koppel Gutheim. Rabbi Heller's daughter-in-law, Mildred, became one of Edith's dearest lifelong friends.

With Edgar's family so deeply involved in the artistic and spiritual growth of New Orleans, it was hardly surprising that both Edgar and Edith, though not observant in any conventional sense, should be swept up in these manifestations of Jewish life. Edith, with her usual thoroughness and curiosity, studied the details of Jewish history, especially as they pertained to New Orleans, and found herself both surprised and delighted. She was astonished to find that Ezekiel Salomon, son of the great Polish-Jewish patriot of the Revolutionary period—Haym Salomon—lived in New Orleans and served there as governor of the United States Branch Bank until his death. And Edith was struck also by the story of another prominent Jew of New Orleans. Different as their life-styles were, Edith felt a special kindred to Judah Touro. Reading his biography from the Jubilee Book of Temple Sinai, she felt drawn to him.

> In the history of American Jewry no name shines with a purer luster than that of Judah Touro; two-thirds of his life were passed in New Orleans. A certain pathos is bound up with his personality, a personality of strange habit, modest reserve and a strong taste for refinement. There were virtually no Jews in New Orleans when he came there in 1803, with the "Black Code" still in force; his most intimate associations seem, almost throughout his life, to have been with non-Jews, among whom he met with devoted friendship. Yet he, the son of a pious Chazan [cantor], deeply attached to his brother in distant Boston, reared after his father's death at the home of his uncle Michael Moses Hays (where he is said to have fallen in love with a cousin, but failed to gain his uncle's consent), he, the lonely bachelor, living in a modest apartment, guiding large enterprises from a small corner in an office, must have yearned now and then for the venerably poetic religious symbols and atmosphere, redolent of his historic associations, that had formed the environment of his early years.
>
> In New Orleans he was one of four bachelors, all of whom lived into high old age, who were said to own, among them, one-eighth of the city's real estate. Like the other three, he was eccentric; he never left New Orleans for one day, except to go to the battlefield of Chalmette; he

would never ride in a carriage after his brother had met with a carriage accident; he never once visited any of the fine shops that served his business. He is described as "not a man of brilliant mind." On the contrary, he was slow and not given to bursts of enthusiasm. He was little fond of hazardous speculation and used to say that he could only be said to have saved a fortune by strict economy where others had spent one by their liberal expenditures. But his saving was not parsimony; only that he had no taste for the wasteful outlay of means on enjoyment which he had no relish for. He had thus the best wines always by him, without drinking them himself; his table, whatever delicacies it bore, had only plain and simple food for him. Of his business methods another friend tells us that "the most tempting opportunities of gain from shattered fortunes which were floating around never caused him, in a single instance, to swerve from the path of plain, straightforward, simple, unbending rectitude." He was an ardent and sincere patriot. He marched to the battle of New Orleans as an inspector of ammunition; a cannon ball having torn a large piece of flesh from his thigh, he was left listless upon the battle-field and only rescued by his friend, Rezin David Shepherd who nursed him in his own house for a year, the patient having to lie on his face for many months and remaining slightly lame for the rest of his life.

A notable act of Judah Touro's public spirit was his donation of $10,000 for the completion of Bunker Hill monument; his liberality gave rise to the well-known stanza about "Amos and Judah, Patriarch and Prophet" and was recognized on the tablet of the monument by an inscription prepared by John Quincy Adams, Daniel Webster, Joseph Story, Edward Everett, and Franklin Dexter.

Judah Touro's deeply rooted religious temperament came to the fore in his enlightened generosity to his friend "Parson" Clapp. The Reverend Theodore Clapp's "Recollections During Thirty-Five Years of Residence" throws much interesting light on New Orleans conditions of the first half of the 19th century. Though he left the Presbyterian church a heretic, attaching himself first to the Congregationalists, then to the Universalists, he is probably not too self-complacent when he reports that "it was a usual saying among my orthodox friends that the merchants and planters who came to New Orleans during the healthy months to transact business never left the city without going to the American Theater, the French opera, and Parson Clapp's church." It is characteristic of Clapp's religious attitudes that he quotes with cordial endorsement the saying attributed to Dr. [Thomas] Chalmers, the great leader of the religious secession in Scotland, that "all right-hearted persons are pious in the sight of God, whether Hebrew, Christian, Pagan or Deistical in regard to mere creed or abstract opinion," a saying which bears a striking resemblance to the old Tosefta principle which teaches that: "The pious of all nations have a share in (the blessing of) the world to come." Mr. Clapp often heard Touro say that "though an Israelite to the bottom of my soul, it would give me sincere pleasure to see all the churches flourishing in their respective ways, and I am heartily sorry that they do not more generally fraternize with love and help each other."

Judah Touro proved the sincerity of these broad sentiments by rescuing his friend's church from debt when it became known that the First Congregational Church was in dire financial straits. When the congregation's efforts to cancel its heavy mortgage proved inadequate, he prevented foreclosure by providing the needed sum; he never called his loan, but gave further assistance, befriending, to the end, the minister who had his confidence and admiration. It was pathetic, under these circumstances, that Judah Touro should not have been able "to fulfill his wish for a place to perform his devotions" until he had reached the age of seventy-six. "The day of the consecration of the Touro synagogue," claimed Rabbi Gutheim at the dedication of the second edifice, "was the proudest day in his life." Judah Touro became a regular attendant after his inconspicuous fashion. Declared Clapp, "This gentleman was the humblest man whom I have ever been acquainted with."

He died in his 80th year, having been confined to his bed about ten days. During the days of his apparent unconsciousness, the *Shema* was often recited to him and very frequently he appeared to recognize the sacred sounds and to take part in the solemn exercises. "The funeral," the New Orleans Bee reports, "was, by his directions, marked with utmost simplicity. No invitations were issued (referring, probably, to the Creole custom of mailing black-bordered notices). The offered military escort was declined and no regular pall-bearers were appointed. The coffin was destitute of all ornaments and trappings: yet the funeral train was immense, every carriage in the city was engaged." There was a far more elaborate funeral at Newport whither the body was transported. In the meantime, the will of Judah Touro, a most notable instrument, had been published. It disposed of a large fortune in a manner which bore out the loyalty of the decedent's friendship and the catholicity of his interests.

It is worth noting, after one surveys the wide and varied scope of this beneficence, that the will devotes to Jewish work $205,000 and to Christian non-sectarian causes $148,000. The residuary legatee was Rezin D. Shepherd, who planned to devote his legacy, some two to three hundred thousand dollars, to the "improvement of Canal Street and the establishment of almshouses." A little earth from the Holy Land, a present from a Christian friend, was placed into the coffin. Over the grave a granite obelisk was erected which bears a Hebrew inscription and this epitaph:

> The last of his name
> He inscribed in the Book of Philanthropy
> To be remembered forever.

Edith was deeply moved, as Edgar had always been. Though such humble simplicity was not their style, they always offered the best of human kindness to their friends and guests. All of their servants remarked on the fact that they could eat anything they wanted in the house, and no special menus of foods diminished in quality were ever given them, as was frequently the case in the service of other homes. Patriotism had always been a part of both their lives, and nonpartisan support to all worthy causes had helped shape both their personalities. Soon it would be seen that when it came to the enhancement of the beauty of their beloved city, no commitment would be too much.

The rich heritage of New Orleans' past and the enjoyment the present offered were constant nourishment for Edith's development. Not parsimony, but a kind of puritanism, enforced especially by her mother, was a trait of her upbringing. The children at home might have poked a little good-natured fun at their parents' frugality, but they seemed to understand the underlying values.

Edith was fond of telling what may have been an apocryphal story about the winter she lost one of her warm gloves. She was too apprehensive to report its loss at home, so she switched the remaining glove back and forth from one hand to the other "till spring crept over the window sill." There was no hint of resentment toward her parents in this or any of the other such stories that all the children had to tell.

On her way to Vassar, for example, Marion stopped over for a brief visit with Edith in New York. The elder sister scrutinized the collegiate wardrobe. *"Those* are your clothes?" she asked incredulously, though she was quite familiar with her mother's homespun touches when it came to "made-over serviceable clothing." Without further ado, she spirited Marion straight to Manhattan's most fashionable stores, acquiring what she later termed "decent clothes" for Marion. That evening, she phoned Chicago, apprising her parents that a number of bills were on the way, following the completion of a successful shopping spree. No word of recrimination materialized.

Quite the contrary, it became a matter of some amusement and was generally applauded. There was already a strong hint of the fierce independence and the loving stubbornness beneath Edith's alluring surface. She was to perform a similar service for Marion a few years later when she bought her a stunning yellow cocktail dress, which Marion still remembers fondly, fussing with the latter's coiffure until it met her rigid standards. When she also removed her sister's eyeglasses, Marion demurred, "But I can't see." The peremptory retort was, "You don't have to see; they have to see *you.*"

If the tale of Judah Touro evoked empathy, the story of another leading Jewish personage caused Edith some disquiet. This tale, too, she found in its essential outline in the Jubilee Book.

> The other eminent Judah, Judah Benjamin, who adds luster to the chronicles of New Orleans ... brilliant jurist, statesman and writer, probably never belonged to a Jewish (or any other) congregation. While he was proud of his Jewish descent, his adult years seem to have known little of sectarian beliefs, though he was not without religious convictions. He came to New Orleans at the age of 17 with less than five dollars in his pocket, unable to finish a course at Yale. He coached pupils while learning law; at the age of 21 he married one of his pupils, a Creole girl, beautiful, witty and accomplished, a devout and ardent Catholic. He rapidly mounted to undisputed preeminence at the bar and rose by swift stages until he retired to sugar planting. In 1852 he returned to a political career to the U. S. Senate and was declared by Charles Sumner "the most brilliant orator in the United States."

To touch briefly upon his career during the Civil War, he rose from the position of Attorney-General in the Confederate cabinet to that of Secretary of State. In that role he became President Davis's chief confidential adviser. In the ghastly dissolution of the "Lost Cause" he considered himself a homeless outcast, spending 23 days in an open boat, without shelter, foundering off the coasts of Florida, the Bahamas, and Cuba, finally crossing the Atlantic and reaching England. In the annals of jurisprudence it ranks as a unique experience to find a man who had reached preeminence in his field in one country, distinguishing himself at the bar of another highly civilized country to whose law schools he had come as a student in his 55th year. Moreover, he passed his courses in less than five months; two years later he published a treatise, "Benjamin on Sales," which ranks as a classic on both sides of the Atlantic. Seven years after his arrival he became Queen's Counsel, the only man of whom it can be said that he held conspicuous leadership at the bar of two countries.

Edith could well understand the rapid rise of Judah Benjamin in his chosen profession, along with the unquestioning loyalty he gave to country and cause. But Judah Benjamin had also written on slavery, and that was more problematic. While jurisprudence consistently classified the slave as property in the enjoyment of which the master must be protected, Benjamin quoted Roman law to the effect that "slavery is against the law of nature, and, although sanctioned by the law of nations, it is so sanctioned as a local or municipal institution of binding force within the limits of the nation that chooses to establish it, having no force or binding effect beyond the jurisdiction of such nations." That part was to the good. But Benjamin was a slaveholder on his own plantation, though it is said "he left none but kindly memories and romantic legends of the days of glory on the old place." To Edith, a product of the Middle West and a frequent visitor to Tuskegee, that was an enigma. While she absorbed the biography of the man and left it to be dealt with at some later date, on a personal level, she was already beginning to frame it in terms of a larger question.

Mardi Gras represented the apex of New Orleans' social life. Edgar took for granted the ease with which he moved among his non-Jewish friends, but he understood, too, that this did not include forays into the realm of Mardi Gras activities. The tacit "off limits" signs were likewise unquestioned by all native sons and daughters, and as soon as the revels ended, it was equally assumed, the barriers would once more come down. Much as Edith loved New Orleans' beauty and gentility, its appreciation of the arts and all that it had to offer, she resented this flaw.

Once more, the recollection of her father's activities gave direction to her thinking. Julius Rosenwald was approached in 1910 for a donation to a building fund for a Young Men's Christian Association that would serve blacks in Chicago. In those days, when no blacks could eat in white restaurants, much less spend a night in a decent hotel in most parts of America, this proposed YMCA would provide a place where blacks and whites could meet, and where prominent visiting black artists, scientists, and educators, among others, could find decent overnight accommodations. Rosenwald's reply to the committee that called on him came as a shock to its members: "I will give you $25,000 for a YMCA building for colored people in any city in the United States where an additional $75,000 is raised among white and colored people."

Reminded by the committee that no Jew was allowed to serve on the national or local boards of any YMCA, he said that he nevertheless wished to help and would encourage other Jews of means to render financial support as well. When the Negro "Y" in Chicago opened, Rosenwald's speech made a deep impression on those gathered:

> The man who hates a black man because he is black has the same spirit as he who hates a poor man because he is poor. It is the spirit of caste. I am the inferior of any man whose rights I trample under my feet. Men are not superior by accident of race or color, they are superior who have the best heart, the best mind. Superiority is born of honesty, of virtue, of charity, and above all, of the love of liberty.

Rosenwald's offer attracted national notice and garnered praise from many, including President William Howard Taft, who wanted a similar "Y" for Washington, D.C. Rosenwald soon expanded his offer to include funds covering a quarter of the cost of buildings for black women as well as men. In the course of the next ten years, he donated $712,000 in twenty-five communities; in response to his challenge, some $6,000,000 was raised for this work.

In light of this, Edith could hardly accept the presence of prejudice. She was never afraid to display the power of her convictions and in later life would have the courage to dine openly with Clay Shaw when the latter was wrongly charged with having played a part in the assassination of President John F. Kennedy.

A little-known fact concerning Julius Rosenwald is that he was among the first to contribute to the Leo M. Frank defense fund. Frank, a Southern Jew, had been accused of the murder of a fourteen-year-old girl who was an employee in his uncle's factory. The sentence was commuted by Georgia's governor, John Slaton, as the evidence pointed more to the fact that Frank was falsely accused because he was a Jew than to any real wrongdoing. Despite that, Frank was lynched by a mob in Atlanta in 1915. Sixty-seven years later, in 1982, an eyewitness admitted that he had been afraid to come forward and name the true culprit at the time. J. R.'s interest in the Frank case may have been yet another reason that Edith felt so adamant about dining with Shaw so many years later.

Nor was Edgar unmoved by the participation of his in-laws and the feelings of his wife on the question of equality. As president of the New Orleans Cotton Exchange, he was weighted down with a multitude of responsibilities, yet he felt inclined toward one more when he was offered the trusteeship of Tuskegee Institute. The world was becoming smaller in some ways, though the barriers would not be broken down, at least in legal terms, until the second half of the twentieth century and the advent of the civil-rights movement. Direct trans-atlantic communication had also become possible, and Edgar was very much aware of it. He was the first to make a telephone call from New Orleans to England when he talked from the floor of the New Orleans Cotton Exchange to the Liverpool Cotton Exchange.

It would be some time still before Edith would remove her kid gloves to fight tough in the political arena for the causes she believed in. But the values that would cause her to fight were deeply instilled in her already. Had not her father termed her "the lion of my flock"?

Edith in her early twenties, posing
in her electric car.

EIGHT

Newcomb School

*T*HOSE WHO ARE CRITICAL of the wealthy and privileged accuse them of pursuing selfish pleasures while entrusting the care of their children to nurses and governesses. Edith Stern was perhaps not the most maternal of mothers, if the word conveys an image of a woman who cannot bear to be out of range of her children or who constantly fusses and fawns over them. Yet there appears to be a double standard in evaluating the degree of parental caring as applied to the wealthy compared with the impecunious.

If a mother works outside the home to augment the family income, or to provide for her children's education, she is praised as unselfish. When a woman for whom financial concerns have been removed determines that her children may best be served by having a well-trained person care for their physical needs, she is frequently condemned. It is, unwisely, overlooked that such a mother may still spend whatever time remains in a meaningful way with her children, even as she pursues her chosen occupations.

Edith Stern totally involved herself in anything she undertook, perhaps to the point of "overprogramming" her children and grandchildren. Bill Hess, her grandson and the "apple of her eye," remembers visits to the stately Stern mansion in New Orleans. Complete lists of activities were planned for the duration of their stay. Picnics, plays, games, the circus—all with children of their own age and every detail thought out well in advance.

His memory may shed light on Edith's motivations much earlier when her own children had reached nursery-school age. She took a long and hard look at the options available and was pleased with none of them. Unlike many of her affluent friends, she did not take the line of least resistance and simply turn over her children to a governess. Although nurseries for preschool children in New Orleans were unknown at that time (aside from the custodial care provided for the underprivileged at a settlement house), Edith was aware that small children need the company of their peers and she realized how beneficial this could be to a child's intellectual and physical development. With the help and participation of some friends who found themselves in a similar position, Edith set out to pioneer such a school.

One member of this coterie, Lillian Feibelman, recalls how the head of Newcomb's Philosophy Department, Dr. Martin TenHoor, took umbrage at the thought of well-to-do ladies disposing of their offspring in this manner from 9 AM to noon each day. Castigating them in a newspaper editorial, he described how "the leisure ladies park their babies while they golf, play bridge, etc., etc." Such attacks, notwithstanding, the school developed and prospered, its waiting list eventually numbering in the hundreds.

Edith's friend Irma (Mrs. Herman L.) Barnett described the decisive way in which Edith worked to create the school.

> Edith discovered and took a lease on a small building not in use, adjacent to Newcomb College campus. Some dozen of her friends' children were enrolled. Graduate students from the Newcomb School of Sociology were hired to supervise the children. Thus the New Orleans Nursery School came into being in 1926, the first of its kind south of the Mason-Dixon line and among the first in the entire

country. Two years later, Edith acquired a five-room cottage, helped to equip it, and it still stands under a row of shade trees on the corner of Plum and Audubon Streets, across from Newcomb College.

Edith went beyond providing funds for the school and the playground. She was ready at any time to confer with parents or teachers, especially Rena Wilson, who subsequently became director of the school. Through long association they became friends, and Miss Wilson turned to Edith when problems arose. Although not a trained educator, Edith had a healthy grasp of the fundamental needs of small children. She understood that a child away from family and home for the first time had to learn to associate comfortably with other children. She required a place where children would have a large, safe playground; would be exposed to fresh air and sunshine; and would be as free as possible from adult supervision. Nonetheless, she desired that the children be under constant, though unobtrusive, surveillance. The school became a place where flights of fancy were encouraged, where old packing cases became ships and horses, where play with others was fostered, and where a sense of sharing and obedience was firmly instilled.

When, in the spring of 1929, Rena Wilson, a young psychology student working in the nursery school, met the president of the board, she was understandably nervous. She was somewhat awed not only by Edith Stern's stature but also by her keen understanding of young children, an expertise usually reserved for professionals. She soon learned that she could relax and developed confidence as the conversation took a more spontaneous and animated turn. Edith, in turn, was impressed by her keen intellect and obvious love and dedication. Such meetings would continue for the next forty-one years. When the Depression threatened the operation of the school in 1933, Edith and the board provided Rena with an alternative. She could operate the facility privately, separate from Newcomb. Rena wrote of this in later years:

> It was during the period when I operated the Nursery School privately that I came to know Mrs. Stern best. In every way she offered her support during those fragile

Depression years. With her encouragement and advice and her financial assistance, she made it possible for members of the staff to study each summer. During the school year, 1939-40, Dr. Frederick Hard, Dean of Newcomb College, with the authority of the Tulane Board of Administrators, sought the incorporation of the Nursery School as part of Newcomb College. This was envisioned as an adjunct to the Psychology Department. With joy I communicated this great piece of news to Mrs. Stern and we rejoiced together. . . .

In 1957, when the school's need for a new home became obvious, Edith Stern was again in the forefront, and a message greeted Miss Wilson on her return from vacation: Mrs. Stern would make a challenge grant.

I floated on a little pink cloud while waiting to burst upon the Dean of Newcomb College with the good news: Mrs. Stern had decided to make a challenge grant of $75,000 which carried the stipulation that the amount of $7,500 was to be raised among parents and friends of alumni to help equip the new school. It reflected Mrs. Stern's exact thinking as to gift-giving. It did not take long before the amount was over-subscribed.

The new building was completed and dedicated in May 1959. Edith had taken a hand in its planning, along with Polly Stern, her son Edgar's wife. Edith was delighted that Polly had displayed a deep interest in the school, and all who worked with the young matron praised her quiet, winning ways and the total dedication she brought to the various tasks she undertook.

The architect of the new school was Dr. John Dinwiddie, and Rena Wilson brought to the project many of her own innovative ideas. Rena retired in 1970 after four decades of nurturing young people in their first stirrings of intellectual curiosity, at a time when she could see the offspring of the children who had initially been entrusted to her care. She stood with tearful pride in a flower-filled room receiving the grateful accolades she so richly deserved. Sharing the moment with her was the woman who so long ago had recognized in that young psychology student the potential of a great teacher.

Four years later Miss Wilson had occasion to call again on Edith Stern. This time she came to offer what comfort she could. Edith had just suffered the grievous loss of her daughter Audrey. Rena Wilson, sensitive to intrusion at such a time, did not plan to stay long. It was Edith who detained her.

As the two women spoke, their talk turned to children— their ways, their moods; then to Audrey, the round-faced, chubby little girl in a light dress, coloring reams of white pages in an effort to give expression to the unbridled fantasy and talent of her childhood dreams. Before them opened vistas of long ago, of children playing in the sun-dappled garden of the new nursery school, when all of them—Edith, Rena, and the children—had seemed so young, so full of visions and ideas. Dusk fell over Longue Vue as the two embraced and bid each other an emotional farewell.

Julius and Augusta Rosenwald.

NINE

Country Day

J ULIUS ROSENWALD, in 1928, apparently was giving much thought to the future course of his philanthropic endeavors. Shortly after it was written, Edith received a copy of the letter that gave new direction to the Julius Rosenwald Fund and gave Edith a new awareness of her father's work.

Chicago, Ill.
April 30, 1928

Trustees, Julius Rosenwald Fund

Gentlemen:

I am happy to present herewith to the Trustees of the Julius Rosenwald Fund certificates for twenty thousand shares of the stock of Sears, Roebuck & Co.

When the Julius Rosenwald Fund was created and sums of money turned over, it was provided that the principal as well as the income might be spent from time to time at the direction of the Trustees and it was my expectation from the beginning that the entire principal should be spent within a reasonable period of time. My experience is that Trustees controlling large funds are not only desirous of conserving principal but often favor adding to it from surplus income.

I am not in sympathy with this policy of perpetuating endowments and believe more good can be accomplished by expending funds as Trustees find opportunities for constructive work than by storing up large sums of money for long periods of time. By adopting a policy of using the Fund within this generation, we may avoid those tendencies toward bureaucracy and a formal or perfunctory attitude toward the work which almost invariably develops in organizations which prolong their existence indefinitely. Coming generations can be relied upon to provide for their own needs as they arrive.

In accepting the shares of stock now offered, I ask that the Trustees do so with the understanding that the entire Fund in the hands of the Board both income and principal be expended within twenty-five years of the time of my death.

Sincerely yours,
Julius Rosenwald

Edith and Edgar had special reason to be concerned with this communication. Aside from her father speaking openly of his mortality, there was the fact that Edgar B. Stern, president of the New Orleans Cotton Exchange and chairman of the New Orleans Community Chest, had also been appointed as one of the nine trustees of the Julius Rosenwald Fund. Edgar would have input as to the expenditure of the vast amounts that the Fund now represented, an awesome responsibility.

The Fund was indisputably a force for good. It instigated, for example, the research that ultimately led to the establishment of such crucially needed health services as the Blue Cross. But it was just one of the many ways in which Julius was reaching out to help others. At Sears he organized the first profit-sharing plan for employees, and, as far as is known, the first pension plan. Both became models that other large corporations followed to the great benefit of American workers. Nor did this kind of work go unrecognized. In the fall of 1928, eight distinguished pioneers of American industry were honored. The list read as follows:

George Eastman—Photography
Henry Ford—Automobiles
Orville Wright and Glenn H. Curtiss—Aviation
Thomas A. Edison—Invention
Charles M. Schwab—Iron and Steel
Henry S. Firestone—Rubber
Julius Rosenwald—Merchandising

As Jacob Schiff, the renowned New York financier, had declared earlier, "I believe there is no one who has done so much to make the name of a Jew respected, to raise it, not only in the eyes of our countrymen, but everywhere, as Julius Rosenwald."

About that time Edgar Stern received the letter that would prove a catalyst for one of his chief interests. On the surface it was routine enough. Dozens of similar letters crossed his desk in the course of a week. Yet this particular appeal for money was also quite different. There were two Negro colleges in New Orleans: Straight College on Esplanade Avenue (subsequently on Canal Street) sponsored by the American Missionary Association; and New Orleans College, under the aegis of the Methodist Episcopal Church. Both were inadequate within their existing framework and felt the need to merge and relocate. The letter that reached Edgar Stern was dated March 1928, and written by President O'Brien of Straight College, who asked that Edgar consider making a contribution of $500 to an emergency fund for the school. Edgar replied promptly:

> I am favorably inclined about what you are doing. However, if $500 is all you need, I should think your church boards could provide it. If you are ever interested in bigger things, you'll find me ready to help.

Edgar was a Southern gentleman from the spats on his high gloss shoes to the tip of his cane. Despite a fine, open mind, honed by the Harvard years, he could by no means be called a liberal. Yet he had strong convictions about right and wrong, along with a keen perception of social injustice, the debris of which was all around him. He was now married to a woman whom he lovingly called his "Yankee Creole" and who was never reticent about expressing her opinions. And he had been amply exposed to Julius Rosenwald's "radical" ideas. But few things peeved him more than the intimation that his involvement in providing quality education for blacks came on the heels of his marriage or his exposure to his father-in-law. In fact, his interest in the Tuskegee Institute was of long standing by the time of his marriage. And he, along with Monte Lemann, had been a student of Dr. James Dillard at Tulane.

While at that university, Dillard, a Greek and Latin scholar, became concerned with the city's need for a new public library. He chaired the fund-raising committee and succeeded in collecting the necessary monies with the help of the Andrew Carnegie Fund. Only after the library was completed did Dillard learn, to his astonishment, that it was open to whites only. He returned to the Carnegie Fund and obtained more money for a branch library for blacks.

When he resigned from Tulane, it was to become director of the Anna T. Jeannes Fund, set up in Philadelphia to help Southern blacks become better educated. Dillard spent twenty-five years in this position, once remarking, "I spent all that time persuading county politicians." The results of his work, however, did not go unnoticed: the new black university to succeed Straight College and New Orleans University was to be named Dillard University.

Upon receipt of Edgar B. Stern's challenge, the two church boards, Congregational and Methodist, asked Edgar to serve as chairman of the board and to direct the fund-raising activities for the new university. From 1930 to 1935, while the plans were laid and the funds raised, the two colleges continued to operate. Under Edgar's direction, a grant of $500,000 was obtained from the Rockefeller Fund; another $500,000 was forthcoming from the Congregational and Methodist churches; the Rosenwald Fund gave $250,000; and another $250,000 was raised in New Orleans. Edgar later observed that he had been chosen chairman principally because "The Congregationalists and the Methodists didn't trust each other, so they elected a Jew."

It was decided from the outset that Flint Goodrich Hospital would be the first unit of the new university. Its goals and objectives were clear and simple. Planning for a vital school of higher education took far more consideration, however. Searching abroad, the board considered thirty applicants for the position of director of the hospital, deciding, in the end, to bring Albert Water Dent from Atlanta's Morehouse College, where he had served as secretary of the alumni.

Even at age twenty-seven, Dent was an imposing, majestic presence. He carried his six-foot frame with a ramrod agility, and his finely drawn facial features were those of an urbane, highly intelligent man. Added to this, his resonant voice imparted quiet authority to his words. He remained an imposing presence until his death in 1984.

On the part of the board, it was a daring move. Dent was considered, even by some of the board members, to be a "young upstart with no experience." Moreover, he was being placed in a position usually reserved for medical men; the choice of a superintendent for a hospital rarely, if ever, went to a lay administrator.

But if it was daring on the part of the board, it was equally daring on his part to accept the position. He arrived in New Orleans with a wife who was six-months pregnant, and taking a cut in salary—$3,200 as opposed to the $3,900 he was earning at Morehouse. But he took the risk willingly in exchange for this challenging opportunity.

The Flint Goodrich Hospital opened its doors on Louisiana Avenue (where it stands to this day) on February 1, 1932. Dent offered postgraduate courses of study for practicing physicians each summer; and within five years some twenty percent of the Negro physicians from an eight-state Southern region attended at least once. Dent brought distinguished black doctors from around the nation as faculty so that no one would think that blacks would be taught only by white men, but his faculty also included white physicians and professors from Tulane and Louisiana State University medical schools. In the early 1930's, salaries and tuition were low. Faculty members received their travel expenses and free room and board. Dent treasured a renewal pledge made by Edgar B. Stern to Flint Goodrich Hospital that arrived on a postal card written from somewhere on the Sterns' trip around the world.

In 1936 Dent's position was expanded to include the business management of Dillard University. For the first four years, William Stewart Nelson served as the first president of Dillard. When he left to accept another position, several important educators turned down the offer of the presidency mainly because the university had no endowment. For one full year the position remained unfilled. Finally, the position was offered to Dent.

Despite his outstanding performance as an administrator, two black trustees of the university voted against Dent's appointment and told him so after. Their votes were influenced by the fact that Dent had no doctoral degree, only a bachelor of arts from Morehouse. Once in the chair, however, even these doubters gave Dent their full support. It was support well rewarded. Dent served for twenty-eight years, resigning in 1969 after a distinguished career. From first to last, he found Edgar Stern a steady support.

One Sunday morning, Edgar called to say that he was bringing visitors to the campus. The first person to whom Dent was introduced was John D. Rockefeller, Jr. The rest, it turned out, were members of the Rockefeller Foundation. As they toured the campus, one man fell behind to talk with Dent. His name was Robert D. Calkins. Calkins asked Dent about major needs of the university. "We desperately need library books; and we should have a science building, but so far neither has materialized," said Dent. The stranger recommended that Dent put all this in writing, which he promptly did, addressing it to Mr. Calkins at the Foundation. In a few weeks a letter arrived from Dent's new friend offering half the science building at $200,000 and half the needed books at $25,000, with the provision that Dent find ways to raise the balance. He reported this news to Edgar Stern, who asked, "Isn't that a bit heavy for you to take on?" Dent replied, "Well, with your help. . . ." And Edgar agreed to think about it.

A short while later, Edgar appeared in Dent's office with a check for $100,000. He asked how the balance might be raised. Dent took a leaf from the Rosenwald/Stern books and suggested that the Stern gift be predicated on matching gifts from each of the two member church groups. Both agreed, and before long Dillard had its science building and its books. Dent observed that Edgar didn't "believe in giving all of what was needed, or asked for. He liked to bargain."

On such bargains, Dillard rose. Dent set as one of his first goals the raising of an endowment fund of $3,000,000. This was accomplished in less than three years. Then he turned his energies to finding more money for the campus and several important buildings. Edgar continued to lend his name and his hand. "He quickly saw and grasped the needs of people," Dent said. "He didn't require convincing."

A depth of mutual respect and friendship grew up between Albert Dent and the Sterns. He was a frequent guest at their home, at a time when blacks seldom were considered fit company in New Orleans society, and few whites had so much as a single black as a close friend. "He always addressed me as Dr. Dent. All the other trustees called me Albert," Dent recalled.

In 1964, at the annual meeting of the Board of Trustees, it was announced that in 1969 the university would be one hundred years old (counting the years of Straight College and New Orleans University). Dent presented a plan to culminate in 1969, a study to include the school's past, its present, and a long hard look at its next hundred years. After the meeting, Edith called to ask about the cost of this study. A short while later, the Stern Fund forwarded a check for the necessary $25,000. Black education had few better friends.

Some might find this a remarkable pursuit for a Southern gentleman. Edgar took it in his stride. He was a man who loved to shop for neckties (it is said he possessed nearly two hundred), who was never without cigars (imported from Cuba in three sizes to match his meals—breakfast, lunch, and dinner); who indulged in two martinis before dinner ("A bird can't fly on one wing," he used to say). This, then, was the man who issued the challenge to his black neighbors to take full advantage of his philanthropic means—the challenge that led to the creation of Dillard University for blacks. As the black chauffeur observed proudly of the many times he drove his employer to the board meetings of the black college, "But, my, he sure looked handsome when he went to Dillard!"

Edith was disturbed in 1928 by the news that her mother, Augusta, needed an operation; nor was the prognosis following the surgery encouraging. The year closed with the publication of John Galsworthy's acclaimed novel *Swan Song;* and the number one song on the *Hit Parade* was "Making Whoopee." It is difficult to imagine two more appropriate titles to close the year of 1928 and open the year 1929. Similarly, in the early days of soaring prosperity of the new year, "Stardust," "Moaning Low," and "Singing in the Rain" were among the most popular songs. For the Rosenwald family it was a year of great personal sorrow. Augusta died in May.

As Edith recovered from her initial grief, she felt instinctively that work and involvement would be the best therapy. She immersed herself in a host of activities. The first and most important of these was the creation of a school that would offer a natural transition from the enrichment and education the Newcomb nursery had given the children. Once more the Sterns gathered a group of parents and set about planning and executing the work. Thanks to a generous contribution from the Sterns, fourteen acres of land were purchased in Metairie, a beautiful wooded section of New Orleans. Edith organized the parents into three task forces. One was to raise money, another to formulate school policy, and a third to find a suitable headmaster.

The work was interrupted abruptly by the collapse of the stock market, which left its mark on both the Rosenwald and Stern fortunes, even though both families managed to keep their losses within reasonable proportions. In fact, evidence reveals that they shared their means generously with those who had lost so much.

Mildred (Mrs. Monte) Lemann, the second wife of Edgar's dearest friend, remembers those days well. She was then Mrs. Lucien Lyons, a young widow with small children. The stock-market crash fairly well wiped out her savings. She had known Edgar before his marriage and now maintained a pleasant, though casual, friendship with Edith. She was one of the parents interested in the new school project. Edith knew of her reduced circumstances and tactfully asked her to become administrative assistant of the school, a position that Mrs. Lyons accepted with alacrity. Before she could assume this position, however, much work remained to be done. The land had to be cleared before construction could begin, a task that enlisted the physical efforts of many of the parents. "There were snakes in the swamps and other crawlies," Mildred Lemann recalls. But the parents worked on undaunted by heat and by tropical foliage that seemed to grow back overnight after a rain.

November came and Edith was struck by an idea. Many children would not be receiving Christmas presents during the coming holiday season. She urged her friends to select among their children's toys those that were still serviceable, perhaps needing no more than a coat of fresh paint, a new ribbon on a doll, or perhaps a new ear on a stuffed toy. The whole collection was brought to one central place and entire families were harnessed to transform them into almost new playthings, enough to delight many children. Men, some of whom were presidents of large corporations or busy lawyers and physicians, could be found wearing old shirts and applying their skills to painting a fire engine or a little wagon with sparkling new red paint. "Poor Boy" sandwiches were served to the assiduous crew. The idea took hold and it became an annual tradition. Henceforth each fall, parents would turn into busy elves in anticipation of Christmas.

The Depression brought about drastic changes in the fabric of everyday life. Many a hitherto pampered lady, who in the traditional Southern manner had been little more than ornamental, was forced to step out into the "real" world to help earn a few additional dollars for the family. Some of them were glad to accept the work that Edith and others sponsored, even killing snakes in the process of clearing swamps to make way for the new school.

The design of the building was Edith's idea. It stands on Park Road at the end of a cul-de-sac, white pillars guarding the entrance. On first glance, it appears to be a plantation home, fashioned of old rosy brick, its low wings rambling to the side and rear connecting patios and long galleries. Flowering bushes set off the facade with its shuttered windows and white front door. The mighty trees around it are covered with drooping Spanish moss that sways gently in the breeze.

The search committee, including Edith, chose as the first headmaster Ralph E. Boothby. By all indications, this young man from Ohio—possessed of a warm heart and genuine love for children—was not only a superb educator but a person of vision. He combined the best of existing traditions with new ideas, fashioning a special brand of education. By way of proof, Mildred Heller points out that her son would come home from college for the holidays, drop his bag in the front hall, and instantly be off to talk with Mr. Boothby.

The school opened with fifty-six pupils, grades one to six, with only seven faculty and staff members. Almost from its inception, and in view of the prevailing economic conditions, it was decided that scholarships should be given.

Along with other friends, Mildred Lemann described the Stern children during the early years at Metairie Park Country Day when she was administrative assistant. Fair-skinned Edgar Jr., who looked most like his handsome father, was something of a dreamer, yet able to ask probing questions even in kindergarten. Once he mused out loud, "Where do school buses go on weekends?" He displayed a natural love and affinity for machines of any kind and would take clocks apart to see what made them tick. His interest in the machines would lead to an interest in communication, which eventually took him into the world of radio and television.

By contrast, Philip was vivacious and constantly in motion. His characteristics more resembled those of his mother. He was particularly adored by his grandfather Julius. Philip was the third of the Stern children, and Edith felt a bit put upon to have had three children within a span of six years. Shortly after his birth, Edgar and Edith went to Europe for several months leaving Philip with a nurse. Later, when Philip's quick wit and incisive mind made him a family favorite, his grandfather observed in jest that he considered it his worst merchandising mistake not to have bought Philip when he could have had him cheaply.

Audrey, the middle child, was a sweet, chubby girl, who fidgeted and wriggled in her seat and was happiest when she could be sketching or painting. Very early, she showed an unusual sense for color and line. The spirit that pervaded Country Day succeeded in bringing out and enriching such childhood interests by permitting free expression. This was one of Mr. Boothby's talents, and it extended through him to the entire school. He advanced the revolutionary concept of requiring no homework until students reached the upper grades, arguing that if children were properly taught at school they would not have to wait for their fatigued parents to explain the lessons to them in the evening. Under a picture of the benign headmaster is a quotation from Ralph Waldo Emerson, "An institution is the lengthened shadow of one man." The statement fits perfectly, though in all fairness it might have been paraphrased to include "and one woman."

Ralph Boothby was headmaster from 1929 to 1956. The progressive methods he instituted eventually influenced almost all the other schools in the city, so that Country Day became a model of progressive education in New Orleans. Today the school extends from kindergarten through the twelfth grade; over the years, buildings have been added so that they now form several quadrangles enclosing the shady, secluded plots where children play and dream and learn.

In an attempt to be of further aid to Mildred Lemann (then Mrs. Lyons), Edith inquired whether "Lady Jane," as she called her, might be interested in solving a problem for her. White Pine Camp, Edith's summer home in the Adirondacks, had become simply too difficult for her to run. She needed help. Wouldn't it be lovely if Lady Jane and her children could have the use of a nice, cool place during the hot oppressive months? She could serve as an unofficial hostess. Lady Jane accepted instantly.

The fact was that Edith had not been well for some time. She had taken on too many activities in the wake of losing her mother. This prompted her to enter the famed Riggs Sanitorium in Massachusetts where she was diagnosed as suffering from an ulcer and exhaustion. Along with the care and rest came the realization that she would have to curtail some of her manifold projects.

TEN

White Pine Camp

*B*EFORE IT CAME INTO the possession of Edith and Adele and their husbands, White Pine had once been placed at the disposal of Calvin Coolidge while he was yet President of the United States. It was referred to as his "New York White House." It was little wonder that Edith needed a competent administrator like Mildred Lyons to direct the facility. A magnificent estate, it consisted of a series of luxurious cabins, each with two bedrooms and two baths. These were scattered among the fragrant pine woods surrounding Oscott Lake, near the Canadian border.

Both the Sterns and the Levys were accustomed to bring members of their regular household retinue, but even this entourage had to be augmented. It took a staff of fourteen to attend to the needs of an average of twenty-four guests. The central building had large living and dining rooms, and, nearby, a tennis court, two boathouses, and a house for the staff. When there was an overflow of guests, they were quartered in the hotel of the tiny neighboring village of Paul Smith.

The two families acquired White Pine in 1930 and owned it until 1946. Friends and relatives looked forward to spending summers there. The prevailing mode was casual, the prime emphasis being on relaxation and fun. One summer, Monte Lemann, in the spirit of the hour, turned his considerable legal talent to the drafting of a set of bylaws for the "White Pine Camp Guest Association, Limited." In this conglomeration of legalese and jest, he classified guests into three categories: Seniors—those who were the "regulars" and had been in attendance at the camp "for not less than two weeks in each of two consecutive years"; Juniors—those who had been guests "for at least two weeks . . . (but excluding mere weekenders)"; and Transients—weekend visitors who "may be referred to for brevity as Worms." The owners or hosts were referred to indulgently as "Conveniences."

The bylaws specifically required that "there shall be no paying guests and no guest will be permitted to incur any expense whatever, except that guests may buy their own postage stamps."

As to a perennial problem of such summer encampments, Monte Lemann specified that "no guest shall be required to hear the same joke or story from the owner or host more than three (3) times in one season." Truly vintage jokes might be "resuscitated by two-thirds vote of the Guests present at a special meeting of the Association after three months' prior notice."

His kindness in this regard, however, was not extended to "Worms," who might be required to listen to repetitions of stories or jokes "without regard to antiquity."

As might be expected, the bylaws were especially strict in regard to the "Conveniences." For example, owners were allowed to use the tennis courts only in the rain or at night "until such time as floodlights satisfactory to Guest Association have been installed by owners." A similar enactment regulated the owners' use of the docks "when their presence would cause congestion."

Naturally, it was stipulated that "owners shall provide all required funds, necessary at White Pine or unnecessary." The document closed with an elegant provision for such future regulations as might be needed: "These bylaws may be altered or amended by majority vote of Senior members at any annual meeting; provided that rights of owners shall never be enlarged."

Edgar Jr.'s birthday on September 1 was always a gala occasion at White Pine. Edith could be counted on to arrange some special event to highlight the traditional outing at Black Pond. Once it was a parade of canoes, another time a stylish boat garlanded with flowers, and yet another time a miniature armada equipped with congratulatory placards rowing the length and breadth of the not inconsiderable pond.

For the rest of the season the family boat, the *RAU*, ruled the waves. It was named for Edith – an acronym standing for "Right As Usual." This appellation the good-natured Edgar applied to his wife frequently; later, it became the name of Edgar Jr.'s plane.

The tradition of presenting family skits, which had flourished in the Rosenwald home, was now transferred to White Pine where it took on new and greater proportions. Edgar Jr. would don any number of sweaters not in immediate service at the retreat, in the process of impersonating his father who had a reputation for always feeling chilly. To the accompaniment of clever lyrics and serviceable melodies, each of the guests, in turn, would come under merciless scrutiny in the course of these miniature musicals.

The entire family seemed to have a flair for the dramatic, or, at least, the melodramatic. A favorite story concerned Armand, Adele's son, who provoked his Aunt Edith's ire at one dinner to such an extent that she asked him to leave and have his meal served in solitude at a small table near the window of the spacious dining room. He had been behaving in such an implacable manner that Edith further admonished him not to utter a single word in his "solitary confinement."

Armand obliged to the letter, but he immediately proceeded to mimic a ride in a railway coach, looking out the window or waving to imaginary people, craning his neck for a better view of the "passing" scene. He conveyed a feeling of swaying with the motion of the moving train, and extended his pantomime, all eyes upon him, while he enacted his wordless capers. Edith could not help laughing as heartily as any member of the assemblage. The upshot: banishment was lifted and Armand comported himself in exemplary fashion for the remainder of the evening.

One of the most welcome guests was Julius Rosenwald who took part in all the sports and games, accompanying the children on nature walks or supervising their swimming.

Another frequent guest, the lawyer Lester Kabacoff, recalled with special poignance his "rags to riches" trip to White Pine Camp. One sweltering hot summer day, he and his wife, Gloria, had traveled the seven to eight hours of the train ride, when a terrible feeling overcame them. Gloria was to have cashed a check before their departure, but it was Friday and they were rushing and she forgot. Between them, they had all of one dollar. Prudently, they had brought Hershey chocolate bars to assuage their hunger, but as these were exhausted they began to worry how they would be able to complete their trip at all. Finally, at dusk, as the broiling sun was setting, the train pulled into the little station. With great relief, they saw Garrett Atkins, the Sterns' chauffeur, there to fetch them in the black limousine. And among the pines a luxurious cottage, replete with such soothing amenities as martinis and silver platters of hors d'oeuvres, awaited them.

Little that could be done for the guests and visitors was left undone. In addition to Garrett Atkins, Edith brought other members of her regular household staff, including Johanna Martin, Minnie (Hermine) Oetjen (who originally came with the Levys and later joined the Stern retinue), Adam Jamet, and Emma Brown, who generally ruled over the kitchen in the late thirties. White Pine Camp remained deeply imbedded in the families' memories long after it was finally sold following World War II.

ELEVEN

Outward Bound

N

O ONE IS QUITE CERTAIN of the exact date, but all who were present describe the night with the same clarity. Certain moments seem to etch themselves into consciousness, as when one instinctively feels that a great event is being witnessed. Edith's cook mentioned that at her church there was a young woman who sang with the voice of an angel. Edith was so intrigued that she and Edgar attended a church service, listened to the young singer, and discovered themselves enthralled.

"Our friends must hear her; the whole world must hear her!" Edith exclaimed, repeating often that the voice was like honey and wine pouring forth from a silver vessel. "We must have a party for her."

Edgar was impressed but skeptical. Such things were simply not done in New Orleans. A black woman could be invited as a performer but not, as Edith intended, as the guest of honor at a dinner. "We'll lose many friends," he stated categorically.

"Well, then," said Edith tersely, "we'll see who our friends are."

Edith promptly set out to make the arrangements for her party. About twenty-five guests were invited; every one of them attended. All sat in rapt silence, spellbound by the beautiful young woman in a long, beige lace dress. She opened her recital with a group of *lieder* sung in a mellow rich alto. "We were absolutely still," Lillian Feibelman recalls, and there were few dry eyes as the singer proceeded with a rendition of Schubert's "Ave Maria." Deeply touched, the Sterns thanked the young woman, Marion Anderson, for gracing their home.

In August 1930, Edith received the news that her father intended to remarry. Julius had chosen Mrs. Adelaide Goodkind, the widowed mother of his daughter-in-law Edith, Lessing's wife. Among the siblings, only Marion remained in Chicago at the time; and only she could know at first hand the loneliness her father had suffered since the death of Augusta. No doubt, for the others, the adjustment was more difficult to make. But in the end, what made their father happy cheered them as well.

In December 1931, a package and a letter arrived at the Rosenwald home in Chicago. Julius was not in the best of health at the time, but the contents of the package lifted his spirits easily. It was an American flag, which, coupled with the words of the letter, sent his patriotic heart beating faster and stronger.

> Thanksgiving Day, 1931
>
> My dear Mr. Rosenwald:
>
> I am glad to send you this American flag that I carried with me on our flight to the South Pole.
>
> With the flag goes my highest admiration, enduring appreciation and warmest regards.
>
> Faithfully,
> Richard Byrd

For J.R., it was more than ample reward for having financed Admiral Byrd's expedition to the South Pole.

A few weeks later, on January 6, 1932, Julius Rosenwald died. A wave of sympathy swept through the country, carrying with it messages to the Chicago home where the family grieved. From the President of the United States to the poor in the streets, from every corner of the world, countless telegrams and letters arrived. Whether in the most elegant style on embossed stationery or poorly scribbled by untutored hands on plain paper, came manifestations of grief at the passing of the man who had taken as his motto "Wellbeing of mankind and investment in people."

The *New York Times* carried a page-long obituary, and in countless temples and churches across the land memorial services were held. To his children, J.R.'s death—or perhaps his mortality—came as an unexpected blow. No child is ever quite prepared for the loss of a parent, no matter how late in life that loss occurs. Like many others who had benefitted so greatly from Julius Rosenwald's philanthropy, those who had shared his life intimately wondered what would happen next.

The Rosenwald children had surrounded themselves with a life-style of beauty, though not on the lavish scale practiced by other wealthy American families. Granted, their homes were beautiful and gracious. Yet their parents' guidance restrained them from idle, self-indulgent pursuits. Of their grandest and most elegant parties, many were given over to causes that served the common good. Their collections of paintings, rare books, and etchings were shared through museums. Perhaps this was the greatest legacy that Julius Rosenwald left to his progeny: a passionate need for sharing.

The year 1932 saw the publication of Erskine Caldwell's novel, *Tobacco Road*, which revealed for the first time in American literature the kinds of conditions Julius Rosenwald had tried so ardently to alleviate. Early in 1933, when Hitler was appointed chancellor of Germany, those able to read early signs might have foreseen the storm gathering. Across the English Channel some took up the pen: George Bernard Shaw wrote *On the Rock*, while H. G. Wells worked on *The Shape of Things to Come.*

All the same, beginning in 1933, large numbers of artists, authors, actors, and musicians left Germany. Among them was Wassily Kandinsky. In his satchel he carried a canvas roughly 28 × 28 inches, painted in oil in 1926, entitled *Several Circles*. It grew out of what he called his fascination with the circle's relation to the cosmos. Of the three primary forms, Kandinsky said, "the circle points most clearly to the fourth dimension."

The Sterns acquired this painting, and it became Edith's favorite, finding a place in the Blue Room, the room in which she spent most of her time. The changing light filtering through the window from the garden seemed to enable the most eloquent view of the painting's varying moods.

On January 23, 1936, Edgar Stern turned fifty. Never one to forget a plan or a promise, no matter how trifling it seemed at the time, Edith reminded Edgar that years before, shortly after they were married, they had spoken of devoting a year to extensive travel and had agreed to do this when Edgar would reach the half-century mark. The time had arrived—they had been married for fifteen years—and the children were of the age at which travel would leave a lasting and beneficial impression.

A German saying aptly captured the situation: *Schlepp mich, ich geh' gern* ("Drag me, I love to go"). In mock horror, Edgar threw up his arms, "giving in" to a battle he had no mind to wage and no chance to win. In anticipation, Edith had pored over their itinerary for months, carefully mapping it out. And this was the itinerary they followed—a journey "to humor Edith."

Yet the scenes and the scenery were such that Edgar fell into the habit of writing copious letters of description and remark home to his family. Upon their return, Edith retrieved these letters and began the process of editing them. She had the resulting draft printed on fine paper and handsomely bound in hand-tooled leather. The title page of the volume read as follows:

A Sentimental Journey through France & Italy
(and other countries)
by Mr. Stern

Fifty copies of this book have been printed, and the type distributed.

Copyright 1938, Mrs. Edgar Stern.
Published January, 1938 [Edgar's fifty-second birthday] and presented with affectionate greetings to those bound to us by love and companionship in the hope that they will enjoy sharing again with us the happiness and good fortune which followed us on our Sentimental Journey. By Edith & Edgar Stern.

Edgar felt compelled to add, "With apologies to Laurence
Sterne," thereby giving credit to the British novelist whose title
he had appropriated for his own recollections.

The first page of the book consists of a photograph depicting a spectacular mountain range. In the foreground is a body
of water on which a sleek white ship—a luxury liner—makes
its way. It is all but lost, a tiny image among the towering crags.
The caption reads: "An ocean steamer sails hour upon hour up
fjords—Norway." An accompanying letter, dated July 17, 1936,
M.S. Kungsholm, elucidates Edgar's thoughts:

> It is a country beautiful beyond man's dreams . . . it is Lake
> Placid which I always thought a rare spot of beauty,
> multiplied 500 to 2,000 times. A good part of the journey we
> were in the land of the midnight sun which means the sun
> never sinks below the horizon . . . you can realize what an
> unbelievable scene results. . . .

He writes of peaks rising out of crystalline waters, bathed
by the evening sun, of dark green forests, of pristine waterfalls,
of lofty images reflected in the water's surface. An immortal
native son gave to generations to come, to all who are young
at heart, a glimpse of this unspoiled land and the people who
inhabit it. In fact, Edgar's next letter was written en route to
Copenhagen, near Hans Christian Andersen's birthplace.
Edgar tells how, while still in Norway, their guide slipped them
into the home of the absent king and queen. Home was the
proper label for the royal domicile, for it lacked all ostentation
save for the family portraits reposing in informal style on the
tables in the drawing room. Among them could be found the
queen's brother, the late King George V of England, and other
kin that represented most of European royalty. It is an extensive letter, and Edgar credits his secretary for having the
stamina to cope with it, lauds her unfailing good humor, her
foresight in bringing along a just-barely "portable" typewriter
in a heavy leather case so that she might make carbon copies
of everything, as well as her proficiency in brewing his beloved
Louisiana drip coffee every morning. This secretary, of course,
was Edith.

Also along on the journey through England, France,
and wherever it was advisable or necessary to be turned

out fashionably, was Edith's personal maid who served in the dual role of Edgar's valet. Her name was Marie, and, according to Philip Stern, she could and never hesitated to swear in seven different languages – a most helpful asset, considering the Sterns' itinerary. Marie's claim to fame was her former employment as personal maid to Douglas Fairbanks and Lady Astor. If Edgar was dissatisfied with Marie's choice of tie or suit,which she laid out for him each day, she would haughtily reply, "Mr. Fairbanks would have chosen that!" Invariably, Edgar would acquiesce in deference to Marie's version of Mr. Fairbanks' impeccable taste.

Rounding out the retinue was Miss Grant, the capable Scottish governess who kept close watch over the children.

The letters continue as Edgar expounds his views on a week spent in Sweden during which the Lemanns joined them. The friends agreed that the Scandinavians were a truly civilized people. Evidently, Edgar had envisioned them as struggling to eke out a meager existence in the harsh northern frontier, a people who had made no significant contribution to the world at large since Viking days. Instead, the letters are filled with praise for the cleanliness and industry of the Scandinavians, the brilliance of their folk costumes, and the generally healthy look of their livestock – every cow seemingly a candidate for a blue-ribbon nomination.

Edgar Jr.–in the company of his uncle and aunt, Dr. David and Adele Levy–left his parents to sail on to Russia, Estonia, and Finland. His impressions of Estonia and Finland were similar to Edgar's, but in referring to Russia, he quoted his uncle, saying it was "a vast place occupied by charity patients I used to treat when I was an intern at Cook County Hospital in Chicago."

According to her husband, Edith was indefatigable, making ambitious plans to see all there was to see. She was extremely fond of Edvard Grieg's music and was taken breathless by the spectacle of Scandinavian countrysides. She made arrangements through the United States Embassy to visit a slum-clearing project in the company of an engineer who had once spent several years in America. After a painstaking inspection she concluded that the federal project she had seen in Atlanta was far superior.

By the middle of August the Sterns reached England. Edgar's letters brim with the pure pleasure of being in Britain. It was as if he had returned to some idyll that his highly cultivated taste appreciated for its charm and quaintness; the comfort he found in it gave him the feeling of being in an ancestral home. "I had almost forgotten how utterly beautiful the English countryside is," he wrote. The Sterns were also delighted by London and their suite at the Dorchester Hotel, where a profusion of flowers sent by the English branch of the Stern family provided a token of welcome. Edgar was much pleased to find that the English reputation for fine stores had been upheld, especially when it came to locating the stylish men's clothing for which the British were famed. With hardly time to catch their breaths, they traveled to Gatehouse, the English Sterns' stately Scottish residence. There, spacious lawns and fine trees looked out on Solway Firth, affording a view of the bay and the gentle coves of the shoreline. Not far away, and usually shrouded in the mists, were the heather-covered moors. Edgar reported to his mother that "we tramped the moors for three hours yesterday and had our first grouse shoot. The children apparently are supremely happy at Miss Grant's home in Moffat, and Maurice is as handsome as ever. His teasing reminds me so exactly of Papa, even to the funny habit of nervously twitching his knees together when he sits down. They gave us a royal reception."

But his personal contentment did not blind him to the realities that surrounded the moment. "We Americans, despite the troubles we've had in the last few years, should thank our lucky stars that our lot has been cast in a country which by accident of geography has been for the most part isolated from the contagion of European entanglements. Whichever side wins the bloody civil war in Spain, it will take years for the country to recover. . . ." And "we have not heard the last word from Russia. America, England and Scandinavia stand out as havens of peace and sanity in a world full of unrest and suffering."

Relaxing in the comfort of an easy chair, dressed in an impeccably tailored Saville Row suit, Edgar pulled out his pipe and sipped his port and occasionally stretched his neck in his collar—a nervous habit—and proceeded to give his version of the fundamental reasons for English stability over the centuries that had seen so many changes. The wealthy elite who for generations had sent their sons to Eton, Oxford, and Cambridge, generally did not waste their precious heritage in idle pursuits, but by and large made a fair return to the nation in positions of diplomatic and civil service. As a result, Edgar concludes, "Masses of people are willing to give and take and trust their rulers and the aristocratic system works well." He adds, "This would be the explanation for the short rule of the Labour Government...."

In a subsequent letter, he underscores this point by reporting on a dance the Sterns attended. It was sponsored by a club whose members were servants and employees of the estate and held in a room above a spacious garage. He describes the self-respect and gaiety of these humble people and their "wholesome satisfaction with life.... Edith made herself very popular by dancing lively Scottish dances with some of the men and received rousing cheers upon leaving."

Promising to return the following spring on their journey homeward, the Sterns left Britain and their relatives and made their way to the Continent. Paris was the next stop, and Edgar could not help comparing it to London. "As stately and over-powering as London is, it is just a sprawling, crude, ugly thing next to this most supremely lovely of all cities. One just cannot believe that the people who created such a triumph of beauty will not pull out of their present difficulties."

It was mid-September and the next letter was sent from the Hôtel de la Paix in Geneva. It bore the news that Edgar and Edith were finally getting the children settled in their respective Swiss schools for the fall semester. Geneva was clean and lovely, and they were pleased that their balcony overlooked the lake.

Audrey was enrolled in the International School, which was connected with the Secretariat of the League of Nations. Both Edgar and Edith approved of the school, the teachers, and the atmosphere, which was permeated by the lofty ideal of brotherhood, the League's ostensible aim.

The boys were enrolled in the well-known Le Rosey school, some twenty miles from Geneva. Its roster of students read like an Almanach de Gotha of the crowned heads of the world, along with the offspring of other prominents. Among the Stern brothers' classmates were the son of General John J. Pershing and the heir presumptive of the Shah of Persia. The boys fell in love with the school — in particular, with the prospect of spending four months in Gstaad, starting in November, when the entire class moved to this location favored by the best and the richest among winter-sports enthusiasts.

But Edgar's letters were still filled with Britain. The Stern children were delighted with their Scottish kilts and hats. Audrey and Philip had taken up Highland dancing with much enjoyment; Philip had a natural flair for this type of dance. In Scotland he had, among other things, learned something of the printer's trade in a print shop belonging to Miss Grant's nephew and become addicted to printer's ink. Edgar Jr., on the other hand, had excelled in the "shoot" and enjoyed a reputation as a superb marksman.

Edith and Edgar attempted to attend a meeting of the League of Nations Assembly, and Edgar observed that the children were bound to be homesick. "We, too, will miss them terribly." But the letter from Switzerland closed on a happier note: they would all be together again for the children's Christmas vacation in Gstaad.

Edgar reported that Audrey's school, despite its association with the League, fell far short of its promise. After conducting a search among more than a dozen schools, Edith found one that pleased her. Here the curriculum was in French and included music, tennis, and horseback riding — pursuits that were among Audrey's favorites. Audrey seemed perfectly happy in this new environment in Lausanne, where among the fortunate students was the daughter of Marlene Dietrich. While Edgar went ahead to Scotland for more grouse shooting, Edith stayed with Audrey an extra week to be sure her daughter was well settled.

Back in Britain, Edgar was shown a copy of the speech delivered by the chancellor of Liverpool University on the occasion of presenting an honorary degree to Harold Cohen.

"It was a masterpiece of English and contained a most graceful, eloquent tribute to the Jews with thinly veiled digs at Hitler." Edgar also reported, somewhat to his amazement, that Maurice Stern would not go hunting on Yom Kippur and that his relative Bertolph, who was alone in Liverpool, spent several hours in temple. It reminded him of an encounter with Abe Friedmann of the Continental branch of his family.

Edgar had arranged for Friedmann to come from Hamburg to meet him in Geneva. Friedmann was a gregarious fellow, and the Sterns liked him immediately. He reported that his business was almost completely ruined by the Nazis. His account of the situation for the Jews in Germany was pathetic, and he was gratified that the two girls, Gita and Ellie, had gone to Palestine to live, thanks to a thousand dollars that Maurice had placed at their disposal.

There was much more about Geneva in the letter from Scotland. Edith and Edgar had, indeed, attended a session of the League of Nations Assembly. They were moved by this "noble experiment" and proud that the catalyst for the League had been an American president. Edgar observed that he could hardly abide the thought of America being left out of this institution created by Woodrow Wilson. "One could not help regretting that somehow the United States had to be missing from such a great gathering. The League has taken some blows recently . . . one cannot help the feeling that sometime, perhaps in the distant future, this ideal of nations sitting down together . . . is going to be more successful than it now appears . . ." At the session, they heard the Ethiopian delegate demand his right to be seated. Edgar said, "It is probably not too much to hope that this rule by crazy dictators is not going to continue indefinitely."

The rest of the letter renders an account of the excellent golf played on famous St. Andrew's course in Scotland. It continues with the information that the Sterns would be spending a weekend with their children in Switzerland before going to Warsaw and then on to Russia, where they hoped to see the "Jewish colonies" in which Julius Rosenwald had taken such a deep interest. Their itinerary necessitated changing trains in Berlin, but the American ambassador there, Mr. William

Edward Dodd, formerly a professor at the University of Chicago, assured him that they had nothing to worry about and offered his hospitality.

It is an exceptional letter. If it were found in a time capsule by some future generation, it could be instantly dated and identified. Viewing it in the 1980's, one cannot but marvel at the innocence with which this generation of intelligent, concerned, and knowledgeable human beings blithely looked, and even traveled, into the very eye of the storm as late as 1936.

Edith's presence is constantly implied in the letters. From the outset, it is obvious that she planned every step of this "sentimental journey." Her arrangements for visiting the League of Nations, for example, point up her probing intellect and, perhaps, the real motivations for the trip itself.

The journey continued. A penciled note, written on a Swiss train, refers to letters received, most of them dealing with the festivities surrounding Harvard's 300-Year Jubilee. One senses Edgar's deep regret at having to be absent. He savored the accounts of the speeches and the pageantry. No doubt, in his mind, he was there on the banks of the Charles. He even writes as if it were so. "It is really the event of the century, and I agree that Harvard is one of the strongest and cleanest and finest things that American life has produced."

As the train rolled into Basel, Edgar added a few random notes about London. "Contrary to old times, there were twice as many dinner coats as full-dress in the theatres, and even a good many men in business suits."

En route from Warsaw to Moscow, October 31, 1936, Edgar reports on their brief stay in Berlin.

> We were in Berlin from Monday afternoon until Wednesday, midnight. I had not wanted to stop on German soil longer than necessary to change trains, but I am now glad that Edith's curiosity persuaded me to do so. On the surface, Berlin looks quite normal and good ... the effect of the "Jugend" movement is very apparent in the splendid youthful healthy looks one sees ... They still use the ridiculous goose step, which makes them look like first-class damn fools. We made up our minds that we would not join the bystanders in the fascist salute when the flag passed by and wondered what would be the result. But nobody said a word. Nothing is left of the old-time

Herzlichkeit. We hardly saw anyone smile, much less laugh, and in the restaurants people talk in low tones. We saw few of the red signs in shop windows, indicating it was an "Aryan" shop.... As to the Jewish question, we heard that Berlin is one of the cities where conditions are not at the harshest.... We left Berlin without having experienced any unpleasantness. Word was evidently given that foreigners should be cultivated (I presume they could recognize us as Jews); nevertheless, we were glad to leave, as one feels subconsciously an atmosphere of restraint hanging like a pall over everything.

There is a postscript to this letter from Leningrad, dated November 4. Among other things, it tells the following:

Here it is late in the evening and the papers say that partial returns from 45 states show Roosevelt has ten million votes to Landon's six million.

Before leaving London we had lunch at the School of Economics with Harold Laski. He has one of the most beautifully clever, logical brains I have ever come into contact with and speaks delightfully. Of course he is avowedly a Marxian Socialist. We told him that people had advised us to risk the dirt and discomfort of traveling third class in Russia in order to meet the masses. His answer: "Don't do it, travel first class and be comfortable; I always do; you know, nothing's too good for a Socialist." We leave in a few minutes for the midnight train to Moscow.

Almost three weeks after the Sterns left Poland, Edgar wrote his impressions of that country to his family in New Orleans. He described exactly what he saw and thought, and evidently it eluded any censor. He wrote of Warsaw, the city that had been in vassalage to the czarist regime of Russia for a century and a half, calling the government the stupidest and cruelest that had ever cursed the world. He gave a short résumé of Poland's unique history, pointing out that after centuries of domination it was free once again. He spoke of the Poles' love of art despite their poverty, and of their excellent taste and style; of their palaces, which they commissioned of skilled French and Italian architects in contrast to those influenced by the boorish German taste. He laments that the Russians, Germans, and Austrians stole most of the treasures of the Polish nation.

When the Russians retreated from Warsaw in 1915, they took away, in a final act of vandalism, over 75 van loads of art treasures. Much of this priceless material was returned in 1920; a commission has been scouring the world for those stolen treasures, and buying them back when possible.

Some were found in Vienna and two magnificent vases were found in the J. P. Morgan collection in New York. When the Polish Commission offered to buy these, the Morgans informed them that they were to take them back without any payment ... as they were not willing to be owners of stolen goods. I am sure the Russians would not believe that a wicked capitalist could be so magnanimous!

Edgar was impressed that the Poles had elected a musician as president; only a country enamored of and dedicated to music could have elected a man like Ignacy Jan Paderewski. On the other hand, Edgar was totally disenchanted with his coreligionists in Poland. The squalor, poverty, and dirt of the Jews of Poland left him absolutely speechless and in an emotional turmoil. He had not one good thing to say about the Orthodox Jews. He abhorred their garb, their looks, and their customs one of which dictated that women shear their natural hair and wear wigs called *sheitels.* At a Jewish funeral he saw Orthodox Jews as well as other members of apparently the same family, who looked much like American Jews in smart clothing and with the women in silk stockings.

Their guide, a Polish woman of obvious good birth and refined taste, took them to all the sordid, foul-smelling alleys of the quarter "where Jewish life has sunk to the bottom of the pit of human existence." If there was any anti-Semitism in Poland, under the circumstances, it did not surprise Edgar. What he observed, he felt, would turn anyone into an anti-Semite. Certainly he could find no shred of personal identification with these Jews who looked "like clowns in their comical garbs." The guide had, for whatever personal reason, neglected to show the visitors the homes and studios of the Jewish intelligentsia who contributed so richly to the flowering of Poland's artistic and cultural life.

Things were otherwise in the Soviet Union. There follows a description of a conversation Edgar had with Harold Laski regarding this. Laski repeated what Stalin told him: "There is anti-Semitism in thought and anti-Semitism in action. Anyone who preaches the first, we would suppress and punish; anyone who practices the second, we would shoot." Edgar alludes once more to the Jews of Poland. Perhaps resettlement in Russia might serve them well, "because there they might get a better deal."

TWELVE

Homeward Bound

I HAVEN'T HAD A WORD from the outside world since I came to Russia November 1; no stock market, no football scores. I just remembered that tomorrow is the Harvard-Yale game, and I'll be on a train bound for Bucharest." In three weeks, Edgar and Edith traveled from the Baltic Sea to the Black Sea. Travel was arduous, much of the time in malodorous trains, the travelers frequently sitting up all night at windows that were broken or in poor repair. They felt cold and unwashed, and considered it a personal triumph if they managed to spend a night in a hotel room comparatively free of bed bugs. The strength of their determination supported them; there was no trace of complaint.

Edgar announced in his letters that he was about to say many favorable things about Russia and the Russians. "Don't think I have gone 'Red.' I still believe that this system is not at all suited to American needs ... and personally it would be a very distasteful form of life for me. I can also state (and Edith shares this feeling) that this visit has been one of the most profoundly stirring and thought-provoking experiences of my life. . . . I frankly admit that our view is necessarily superficial. Russia covers nearly one-sixth of the earth's surface and has a population of 170,000,000; one would need years to study it, to really understand it." He described the beauty of Leningrad and its vestiges of the opulence of past regimes. He tells of the eight days they spent in Moscow; the three days in Kharkov; and the trips to Dnepopetrovsk, Zaporzhie, and Dneprogress – new cities designed to hold mammoth industries. They saw dams and power plants, collective farms and state-run kindergartens. They also included Kiev and Odessa on their itinerary, and managed a visit to a Jewish collective farm. Edgar dismissed as "tommyrot" the much talked about Russian propaganda and the allegations they had heard of visitors being hoodwinked by Russian guides especially trained for that purpose. "Yes, if I see another bust of Lenin or Stalin, I'll be ready to scream," he added, but other than that he felt no pressures placed upon him to accept what the Russians would have him believe.

The Sterns were deeply impressed by one enlightened policy: ex-prostitutes, after extensive reform, were offered a fine education, taught trades, and given – most essentially of all – self-respect. "It was quite evident to us that these girls were happy, normal persons who might marry and lead perfectly normal lives. . . . They have unbounded faith in the ability of an improved environment raising the living standard of all men. I understand that they are still cruel and merciless toward opponents of their socialistic system, but to all others their law and practice is an inspiration."

> The scene in People's Courts must make an American blush when he thinks of our lower criminal courts at home. The trial is held before a judge and two jurors. The panel from which the jurors are chosen is selected each year by the Trades Unions. The jurors are given six months' training. A verdict of two out of three prevails, so the jurors may outvote the judge. In case of conviction the law does not seek revenge but reform. . . . I was told by non-partisans that the prison colonies are model affairs, men learn skills, are paid for their work and visited by their families.

They were enormously taken with the devotion of the workers and the spirit of sacrifice displayed in an effort to make the Five-Year Plan work. Edgar describes the Stakhanovite

Movement named for a man who by special study of the machinery on which he worked was able to turn out nearly four times the daily norm. This dedication to production was dramatized all over the country by means of little red flags indicating which machines were being operated by machinists who emulated Stakhanov. Edgar summarized this situation:

> In these excessively long letters I have said much that is favorable of Russia; you may almost have concluded that I am prejudiced in their favor. I may have over-emphasized their accomplishments. I did it because, before going to Russia I heard prejudiced attitudes against them. They have many faults. They are terribly tied up in red tape. They are stolid, unenthusiastic people which perhaps fits them especially for their collectivist system. They are almost devoid of humor, which makes the task of their propagandist easier. I don't feel capable of making an appraisal of their system nor any prophecy as to their future.... They have made amazing progress in industry and agriculture ... and in the absence of war, they are likely to become a very rich country.... I am tremendously impressed with their social ideas and practices and with their zeal for education. I have one other opinion, and that is that the success of this system in Russia does not clearly indicate its adoption in democratic countries where a fairly broad distribution of property exists and I raise two serious questions about the future of Russia. Their success up to now has been largely due to the unusual leadership and the spartan spirit of sacrifice among the people. In spite of cruelty, fanaticism and tyranny, these leaders are generally agreed to be honest, tireless patriots. Most of them endured tremendous hardships and dangers in the days before the Revolution and in the Civil War. As a consequence, the spirit which moves them is something like that which prevailed in America while it still was governed by Washington, Jefferson, Madison, Monroe and other products of the exaltation of our Revolution. They have yet to face the entry of an Andrew Jackson with the doctrine, "To the victor belong the spoils." One must recognize, too, that the people who are now filled with the spirit of the brotherhood of men are, in spite of their present disabilities, far better off than before the Revolution. In a relatively few years they are going to be rich and probably soft ... generally well educated. What will then be their reaction to the dictatorship of the proletariat and regimentation by the State? Without attempting to answer these questions, I can say with strong conviction that I could not be happy under such a system.

Edgar was astonished to find that a nation that, until twenty years before, had harbored a population between 70 and 90 percent illiterate, had almost wiped out illiteracy. At the opera, the Sterns observed a man "without a collar, deeply studying a book of science during intermission!" They found the public libraries enormous, and the teaching of science universal from the elementary school levels to the universities. When an official was asked how the government could afford to spend so much money on education at this stage of their development, his reply was "We cannot afford *not* to do it."

The Sterns were a long way from home, but what they saw could not help but have a decided impact on them. The distillation of their European experiences would lead them to a redoubling of their efforts in behalf of such causes as Tuskegee Institute and Dillard University on their return.

The travelers were back in Gstaad, Switzerland, in December 1936. Edgar's pen now sketched in the days omitted before in the exigencies of the journey. He focused on Romania, pointing up the deplorable fact that war had transferred the large, important province of Transylvania from Hungary to Romania where corruption and incompetence seemed to be the chief industries. He found their architecture "the worst form of modernity," and the army uniforms the gaudiest outside of comic opera. Yet he praised the food and reported attending a superb concert by pianist Alexander Brailowsky. "Such is Bucharest as we could learn about it in three days. It looks like a country ripe for communism, or any other kind of revolution, except that the people seem too soft and lazy to do much revolting. . . ."

> [Romania's] importance is that, together with Poland, [it forms] a buffer between Germany and Russia. [It is] one of the many pawns being played by politicians in Europe, [in] a game utterly bewildering and incomprehensible to an American. The confusion and political and economic instability we saw in Romania, and to a lesser degree in Hungary and Austria, are in sharp contrast to the definite planning in Russia.

Edgar and Edith were exhilarated to encounter once again the amenities of life once they crossed the Russo-Romanian border: "Clean linen and shining bathtubs!"

Edgar did not fail to remark on the curious experience of changing trains in Kishinev. Boarding the International Wagons-Lits, they considered what the name Kishinev meant a generation earlier when it stood for the site of bloody anti-Jewish pogroms. No doubt Edith, in particular, recalled her father's story of the huge pledge made on behalf of those who suffered, at a time when he could ill afford to make it.

The narrative turned to Budapest where "the architecture is fine, people are properly dressed and gracious, the women chic, beautiful and charming."

> You get a feeling of a very old civilization that has become sound and stabilized a long time ago, and yet holds its own in a modern world. . . . under the benevolent dictatorship of Admiral Horthy, the former head of the Austro-Hungarian Navy who bears the title of Regent, perhaps indicating that he is in temporary possession of the "throne" until a Hapsburg heir can be brought back as king of Hungary and Austria. There would be good economic reasons for that merger, as Hungary is largely agricultural and Austria, on the other hand, industrial. . . .
>
> While both the goulash and the gypsy music are disappointing, the native Tokay wines are truly excellent; and there is also much fine music here; we heard Toscanini conduct a symphony orchestra and had a curious experience about Marion Anderson, the American Negro woman whom we had sing at our house in New Orleans a few years ago, and who has since become internationally famous. A recital was advertised for the day we were to leave, in a hall seating some 2,500 people. We were willing to stay over an extra day to hear her but were absolutely unable to buy a seat.

This last, matter-of-fact statement reveals something of the Sterns' character. Apparently, it had not occurred to them that one phone call or message to Marion Anderson would not only have assured them of seats but in all likelihood of the best seats in the house. If they refrained from making such a call by design, that very decision set them apart from most "do-gooders" in the world.

If the travelers had appreciated the charms of Hungary, their delight knew no bounds when they arrived in Vienna. Edgar noted, "I never thought to see any city to rival Paris, but Vienna does. Vienna seems to me like a Johann Strauss waltz, full of gaiety, rhythm, beauty and charm. The women are very good-looking and know how to dress. The Austrians have the neatness of the Germans with none of their pompousness or arrogance. They have the sparkle of the French with more dignity. . . ." Theater, music—"They are not only music lovers, but music is the biggest thing in their lives." The magnificence of the Hapsburg palaces of sweeping grandeur and rococo detail rendered in exquisite workmanship, and the heavenly cuisine—a trifle richer than the French while not quite as heavy as the German—Vienna had it all. The goose liver pâté was unexcelled; the Wiener schnitzel worthy of paeans; strudels and pastries and torten were unsurpassed. Above all, the Sterns were aware of Vienna as a cultural Mecca, a city that drew young intellectuals from all over the world. It was famed for its medical research, especially; and here legendary names from the arts and the sciences casually crossed paths. Mostly Jewish names at that, a fact in which the Sterns took special pride. This, after all, was the home of Gustav Mahler, Franz Werfel, Sigmund Freud, Béla Bartók, Emanuel Feuermann, and Béla Schick, to name but a few.

The Sterns were entertained in the salon of Madame Irma Freyhan Weiner, whose husband was an important banker. There is a description of her lavish life-style, coupled with a surprisingly modest demeanor. Edith and Edgar were pleased, too, to see the vast modern hospital, which accommodated as many as four thousand beds; and the dental clinic with children's crèches, where medical research and social conscience admirably joined forces. Nevertheless, Edgar's astute eye led him to observe, "People are nervous here about their political future, especially about the threat from Germany." As they took one last look at the magnificent Habsburg palaces, now only echoing the strains of the last waltzes played in them, at the muddy Danube which poets had myopically invested with blue waters, they could not help but wonder what was to become of this glittering capital.

Now, in Gstaad, having completed visits to eleven countries, they rested in reunion with their children. All three had thrived in this environment, having noticeably grown inches and now chattering in perfect French, Philip's accent being decidedly Parisian. In fact, the young people poked fun at their parents' French, particularly their mother's inflexible American-style "r," which was a constant source of amusement. They skated on the lake and skied on idyllic slopes. When fresh snow fell, the powder shimmered with magical brilliance in the bright morning sun, transforming the landscape into an enchanted wonderland. The Sterns agreed that they had never witnessed anything more breathtaking. And the evenings were afire with the *Alpenglühen,* the spectacular glow that bathes snowcaps in red and purple light.

In February, Edgar wrote from the *SS Lamartine* en route to Istanbul. There had been a brief interlude in Italy, and Edgar made a note that the treasures they had viewed there were tantalizing enough to merit a later, more exhaustive visit:

> Edith more than I, has come to feel that we are getting near the saturation point in receiving new impressions. We decided that Italy has so much to offer that one ought to go there fresh indeed. We had planned to use it mostly to explore Italian gardens. After we saw a few, though extremely beautiful in their way, they are too formal and give us no inspiration for use at home.

They had the pleasure of seeing Leonardo da Vinci's *Last Supper,* and Edgar noted that it was "an amazing piece of work, but unfortunately was painted on the plaster wall of an old monastery and time has made sad ravages."

In Belgrade, he reserved his praise for the excellence of the native brandy called slivovitz, "decidedly the best thing ever to come out of a prune."

Early in the morning, on the captain's invitation, the Sterns had a grandstand view from the bridge, enabling them to observe the ship's entrance into Istanbul harbor. Considered one of the most beautiful harbors in the world, the domed and minaret-studded city (there are 365 mosques in Istanbul) is situated on several hills sloping down to where the narrow Bosporus meets the Sea of Marmara and an inlet of the

Bosporus called the Golden Horn divides Europe from Asia. In 1927, President Kemal Atatürk, a benevolent dictator at the helm of the government, was trying to bring the country into the twentieth century. Yet for all that, the city, the country, and its people seemed still under the power of the sultans who had reigned supreme for centuries. It was still the same Istanbul that had formerly been known as Constantinople and once as Byzantium.

The Sterns reveled in the Bazaar, which appeared to hold treasures right out of *A Thousand and One Nights:* carpets, jewels, brocades, sapphires, rubies, and pearls. They were intrigued by Turkey and curious to see how long it would take before the fez-wearing men and veiled women would feel comfortable in Western dress and whether indeed they would be happy in their new life-style.

Edith and Edgar both felt that the world knew too little of Turkey. The Turks had been a race of warriors who conquered much of Europe, yet they left startlingly few traces of their civilization. They apparently were only fighters, never colonizers; thus destroyers rather than builders and artists. What place would they eke out for themselves in the modern world?

That question still reverberating in their minds, the Sterns embarked for Greece—Turkey's bitter, longtime foe. The pages vibrate with Edgar's impressions: "All my life, I had such an ideal vision of the Acropolis that I was really nervous about approaching it; a horrible feeling that a childish illusion is about to be rudely shattered." But they visited the Acropolis again and again, saw it in every light and perspective, marveling at its timeless beauty, which moved them finally to tears. They visited Delphi and played tennis against a backdrop that caused Edgar to remark that "the Greeks located their temples in the most glorious places."

"We enter tomorrow night the land of our ancestors." Edgar's terse statement comes almost as a recognition of an obligation to be borne and, if need be, to be suffered with fortitude and requisite dignity. Perhaps Edith shared this view of their next destination; perhaps not. However, in a letter dated February 27, 1937, Edgar indicated a change of heart: "Let me say right here that Palestine was for us a series of very agreeable surprises. We really hesitated long before deciding to go there and went, principally, out of a sense of duty; for one thing, to compare with our impressions of the Jewish colonies in Russia."

Edgar's own point is telling. He had been raised by a family devoted to Temple Sinai, with a tradition of service to that house of worship, yet he and Edith had made no real attempt to come to terms with their Jewish identity. They were Jews, and they fiercely defended that heritage with all their pride and dignity. Nonetheless, they had long before given up making even perfunctory appearances at Yom Kippur services, the most important of the year. Their children, given every other cultural advantage, were never truly exposed to their religious heritage. This was surprising in that both parents had imbibed their philanthropic instincts precisely from this font of values, the Jewish experience. Perhaps they sought to "spare" their children the suffering that supposedly was attendant upon having Jewish roots. But this would only be a fractional explanation, at best. And there is no clue that they ever even considered rejecting their Judaism.

> It happens that the few times that I have been to temple on Friday night it always seemed to be the third Sabbath of the month on which a special section is read, "Like the dews of Mount Hermon falling on the plains of Lebanon." If I ever go to temple again I shall never hear the phrase without recalling this beautiful sight . . . and understand the scriptural "dews," meaning the melting of snows. . . .
>
> Neither of us has ever been a Zionist and we had expected to find an ugly land, dreary and an unpleasant incident of our travels. We now feel that it is one of the very high spots of our whole trip, exciting and thrilling. The Jewish colonies (*kibbutzim*) have forged fertile farms from the rugged terrain. It is not difficult to realize why such a rugged and inspiring landscape should have stimulated the imagination of spiritual leaders . . . it is equally easy to understand why the Jews of the present day passionately love this land. It is definitely not just another country. Jerusalem is a unique city. I shall never forget our arrival there at sunset. . . . Built on hills, one gets a marvelous view

of the whole countryside, of churches and mosques, the Jewish University [sic], and the hospital on top of Mt. Scopus. The weather-beaten walls are a sight of rare beauty. Cosmopolitan is a very tame word to describe the population and architecture. . . . We met Miss Henrietta Szold, a great friend of Mrs. Rosenwald's and at 76 still working 16 hours a day, a grand old warrior. We presented letters and renewed acquaintances with a few of the leaders. Col. Kish, formerly of the British army, who dined with us in New Orleans, is now married to a beautiful cultured English Jewess; Dr. Magnus, who gave up the pulpit at Temple Emanuel in New York to become President of the Hebrew University, is married to Louis Marshall's sister; Edwin Samuels, son of Sir Herbert Samuels, the first British Lord High Commissioner of Palestine, is married to a perfectly delightful girl born in Palestine of Russian-Jewish parents. It would be impossible to describe to you the rare quality of all these persons. They are all high idealists, devout believers in their cause, but they have avoided, entirely, the annoying qualities usually associated with missionaries. They spare you all propaganda. One hears no mention of the obvious sacrifices they all have made in leaving comfortable and even high places in their former homes. They have evidently been through perfect hell and real danger during the Arab uprising (and even now one is advised not to motor in the country after dark). One hears no complaints from them, nor boasts of their bravery, although we know that there were some barbarous atrocities. They are of course waiting with great anxiety for the decision of the Royal Commission which is considering the future relations of Jews and Arabs. They all believe that at the worst this decision could only stop, or postpone further, Jewish immigration. They are entirely confident that the 400,000 Jews that are there, dug themselves into the land so deeply by their roots that nothing will get them out.

Edgar goes on to tell of the Sterns' experience in attending a concert given by a new symphony orchestra. Though it was only two and a half months old, it already had the reputation of including the finest strings in the world, and the honor of having seven *Konzertmeisters* from the leading orchestras in Europe.

You may have heard that Toscanini volunteered to be their first conductor and refused to accept a penny for his services. While he was in Palestine he received a cable from Germany. Hitler wanted him to conduct a leading orchestra. Toscanini's answer: "I only conduct in countries that are free." And turning it over to his secretary, he directed him to route the cable through Milan where he had also refused to conduct for the same reason.

The audience for the concert numbered no fewer than 1,600 people, nearly all Jewish. "It is striking to see how, in this free atmosphere, they have lost their nervous high-strung qualities. We have never seen a more quiet and dignified audience."

> Lady Downs, who was with us at the symphony concert is a distinguished aristocratic-looking Englishwoman, sister of Lord Allenby, Commander of the British forces in Palestine during the World War. She has built a home in Haifa and spends a large part of the year here. She loves Palestine and its people and added, "You'll find the rest of your trip dull after leaving this country." She told us, further, that no one will ever know how heroic the Jews were during their troubles with the Arabs.
>
> We had a spontaneous long laugh when we found that the Ford agency had its sign printed in Hebrew. I was careful to photograph it. You might remember that after my visit to Poland I wrote you of my deep humiliation at the sight of the degradation to which the Jews have sunk. What a contrast is seen here. Nowhere else have I ever had such a feeling of pride in belonging to this people, or so much confidence in their inherent qualities.... Here one sees strong, happy, young Jewish boys and girls working right out in the fields. One can almost see the new vigor they are getting from the contact with the soil which has been denied to them for so many centuries.... Of course the contrast between the farms of the Jews and the Arabs, as well as every other phase of their lives, is the difference between day and night.

In Poland, Edgar had remarked on the tenacity with which the Poles had kept their language, their culture, and their tradition intact for some one hundred fifty years; and their great courage in restoring their nation. "That now seems like child's play compared to this Jewish renaissance."

> These young Jews ... are not chauvinistic nor rabbi-ridden. Their love for this country is translated into planting a million and a half trees already, in a country denuded for more than 1,000 years; building dams and power plants, bringing a modern social program into a country that had, for centuries, known only filth, disease and degradation of the Orient. We shall not soon forget the serene joy on the

faces of girls and boys brought here from Germany last year.... Just one little story: At one of the colonies we found two school buildings—one brand new, modern, concrete building, the other weather-beaten, old, made of wood. The latter was crowded with children, whereas the former was empty. We asked the reason. The answer: "Oh, we're saving the new one for the German children who are coming soon. They are used to better things, our children are not."

Even as they studied the land and the people, Edgar and Edith were reevaluating their attitudes:

I used to think that it was a pity that such heroic effort should be wasted on such a barren, unattractive section of the world. Better to follow [Israel] Zangwill and found a new Jewish land in some good part of Africa. I can see now that the sentiment connected with the ancient, historical association of this country is a great source of strength in fortifying these people against the hardships with genuine emotional patriotism. After this long recital, you are probably labeling Edith and me as Zionists (for she fully shares my view) but we are not much interested in labels. What we saw in Germany and Poland drove home forcibly to us the fact that the necessity for finding a refuge for Jews is no longer an academic question.

From Palestine, the Sterns traveled to Egypt, reversing the exodus of their people. They were so caught up in sightseeing that Edgar's impressions were not posted until March 18 in Paris. They found Shepherd's Hotel in Cairo to be comfortable and the pyramids to be awesome. They were stirred by the tombs of the kings and the untold riches they contained. Edgar was astonished to learn that King Tut was only sixteen years old when he died and of relatively little importance in life, yet the magnificence of his tomb's treasures would belie his earthly achievements. Once more, his keen vision was turned to the people and the land.

It was of much interest to me to note that in observing the rule to veil their faces, those of the Egyptian girls who are pretty arrange to wear veils which are highly transparent, whilst the fat old ladies still wear very thick veils. Before we left Egypt we had several hours' journey through the dreary desert where Moses is said to have wandered for forty years before coming to the Promised Land. Edith wondered why he had not had sense enough to lead his people to the seashore and find his way straight up the coast. It is too bad that she was not there to run the show for him.

THIRTEEN

Final Visits

*F*ROM PARIS IN APRIL, Edgar jotted down a few random
thoughts concerning Egypt and the Suez Canal. "We saw
numbers of English soldiers whose departure is scheduled for
some date still in the future.... The ambitions of Mussolini in
the Mediterranean and his occupation of neighboring territory
make it appear probable that, in fact, England will keep a pretty
close control over Egypt."

After outfitting herself with a Paris wardrobe suitable for
the spring, Edith went to Venice with Edgar to meet the children
for their Easter holidays. The whole family delighted in the
galleries in Venice, Florence, and Rome. Edgar, with engaging
and disarming frankness, admitted that heretofore he had little
interest in paintings, especially those of religious content of the
kind that form so large a part of the collections in Italian
museums such as the Uffizi. Confronted by these remarkable
originals, his innate good taste and discernment came to the
fore. Candidly, he expressed his feeling that one need not be a
student or expert to be moved by the greatness of the likes of
Michelangelo, Titian, Raphael, Tintoretto, and Leonardo da
Vinci. Speaking of Rome, he saw into the nature of the place:

As I walked around the Forum and the surrounding Capitoline and Palatine hills and the Circus Maximus, these names and associations long forgotten gradually carried me back over the span of a generation and brought back the memory of high-school Latin and History. Since then, H. G. Wells and other liberals have opened my eyes to the bloody ruthlessness of the insatiable ambitions of Imperialistic Rome. And one still sees reminders, as indeed one does also in Egypt and Greece, that their glories rested on the sweat and blood of innumerable slaves.... Mussolini, of course, is trying to revive in the modern Italian the sense of Rome's destiny to rule an Empire, and finally the present status of Italy's imperial possessions, with an obvious hint as to what the next map will show.

The family left Italy—it was unusually cold for that time of the year, the weather suited to sightseeing but not to bathing—and repaired to the French Riviera, finding sunshine and relaxation at Juan-les-Pins. After months in the wintry mountains of Switzerland, the children relished the warmth and the beaches of the Côte d'Azur. Their parents took such vicarious enjoyment in being able to watch the children disport that, according to Edgar, "We went to the Casino in Cannes only once, which was plenty enough." There was regret in departing from the children "for they have now come to an age where it is hard to give them up."

Edgar added a note to the family back home to indicate that the trip was now nearing its conclusion.

> You have all been very patient in reading these long letters ... this will probably be nearly the last, as Edith and I feel that we have worked enough in sightseeing.... We expect to remain in Paris until the first week in May, going to the country for weekends; then we will go to Holland to see the tulips and will arrive in London on May 8, where we have leased a house at 42 Upper Grosvenor Street, for six weeks, and expect to have the Liverpool Sterns visit us there. We have tentatively booked our return passage on the *Conte di Savoia* on the 22nd of July.

The house on Upper Grosvenor Street proved to be a stately, distinguished English home, its furnishing and paintings in the best of taste, and its rental including an excellent cook and competent staff. Writing from this fashionable location, Edgar reviewed the weeks preceding their arrival in London.

In Paris spring had come late, but compensated for its tardi-
ness with the most extravagant abundance of flowers, in
Chantilly, St. Cloud and the Luxembourg Gardens. The
horse chestnut trees in full bloom lining the Boulevards
transformed the city into a bower of beauty.

Edgar found the French jittery and nervous, despite the
serenity of springtime. He attributed this to the fact that the
wealthy and titled classes held a very reactionary view toward
the masses. "There has been far less distribution of wealth than
in Great Britain or America." Few of the wealthy had given real
service to France in public life, many were hiding their wealth
and transferring it to other countries in huge amounts, and to
a person they seemed to have "a very arrogant attitude toward
the working classes." As it was expressed to him, "France is
enormously wealthy but the government is bankrupt."

> In the midst of this delicate situation, Blum has maintained
> himself as Prime Minister longer than anyone could have
> believed possible. Wealthy classes naturally dislike him,
> but believe in his personal honesty. So far he has been able
> to control the extreme radicals in his group.

In this opinion, as in most of his political observations,
Edgar proved himself an astute student of the countries in
which he sojourned. He was now to escort Edith to the coronation of the new king of England. It was not the coronation
they had expected to attend when their journey began, for King
Edward VIII had renounced his throne for the woman he
loved, and the festivities were given over now to his younger
brother, the Duke of York, who would be crowned King George
VI. Nevertheless, as Edith had hoped, the Stern children who
were brought to England for this event, were profoundly
impressed. The Stern family spent the night before the coronation dining and dancing at the Savoy, not leaving there until
2:30 A.M., as a rain began to fall.

> We had to walk all the way home in our evening clothes, and
> already at that hour the sidewalks were lined with people,
> taking their places for the next day's procession. Children
> sleeping in their mothers' arms, young people dancing in
> the streets. We in America will never be able to understand
> the attitude of the British toward their royal family: A
> mixture of reverence with deep-seated affection. It is a great
> tribute to the English aristocracy that they have been able

to keep the confidence of the people through a display of "noblesse oblige." Think of it, the audience in the Abbey for the Coronation, except for members of the House of Commons and visiting ambassadors, was composed entirely of peers and peeresses of the realm. There was not the slightest resentment at this among the people. On the contrary there was only cordiality toward these peers and peeresses as they drew up to the Abbey, magnificently clad in red velvet and ermine capes, carrying their coronets. In spite of the tremendous change in the world, it may be said that every Englishman still loves a lord!

From their excellent seats near the Abbey, the Sterns watched the spectacle of the coronation. No people on earth, it seemed, could mount a show as the English could—even after the bitter disappointment caused by a man they had hoped to crown and whose abdication left them stunned and bewildered. But now they had a new king, a queen, and little princesses—a Royal Family with whom they could identify, whom they could emulate, and who possessed all the homely virtues as dear to the English as their afternoon tea.

The pageantry dazzled the eye as the Band of Scots Greys Regiment, all on grey horses with black bearskin saddle cloths rode by and the Life Guards on black horses with white bearskin saddle cloths followed. Brasses sounding, horses stepping high, breast plates gleaming in the sun . . . scarlet jackets and white plumes of the Field Marshals and the brilliant silks and breathtaking jewels in the turbans of the Indian Rajas.

The crowd cheered and the Sterns joined in, as the carriages rolled by with peers wearing coronets and their ladies wearing tiaras. Finally came the state coaches bearing the Royal Family, regal and bejeweled, like a vision from a dream.

They were like pictures out of a fairy tale, from Queen Mary down to the little Princesses; all looked every inch a king or queen. . . .

After the unrest and turbulence we had witnessed in every other country in Europe except Scandinavia, I think England is the one place where one can feel that there is stability and security left. The hearts of the British are in the right place and their heads are screwed pretty squarely on their shoulders. They will slowly take on new ways, but in doing so, they are not going to "burn down the house to roast the pig."

Edgar closes by noting the extra delight in having Edith's sister Marion present for the festivities. They would now be going to LeTouquet for a week, then to Lausanne for the closing of the schools—and, at long last, home.

The *Conte di Savoia* set sail on July 22, 1937. All the Sterns were aboard with numerous steamer trunks and the faithful Smith Corona typewriter—its leather case battered but intact— on which Edith had faithfully typed out Edgar's notes throughout the journey. A year had passed. Edith and Edgar had chosen—was it by uncanny intuition or by charmed accident?—a crucial, unique moment in history as Europe stood poised at the edge of the abyss.

In country after country, they had seen and heard and felt the danger approaching as only outsiders can; while the natives, partly through complacency, blind faith, or resignation, went on with life as usual. From their European relatives and through their trip to the Holy Land, they had glimpsed the many faces of their people, the Jews, and learned something of themselves, their religion, and their heritage.

In the Europe they had left behind, the game was already afoot. Stanley Baldwin retired and Neville Chamberlain became prime minister of Great Britain. Italy withdrew from the League of Nations. Léon Blum resigned his office as premier of France. The Royal Commission on Palestine recommended the establishment of separate Arab and Jewish states. Lord Halifax visited Hitler, initiating a policy of appeasement that would lead Chamberlain to the delusory statement that he had brought "peace in our time."

At this point, as they pursued all the pleasures that a luxury cruise had to offer, Edith and Edgar were reasonably certain that any conflagration could be avoided. But even if not, then surely they and their country would not be directly affected. They were returning to the Land of the Free.

BOOK TWO

BOOK TWO

ONE

Longue Vue

NEW ORLEANS was in hot, sultry summer when the Sterns returned home. Family, friends, the household staff—all greeted them affectionately. The house once more enveloped them, a sense of well-being pervading the rooms. Edith distributed the plethora of gifts that immediately bespoke the many countries they had seen. After all their experiences, their venturesome spirits temporarily sated, they sensed that priceless feeling of those who have wandered far: the security of the familiar.

With the new day, the phone began ringing with invitations for Edith to consider. The children could barely wait to see the new wonder of wonders, Walt Disney's *Snow White*, the first full-length animated film. Fairy tales would not be quite the same thereafter. The world was soon to be stripped of many of its illusions.

For her part, Edith was eager to read a book by a new woman author whose work not only was sweeping the South but characterizing it as well. Among the many portents that popular titles offer, this was by far the most eloquent: *Gone With the Wind*.

Their friends wanted to know more of the Duke of Windsor and Wallis Simpson; it was the juiciest tidbit of international scandal. Was he, in fact, enslaved by sex? Had the Sterns discovered anything in the way of "inside" information during their English sojourn? The Sterns might well have wondered how people could be more interested in the internal workings of the British Royal Family than the consciousness-widening descriptions of Communist Russia or Palestine.

Edgar, as much as he admired all things English, took satisfaction in the good news that the United States tennis team managed to wrest the Davis Cup from England. And good news arrived from Lessing and his wife, Edith. They had become grandparents—a new generation had made its appearance.

The gardens at Longue Vue were fragrant. Edith walked the paths more frequently than ever before, taking deep enjoyment from the blaze of colors, the shades of green, the charming hideaways, the water-lily-crowned pond, and the profusion of blooming shrubbery demarking the outer perimeters of the property. A thought came to her, and she wondered why it had not occurred to her before. Why should the gardens be so removed from the household? Why should there be just one window on each floor of the house through which to glimpse the wonder and beauty they had to offer? She vowed to do something about this.

Edgar, too, was struck by a new awareness. He had reassessed his life's work and now made a sweeping and dramatic announcement. He was resolved to retire. Many among their family and friends were puzzled, if not shocked, by his decision, and what explanations he may have offered went, by and large, unrecorded. His sentimental journey appears to have been a factor. With the paradigm provided by his English country-squire cousins in mind, he may have fallen in love with the life-style of the grand seigneur. Perhaps, too, a stirring of patriotic service was involved and he wished to be free to serve in whatever capacity might be desirable in his own judgment.

Edith reestablished herself as the head of the household. She conferred with her English head gardener at length, complimenting him on the sculptured perfection of the gardens. She expressed her delight at the innovative floral arrangements Johanna had placed throughout the house and henceforth delegated this pleasant task to "Joh-Joh," the first ever to satisfy Edith's own taste and skill in the placement of flowers.

Entering the kitchen, she found that her accomplished and faithful cook, Julia Sonat, was in need of additional help. That important message was flashed "to whom it may concern" by means of Ortique's grocery store. Soon a personable young woman named Emma Brown appeared. Edith took an immediate liking to her lovely, round face and brown eyes, which reflected much kindness and intelligence. Emma was hired instantly as kitchen assistant and given the duties of preparing vegetables for cooking and baking, setting the table in the servants' dining room, and helping with the dishes. Not long afterward, she was taken off the "temporary help" list, became head cook, and went on to garner some impressive testimonials in the course of her career. Adlai Stevenson personally complimented her by saying that her red beans were the best he had ever eaten. Eleanor Roosevelt sent word to the kitchen that she wanted to meet the culinary whiz who had baked "those heavenly biscuits."

Guests from England were received with the most lavish welcome of the Stern household. As the gardens at Longue Vue burst into another fragrant spring, small talk turned to serious discussion. Hitler's hordes had goose-stepped into Austria to an enthusiastic welcome. Edgar and Edith were shocked. How little time had passed since they had watched the passing parade at Demmels, eating Linzertorte before returning to the justly named Hotel Imperial. Now Hitler addressed the crowd from the balcony of that very hotel. Anthony Eden, epitome of the English gentleman, resigned in protest to Chamberlain's policy of appeasement. Edgar understood that stance well. Daily, he took lunch with his close friends Monte Lemann and Moise Goldstein, the architect. As the debates raged on in the British Parliament, the three friends debated as well. What would happen in Europe? And if the unthinkable happened, how should the United States react?

Edith continued to absorb herself in domestic matters. In the early 1930's she had met Ellen Biddle Shipman, the designer of the elaborate landscaping for the Laurence Williams Home at 3 Garden Lane in New Orleans. Edith remembered being captivated by the charming, restful, and seemingly effortless results that were Ellen Shipman's trademark. She was captivated as well by the woman herself, and as they became friends Edith began to call her "Lady Ellen."

In 1935 Edith approached Lady Ellen, asking for a design that would do justice to the potential of the gardens at Longue Vue. The results surpassed Edith's highest hopes. In fact, the gardens now outshone the manor house.

Lady Ellen had little or no formal training as a landscape architect. She was a native of Berkeley Springs, West Virginia. While attending Radcliffe College as an undergraduate, she met Charles Platt, the renowned architect and landscape designer, who took her under his wing. Later she married playwright and editor Louis Evan Shipman and lived for a time in New York City. Subsequently, she was attracted to Cornish, New Hampshire, a center for artists, where she encountered Augustus Saint Gaudens. Inspired to work, she became part of a renaissance in landscaping led by a few visionary women who conceptualized the use of plants in terms of painting techniques. In a 1938 interview, Ellen Shipman already considered it fair to state that "until women took up landscaping, the art of landscaping was at its lowest ebb in this country."

Edith confided to Lady Ellen her dissatisfaction with the house that afforded only dismal glimpses of the gardens. Could not something be done to improve the house in this regard? After extensive study and discussion, agreement was reached that it would be neither aesthetically nor economically feasible to enlarge and equip the house with all the accoutrements Edith now desired. A new house, then! But Edith was loath to acquire a new house, no matter how splendid, because it would mean giving up the gardens for which she had a profound attachment.

The solution was that a new house should rise on the foundation of the old one—a second Longue Vue. But who could design and build a home that would meet Edith's exacting requirements – one that would bow to traditions that had become cherished, afford the luxuries that Edith sought, and yet remain unostentatious? Lady Ellen provided the answer. She suggested William Platt of New York, son of the distinguished architect Charles Adams Platt, who had made his name in the Classical tradition.

William Platt and his brother Geoffrey had inherited the family firm upon their father's demise. They had achieved renown in their own right on projects such as the Chapel for the American Battle Monuments Commission in Paris, France; the first Corning Glass Building on Fifth Avenue and 56th Street in Manhattan; a chapel for Smith College, Northampton, Massachusetts; thirteen buildings for Deerfield Academy in Massachusetts; and more. Longue Vue II would constitute a principal project for William Platt from 1939 to late December of 1942.

During that time much discussion within the Stern circle, as elsewhere, centered on the distasteful subject of the rapidly deteriorating political situation in Europe. To be sure, there were less weighty conversations over the particularly rich harvest to be found in contemporary literature. William Faulkner's *The Unvanquished* received critical acclaim, while Christopher Isherwood's *Goodbye to Berlin* fared less well. Daphne du Maurier's *Rebecca* was published and Thornton Wilder's *Our Town* received the Pulitzer Prize for drama.

Edgar was especially pleased when the Pulitzer Prize for literature went to an alumnus of Harvard, John Philip Marquand, for his brilliant novel *The Late George Apley* which portrayed a Bostonian and his world. Edgar reveled in the work, deriving particular pleasure from the descriptions of Harvard life. "About these halls there has always been an aroma of high feeling not to be found or lost in science or Greek – not to be fixed, yet all-pervading." Edgar Jr. would soon be retracing his father's footsteps among the ivied halls, and Edgar's heart swelled with pride at the thought of a second generation of Sterns sipping from this incomparable font of knowledge. With a mixture of awe, wonder, and surprise, Edgar must have scrutinized the program of that year's graduation exercises. Among the awards was an honorary doctorate for Miss Marion

Anderson, the remarkable contralto they had first heard in their cook's church. Edgar and Edith could easily picture her proudly wearing the crimson-and-gold hood of Harvard.

The year 1938 closed on a dismal note. Hitler was on the march again. Even though Edgar was strongly anti-Roosevelt, in direct opposition to Edith's sentiments, for once they could both agree that it was the appropriate move on the international chessboard when Roosevelt recalled the American ambassador from Germany.

Edgar came home one day to find Edith seated on the floor, totally engrossed in stacks of blueprints. When questioned, she allowed that these were the plans for their new home. Naturally! And, what was even more natural was that Platt had done an incredible job. Edgar succumbed, joining in, finding this an absorbing task and completely immersing himself in it. As the weeks lengthened into months, the building of the new house became an obsession.

Lady Ellen, William Platt, Edgar, and Edith proved a formidable quartet. They all visited famous, as well as less-renowned, homes in Louisiana and elsewhere. Longue Vue II would be erected in the Classical tradition, drawing on examples of indigenous Greek Revival homes and buildings in Louisiana.

The main facade was designed in just that style, incorporating such fascinating detail as a temple pediment with Doric columns and French doors. The oak-lined drive to the house recalled that of Louisiana plantations, and the entrance court was paved with granite ballast and flanked by two small cottages in West Indian style. In the forecourt would be a double-tiered cast-iron fountain restored from fragments that Edgar had found. The original was English, cast about 1840.

The clipped boxwood was to reflect seventeenth and early eighteenth century English styles, while the arching fountains, mosaic sidewalks, and container plantings were to be reminiscent of the Alhambra Gardens in Granada, Spain. The totality was to have the appearance so often found in "unplanned" English gardens. The suggestion was made that the old house not be demolished, but sold instead for $5,000 and moved intact down Garden Lane to the vacant property of its new owner.

At the same time, in Europe, the tense and volatile political atmosphere reached a flashpoint on September 1, 1939. Hitler unleashed the fury of war. Poland lay prostrate within eighteen days, torn to shreds and devoured by two predatory neighbors, Germany and Russia. Some of the towns and cities through which the Sterns' train had taken them not long ago were smoldering heaps of rubble. Even the fairy-tale Finnish countryside now under Soviet dominance was difficult for Edith and Edgar to visualize.

Concern for the safety of their British relatives was allayed by frequent communications. While the Germans sang out a strident challenge in "Bomben auf Engeland," the plucky British countered in a lighter, if ingenuous vein, with "We're going to hang our washing on the Siegfried Line."

The most popular song written in America that fateful year was "God Bless America." And there was much to be thankful for in the small bits of good news. Monte Lemann reported that his good friend Felix Frankfurter had been appointed to the Supreme Court by President Roosevelt. And Judy Garland's voice came over the air waves with the haunting promises of "Over the Rainbow."

One day the preparations were complete: Longue Vue I was ready to be moved down the street. New friends, neighbors of the Sterns, Albert and Maxine Wachenheim, were on hand for the move, fascinated by the spectacle. From the Elsas home, also on Garden Lane, they watched Longue Vue in the process of being towed to its new site. Suddenly, Edgar came tearing around the corner, obviously in great agitation, shouting at the movers to "stop this immediately!"

The whole affair came to a halt. Edgar climbed up the structure, threw open the doors, ran into the house, and emerged shortly thereafter, triumphantly waving a tuxedo and several other items of clothing that apparently had been forgotten in one of the closets. He smiled sheepishly to his astonished neighbors. "We all laughed so hard that tears were rolling down our cheeks," said Mrs. Wachenheim, "and that laughter cemented a warm, long-lasting friendship."

It was one of many friendships that Edith and Edgar enjoyed in Garden Lane. There was, for example, their close relationship with John Labouisse and his wife, Olive May. Edith and Edgar had known young Labouisse since he was a small boy, when John's father was a business acquaintance of Edgar's. Even then, the two held one another in great esteem, and, in time, the Sterns found the younger Labouisse family most companionable.

Olive May also held a special place in their hearts. The Sterns had given a memorable party in honor of her debut. In keeping with her reputation as a hostess *par excellence,* Edith outdid herself on that occasion. Guests were required to attend in children's clothing, and, in order to get into the ballroom, they had to slide down a precipitous chute. They were met at the bottom by their laughing host and hostess, and rewarded for their daredevil exploit with a baby bottle filled with stern stuff. Trying to imbibe the liquor through the nipples produced further hilarity.

When John and Olive May married in 1933, at the depth of the Depression, money was scarce. Edith stepped in, again, to provide the bridal finery. And when the Labouisses' first daughter, Jeanne, was born, Edith sent a gift elegantly wrapped. Inside was one little bootie. The family was baffled. One bootie, no matter how beautiful, was not very useful. However, closer scrutiny revealed that the bootie contained a memo. Enclosed were five shares of Sears, Roebuck stock, and the note explained that Jeanne was now the youngest Sears stockholder. John Labouisse, writing of that incident many years later, added that his daughter still cherished that single bootie along with the certificate, which, by then, had grown to 244 shares.

The Elsases, the Labouisses, the Legendres—all the neighborhood—watched with delight as the walls of Longue Vue II went up. More than the sure knowledge that the value of their own real estate was also going up was the pleasure in knowing that Edith and Edgar had chosen to remain close by.

Edith's forty-fifth birthday fell on Memorial Day, 1940. While she sat in her flower-decorated chair receiving congratulations from family and friends, a brave small armada composed of everything from chug-boats to luxury vessels was challenging the turbulence of the English Channel in an effort to evacuate the British forces, some 340,000 strong, from Dunkirk. Winston Churchill, the "alarmist," had become prime minister of England and could offer his people nothing but "blood, toil, tears and sweat" on that glorious spring day.

Edith and Edgar regarded their children. Edgar Jr. would be eighteen in September. He expected to celebrate his birthday at Harvard. Audrey—charming and effervescent, a gifted young lady—would turn sixteen in July. And Philip—delightful, quick-witted, and sensitive as always—would soon be fourteen. When they all had dined at the Dorchester in London not long ago, could they have foreseen the risks to which the flower of this next generation would be exposed?

On Friday, June 14, Paris fell. The Nazis marched through the Arch of Triumph. A small airplane with German markings on its wings stood in the middle of the Place de la Concorde. Men far less emotional than Edgar Stern wept freely.

Edith soon left for New York to spend some time with her sisters Adele and Marion. David Levy, Adele's psychiatrist husband, could no doubt offer much insight into the world situation, as could Max Ascoli, Marion's new husband, an urbane and erudite Italian-born political analyst. Perhaps she could find a point of view from which the European news might not sound so terrible. And, of course, she wanted to go shopping with Lady Ellen in search of acquisitions for the new house.

New York City was oppressively hot under the unrelenting sun of the summer of 1941, hardly better than the caldron of steam and humidity that was New Orleans in July and August. By contrast, White Pines Camp, with its lakes a shimmering golden mirror reflecting the tall pines along the shoreline, offered welcome refuge. The Sterns and Levys, with most of the domestic staff imported from New Orleans, made their way to the Adirondacks. There was a new and welcome addition to the staff that summer in the person of Adam Jamet, a dashing black man whose friendly smile and consistent good humor dispelled any lingering gloom. A fine driver, he became the general factotum of the Stern household, holding that post for the next thirty-nine years.

Construction on Longue Vue II was proceeding well. William Platt was doing a superb job, aided by the contracting firm of John O'Brien and by Philip Bradbury. Edith was particularly pleased that Bradbury was performing with considerable panache, justifying her faith in his competence, which had overruled Platt's objections, so that Platt finally had to admit that Edith was "right as usual," and that it was no accident that Edgar referred to her as "RAU."

Philip Bradbury was born in New Orleans in 1897. He left school after the third grade and went to work for a saddle-maker named Weiss. He emerged as a skilled carpenter, and, as legend had it, if Phil Bradbury could not fix something, it might as well be junked. In the late 1920's, Bradbury had been engaged in some work at Longue Vue I, when the governess, Miss Grant, asked whether he could fix a phonograph turntable that had defied all efforts at repair. In a short time, Phil Bradbury had the turntable apart and analyzed, then fixed. What is more, he refused remuneration, saying that he had enjoyed the challenge.

From that time, whenever Edith conceived a project, she relied on Philip Bradbury to transform it into reality. One day, Edith asked him to build a six-foot platform around a large shade tree. "But don't paint it, Philip," she admonished, "just prepare three tomato cans of paint and some brushes. I'll send you the painters."

The following day, Audrey and her two brothers appeared on the scene clad in coveralls and launched themselves furiously into the job at hand. Their enthusiasm was far greater than their skill, and equal amounts of paint wound up on the coveralls as on the platform.

When it came to contracting Longue Vue, Edith insisted, over Platt's complaint that Bradbury could not read architectural plans, that Phil Bradbury be placed on the project. Bradbury set himself the task of learning the intricacies of blueprints and successfully saw the construction through from start to finish. His incomparable workmanship and close attention to detail became legendary. Once they arrived from the foundry, he fit the curved stair railings, running over three stories, with watchlike precision. He took part in every aspect of the project.

Upon its completion, Edith and Edgar offered the custodianship of the impressive mansion to Phil Bradbury. He stayed on for thirty-two years, hardly taking any time off from his all-consuming work, which, as far as he was concerned, also constituted his leisure. He was ever prepared to create decorations for numerous parties; it was he, at twilight, who threw the switch that lighted every bulb at Longue Vue. Once, when Edith confided that she was apprehensive about how a wallpaper she had chosen would look, he built a miniature room papered with the design in question and presented it to Edith for her inspection.

The fine millwork used on the interior of the house was made in Bronxville, New York. The window sashes were made of mahogany; as a special touch, the doors in the formal rooms of the main house were of Honduran mahogany, while Brazilian rosewood was used for the floors. Edgar's study and the Blue Room were floored in white oak. Hardware and steel arrived from New York City, and Angelo Angeleosi produced the friezes and plasterwork details in the ceilings. Corning Glass provided the remarkable glass curtain wall in Edgar's bathroom. Longue Vue was one of the first homes in New Orleans to be centrally air-conditioned, and the unit chosen was an eighty-ton mechanical wonder. Almost none of the firms that contributed custom services to the creation of Longue Vue are in existence today. The fine craftsmen of that era are hardly to be found; nor would there be a large market for their consummate skills. Edith no doubt was correct when she observed, toward the end of her life, that Longue Vue was the last great custom-built house in America.

The Stern family—Edgar, Edith, Edgar Jr., Philip, and Audrey—at Biarritz in the early 1930's.

The Stern family in the late 1940's. Standing (left to right) are Philip, Edgar Jr., and Thomas Hess. Seate are Audrey (holding William), Edgar, Edith, and Polly (Edgar Jr.'s wife).

TWO

Home and Friends

WHEN ON SUNDAY MORNING, December 7, 1941, Japanese war planes attacked Pearl Harbor, the Sterns, despite their privileged knowledge of and exposure to foreign affairs, despite endless conversations dealing with potentially dire political possibilities, were as unprepared and astonished as the rest of the country. In the days following the declaration of war, hysteria and fear swept the nation. There was panic buying of food supplies; many people considered bombing raids on the American Mainland to be a distinct possibility. Following the model set in Britain, many looked for safe havens in the countryside for their children. The initial shock wave subsided, however, and a certain routine set in as people began working for the "cause" and their inordinate fears diminished.

Edith was asked to take a high-level position in the Red Cross. She soon became a ubiquitous presence in her natty uniform, teaching, exhorting, and inspiring groups of women to work for the organization and to sell war bonds. She proved indomitable in pursuit of such activities.

Soon after President Roosevelt's "Day of Infamy" speech, Edgar decided to go to Washington to offer his services as a "dollar-a-year" man. He was prepared to put at the disposal of his country his efforts, his experience, and his considerable means. Edith accompanied him. Edith and Edgar subsequently commuted between Washington, New Orleans, New York, and Chicago, with an occasional stop in Boston to see the children. They worked tirelessly in behalf of the war effort, keeping up a vast correspondence with relatives and friends. Even so, the conflict was brought much closer to them when Edgar Jr. enlisted.

In Washington, the Sterns met Eva Hertz, daughter of Edgar's second cousin who lived in Lucerne, Switzerland. Eva was studying in London when the war broke out and made the hazardous crossing to the United States in a convoy at the height of the war in 1941. Soon after her arrival in New York, she met and married Kurt J. Hertz. An immediate rapport developed between the older and younger couples. Edgar and Edith invited the newlyweds to spend their honeymoon at Longue Vue: the New Orleans mansion would be at their disposal under the care of the staff.

Eva Hertz remembers how she and her husband committed their first *faux pas* when they alighted from their car, opened the trunk, and began to retrieve their own suitcases. The houseman appeared; raising a quizzical eyebrow toward what he must have considered "country bumpkins," he removed the luggage from them, his stoical mien betraying little of his assessment. Edith had sent instructions that the honeymooners be assigned the master-bedroom suite. A maid appeared almost instantly, much to Eva's discomfiture, and proceeded to unpack the suitcases. A tour of the house and grounds left the newlyweds overwhelmed. In light, especially, of the war-time austerity that Eva was used to, Longue Vue seemed like paradise.

For the first time, the couple slept between luxurious silk sheets, had their nightgowns and pajamas ironed daily, and were greeted each morning by a fresh corsage for Eva, accompanied by breakfast in bed. This last a delicate problem: As Orthodox Jews, Eva and Kurt could not eat until the morning prayer ritual had been completed. Kurt, accordingly, rose early, dressed, and prayed in the prescribed manner, wearing his prayer shawl and phylacteries, then quickly disrobed, climbed back into bed, and allowed Eva to ring for the maid to bring breakfast. They were too young, too shy, and too inexperienced simply to leave orders that they did not want breakfast in bed.

Many years later, the Hertz's son-in-law Dr. Rolf Lederer attended a psychiatric convention in New Orleans. Remembering the stories of his in-laws' honeymoon, he took the opportunity to tour Longue Vue (which, by then, was open to the public). Listening to the docent who escorted his touring party, he felt the urge to add some details of family lore. But he chose instead to reserve them for his sons back in Toronto, and for his nephew and niece in Israel, who listened in wry amusement and considerable awe to the tales of their grandparents' honeymoon.

The Sterns enjoyed tennis as recreation from their wartime labors. And several of their friendships revolved around the courts. With the children away from home, they "adopted" a young Army officer named Lester Kabacoff, nicknaming him "Kabby," and spent many hours with him on and off the court. Kabby was a skillful player of tournament stature. It was he who formed what was known as the "Racquet and Julep Club" at Longue Vue. Frequently, after their exertions, they took time to enjoy the potent and relaxing powers of the mint julep. Edgar was given the honorary title "Prez," and the name stuck. The friendship stuck, too, so much so that when Kabby and his wife, Gloria, had their first son, they named him Prez in Edgar's honor.

There was the time when Maxine Wachenheim, working as a volunteer nurse's aide at the Charity Hospital Burn Center, was surprised to discover a familiar face in the course of her daily rounds. To her dismay she realized it was Kabby, who had just had a tonsillectomy. After cleaning him up and making him comfortable, she ran for ice to minimize his pain. Maxine immediately notified Edith, and the young man's "foster mother" wasted no time in supplying the patient with her own proven panacea: chicken soup and affectionate concern. She was at her best when she felt needed, taking full charge of any situation. It never occurred to her to call a servant to perform unpleasant tasks when one of her children or her grand-children was sick.

Edith had a special knack of making friends of all ages. Thus, Marilyn Barnett, daughter of friends of the Sterns, became a frequent visitor to the Racquet and Julep Club. The Sterns appreciated her keen intelligence and delightful wit, at the same time finding her exquisitely beautiful, as well as athletic. Following several sets of tennis, all would sit bundled up in sweaters with towels around their necks, relaxing over frosty juleps or Johanna's brandy milk punch. Edgar would light his aromatic pipe, and stories would unfold. Marilyn recalled how Edith entertained a somewhat flashy, wealthy Texas lady at lunch one day. Afterward, during a leisurely stroll through the gardens, the lady from Texas noted a golf course (the New Orleans Country Club course adjoins one side of the Longue Vue grounds). Seeing the manicured field, dotted with a few players, the lady from Texas remarked, "Oh, Edith, you have a golf course, too! Ours is nine holes—what's yours?" Without a moment's hesitation and in her marvelously con-trolled manner, Edith replied, "Eighteen, dear."

Another charter member of the club was Francis Soyka. In impeccably tailored whites, floppy matching hat perched on his head, exuding outdoor vigor, and smiling his courtly smile, he was a charismatic presence. Though he was physically small, people spontaneously addressed him as "Mr. Soyka." Born in Prague in 1892, when the city was still part of the Austro-Hungarian Empire, he was named for the beloved Emperor Franz-Josef. Young Soyka served in the emperor's army in World War I, fighting valiantly on the Russian front. He was decorated for bravery by the emperor himself. To the end of his life, a picture of this monarch occupied a place of honor in his bedroom, even though Soyka had become a proud American.

Francis was the scion of the renowned Soyka family that owned one of the largest champagne bottling companies in

Czechoslovakia. He began playing tennis at the age of eight, and took to this elegant sport with a passion. He had played the "sport of kings" against King Peter of Yugoslavia, Queen Marie of Romania, and King Gustaf of Sweden. At the Sterns' courts he would sometimes reminisce for the benefit of Marilyn Barnett. In his arch, accented voice he would recall how in his golden youth, from 1925 through 1935, he had led both the Czech National Amateur Team and the Davis Cup Squad in matches on the Continent and in South Africa. In 1939 he fled Nazi-dominated Czechoslovakia sans sports car, tailored suits, and tennis rackets, arriving in New York with no connections whatever.

To improve his pronunciation of English, he read segments of the *New York Times* aloud. In the course of one such exercise, he learned that two Czech comedians were giving a performance in the city. He had no job at the time, his total financial resources amounting to five dollars. To attend this benefit performance would reduce his capital by twenty percent. After some deliberations, he concluded that the dollar would make no difference in his overall affairs. It was a fortuitous decision. At the performance, he met a kinsman from Prague who lauded his achievements on the tennis courts to a lady who found Soyka a job as a tennis instructor at a Maine summer camp. On Parents Day, the youngsters sang their instructor's praises. The parents of one of the boys he was coaching were from New Orleans. Tennis, they noted, was played there all year round, and they offered to investigate job opportunities for him.

Through the good offices of Miss Ruth Dreyfous, an alumna of the Newman School and the school psychologist, Soyka was offered a position as tennis instructor, arriving in New Orleans in 1941. In later years, as his Soyka Method for teaching tennis earned him a certain degree of fame and fortune, he did something marvelous in repayment of what he considered his "debt." Before his death in 1979, he gave half of his not inconsiderable estate to the Newman School, one of the largest bequests ever received by that establishment whose many loyal, successful graduates consider it "one of the most extraordinary educational institutions in the country."

During those years, Edith and Edgar put their newly finished home at the disposal of diverse organizations geared to the war effort. On Tuesday, November 22, 1944, the *New Orleans Item* apprised its readers that an auction sale to be held on December 5 at Longue Vue would be jointly sponsored by the Garden Clubs of New Orleans.

> The funds realized from the donated heirlooms will go to beautify the grounds of the military hospitals of the city. Mrs. Stern is President of the New Orleans Garden Study Club; she is also on the Conservation Committee of the Garden Clubs of America and has held two meetings with the presidents of 17 garden clubs to plan for this big benefit sale. Every Wednesday, Mr. and Mrs. Stern entertain servicemen and their dates.

Among the donated treasures at the auction, Edith spotted a photograph of Francis Soyka playing tennis with King Gustav of Sweden. Realizing that this was one of the few keepsakes Soyka had brought along when fleeing the Nazis, she asked her friend Lucille Blum to bid for it. As soon as Lucille gained possession of it, Edith asked Lucille to restore it to its original owner. Francis Soyka never caught on that Edith was behind this gesture.

Edith and Edgar continued their work in Washington, without disrupting their family involvements. From the nation's capital, Warren Stern, son of Edgar's brother Walter, received a warm congratulatory letter from Edgar on his graduation from Tulane University. It was filled with avuncular concern. Edith wrote to Clara Guttman, an elderly relative, to thank her for the gift of a bag done in needlepoint. She noted that the bag, with its exquisite workmanship and choice of colors, made her the envy of her friends at the Red Cross functions. The bag, it should be noted, was an expression of appreciation to Edith for having, in effect, saved Clara's life and the life of her immediate family by helping them to flee Germany in the nick of time.

Edith continued to enjoy herself by completing the decorations at Longue Vue, buying many fine eighteenth and nineteenth century pieces. Most were not museum quality; in this, Edith heeded the advice of Elsie de Wolfe, who decreed, "Good reproductions are more valuable than feeble originals." Formality was largely abandoned to comfort and convenience. Dining-room pieces were used in sitting rooms if they served a practical purpose; bedroom pieces were sometimes used to advantage in formal rooms. Lady Ellen engaged Euphane Mallison to supervise the interior design. Miss Mallison went to great lengths fashioning models for furniture placement, executing the stencil decoration for the sleeping porch, and mixing paints. While supervising the project, she lived at the adjacent residence of Victor and Bertha Elsas.

The dining room was Edith's special pride and joy, combining her own taste with the taste and skill of Ellen Shipman. The wallpaper consists of three Chinese screens originally bought for Mrs. Shipman and hung on the walls of her New York home on Beekman Place. The Sterns later bought the Beekman Place home and had the paper painstakingly removed to grace the dining room walls at Longue Vue. They further enhanced the warmth of the dining room by placing two easy chairs to flank the fireplace. A smaller table, used for more intimate dining than the main table could afford, is set in a bay window framing one of the loveliest and most charming gardens on the estate, the Pan Garden. The statue of Pan, the centerpiece of this quiet haven is the work of Josephine Knoblock, an English sculptor. Nothing pleased Edith as much as this view replete with azaleas, magnolias, and a stately rose tree. And it was in this particular garden, on a wall, that Edith had affixed a plaque, which reads:

> Ellen Shipman
> Creator of beauty
> With love and gratitude.

Every piece selected for Longue Vue seemed to have a story of its own, none more interesting than the Karabash rugs from Russia. By royal decree, the rugs from this province had been designated exclusively for the family of the czar. After the Revolution, much of the czar's personal property found its way into the open market, where Mrs. Shipman discovered these rare masterpieces in a famous auction house. They were to remain the only ones ever to surface. Apparently, the Bolsheviks realized what they had done and clamped the lid on such exports.

It was a feat of daring when Edith installed the Disney Corridor containing seventeen celluloid paintings from diverse Walt Disney productions, including *The Reluctant Dragon, The Country Cousins, Snow White and the Seven Dwarfs, The Brave Little Tailor, Fantasia, Ferdinand the Bull,* and *The Ugly Duckling* – all completed between 1935 and 1938. The cast of irrepressible characters cavorting in those otherwise staid surroundings imparted an infectious sense of mischief and good fun, astonishing many distinguished guests, who would gaze at the walls in disbelief while making their way to the drawing room.

And who but Edith would ask for a wild garden in a remote corner of the property, devoted to flowering trees, a pigeonniere, a wildflower walk of hydrangea, Louisiana swamp iris, wild azaleas and Spanish moss – the whole completed by a replica of an outbuilding? Edith's special personality was captured, too, in a room found in few, if any, private residences, the "Package Wrapping Room," where custom cabinets of gumwood held wrappings and decorative frills to prettify gifts for any occasion. Edith used it extensively through all the seasons of the year.

The Playhouse across from the Japanese yew-screened tennis courts was a replica of a colonial Virginia barn that paid special homage to the long tradition of amateur dramatics in the Rosenwald and Stern homes. In the 1970's, Edith placed *Louisiana Weeds and Wildflowers,* a sculpture by Trailer McQuilkin, on permanent display there. And the "Whim House," a charming guest house reflecting eighteenth century themes, was an escape from the formality of the main residence. It sports a swinging bed that hangs from the ceiling, flowered chintz upholstery, and Murphy beds in its curving walls. From Whim House one could look out on the Yellow Garden, so named for the yellow flowers that bloom there throughout the year, or take a more serious turn into the underground tunnel leading to a bomb shelter beneath the Playhouse Casino. In the winter of 1942, when the German army laid siege to the fortress that was Stalingrad, Longue Vue stood finished and prepared.

THREE

The End of the War

T HE DAY OF JUNE 29, 1944, dawned very hot in New Orleans. The household rose early with an air of happy anticipation. It was Audrey's wedding day. Topiary trees adorned with daisies had been placed in the hall. The dining room was a vision of white. The chairs around the large dining table, as well as those that ringed the several smaller ones, had backrests covered in white and festooned with matching white ribbons.

Heightening the general elation was the knowledge that the young man about to join the family was no stranger but belonged to a clan that had held a common bond of friendship with the Rosenwalds for three generations. Tom Hess, the groom, a handsome, tall, brown-haired, brown-eyed youth, looked dashing in his Air Force uniform. He was stationed in nearby Selma, Alabama, as an instructor of French pilots. In civilian life, Tom was the editor of the prestigious *Art News* magazine. He was the son of a prominent New York attorney, Gabriel Hess, and his wife, Helen (née Baer), and the grandson of Ben Baer of St. Paul, who had been a good friend of Julius Rosenwald.

The Hess family and their children had enjoyed a close friendship with Edith's sister Adele and her family in New York and were frequent visitors at White Pines where Tom's sister, Betty, would team up with Edith to go on botanical "field trips" in search of exotic flowers, plants, and herbs, which they fashioned into miniature horticultural creations on pie plates. They called these their "fairy gardens." Through Betty, Tom and Audrey began their storybook romance in the fall of 1942, when Audrey entered Bennington College in Vermont as a freshman. Audrey spent a good deal of time visiting her uncle and aunt in New York, where Dr. Levy was making a study of the importance of interaction between mother and child in the immediate postnatal period to further his advocacy of early childhood development. When Audrey, eighteen years old, inquisitive and alert, betrayed an interest in child psychology, her uncle commissioned her to do some research for him, inasmuch as Bennington allowed credit for such off-campus activities.

Providentially, when Betty Wolff gave birth to her daughter, Nancy, in October, Audrey had a splendid opportunity for some first-hand observations. Audrey's presence, in return, helped Betty through the postnatal period, made difficult by her Army husband's absence. Tom appeared with astonishing frequency in the Wolff home, until it became clear that his love for his new niece was tempered with a fascination for the young researcher diligently recording each of the baby's moves. Tom's courtship of Audrey was briefly interrupted by his induction into the Army, but the lively correspondence that ensued brought the two closer and closer together. In the end, Audrey asked Betty to be one of her attendants.

Edith marshaled all her considerable organizational resources into making her only daughter's wedding beautiful and meaningful. She was startled to learn that Tom and Audrey had not thought of inviting a rabbi to solemnize their union. "Nonsense," she declared, "of course a rabbi will be present." But when Rabbi Julian Feibelman in going over the details of the ceremony suggested the traditional breaking of the glass, Edith balked at the idea. No glass was to be broken, except perhaps inadvertently, during the reception.

Tom and Audrey voiced plans to live in New York after the war, hoping to enjoy the benefits of that cultural mecca. A glittering future seemed to lie before them, and by all appearances the world was theirs for the taking.

The Allies crossed the Elbe and advanced swiftly toward the Russians. Mussolini was killed by Italian partisans. On April 30, in his bunker in Berlin, Hitler and his mistress committed suicide. Berlin surrendered to the Russians on May 2; Germany capitulated on May 7; and VE Day ended the war in Europe officially on May 8. The end of the war in Europe gave rise to the hope that the war in the Pacific would also end soon. One peaceful afternoon, shortly after VJ Day, Johanna was summoned outside the house. There stood a shiny black Studebaker, bearing a card with her name. Edith had promised her a car of her own if Edgar Jr. and Philip would return unscathed, and now she was redeeming her promise.

With the end of the war, a new truth dawned: the price that had been paid for peace. Europe was in ruins. Bands of refugees crisscrossed the scenes of desolation in search of their former homes, many of them looking in vain amid the rubble. The scene transcended anything the mind could conceive. The familiar, sobering voice of radio correspondent Edward R. Murrow for once lost its measured cadence as he reported, "You will be sitting down to dinner, but after hearing what I have to say, few of you will be able to eat...." Murrow had entered the gates of the Nazi concentration camp at Buchenwald.

As soon as the fragments of the unspeakable horror visited upon European Jewry became known, Adele Levy determined to go on a fact-finding mission. Thanks to the intervention of Eleanor Roosevelt, who shared Adele's concern and pain, Adele managed to be among the first civilians making the crossing to the Continent. Arriving in France, Adele was received and escorted by Paulette Opère, a stunning young Frenchwoman from a prominent Jewish family. During the war, Paulette had performed selflessly and heroically in the resistance movement, saving children at great risk to her own life. Her husband, an officer in the French Army and later a member of the underground, had been engaged in similar heroic exploits when he was caught and executed by the Nazis in the waning days of the war.

When the armistice came, Paulette found herself alone to care for her own two girls, but immediately took up the cause of homeless and orphaned children from all over Europe. A run-down mansion in the environs of Paris provided temporary shelter for these pitiful remnants of Europe's once-proud Jewish communities. It was to Malmaison, onetime residence of the Empress Josephine after her divorce from Napoleon, that Paulette brought Adele for her unforgettable encounter with the children. The two women's paths were to cross many times thereafter. Paulette ultimately came to live in the United States and married Israel Fink of Minneapolis. It was not long before her leadership qualities and experience catapulted her to the position of chairman of the Women's Division of the United Jewish Appeal, where she proved a worthy successor to such women as Adele Levy and Mathilda Brailove.

Adele's gentle personality served as an antidote to the harsh realities of man's inhumanity to man. On her return, Adele began her campaign to enlist the aid of Jewish women all over America in caring for these children and helping to shape their future. They responded by founding the Women's Division of the United Jewish Appeal and electing Adele as its first chairman, in March 1946.

As might be expected, Edith heeded her sister's appeals, quite independently giving high priority to this project. Henceforth, she was a stalwart, unswerving, and generous supporter of the United Jewish Appeal. Not only did she contribute toward the first million dollar Rosenwald gift to the Appeal in 1945, but the Sterns also gave $100,000 in honor of their twenty-fifth wedding anniversary in June 1946.

Edith was in her prime, a woman who had passed the half-century mark, married for twenty-five years to the man she adored. The children were grown and had achieved independence. Edith and Edgar had completed Longue Vue, which they called their "machine for luxury living." They seemed to possess all that one might aspire to: loving family, hosts of friends, health, wealth, stature, and good fortune. Being astute and sensitive, they did not take their position for granted. In support of worthy causes, and in support of the arts, nothing proved too lavish. Now Edith began the fulfillment of another promise, that after the war, when Red Cross and similar duties would no longer claim her time, she would devote energy to the furthering of the Symphony.

On January 23, 1946, Edgar was to celebrate his sixtieth birthday. The event clearly called for something special. While Edgar was dressing upstairs, members of the New Orleans Symphony Orchestra were clandestinely slipping into the house. Karen Makas, principal cellist of the orchestra, remembers Edith going upstairs to return a few minutes later with her husband. As she led him down the grand staircase, Alexander Hilsberg, the conductor, lifted his baton for the opening strains of Mozart's "Haffner" Symphony. It was Edgar's favorite piece of music.

FOUR

Voters' Service

D ELESSEPS S. MORRISON, better known as "Chep," was bright, alert, and thirty-four years old when he completed his military service in the Army. Now, in the latter part of 1945, he was a candidate in the mayoral elections for the city of New Orleans. In the forefront of his volunteer workers were women determined to replace the incumbent administration. In their eyes Chep Morrison brought a new honesty and a worldly wisdom. Among his most ardent, reliable supporters was a woman whose keen intelligence and instantaneous grasp of knotty problems was tempered by tact and the ability to defuse potentially explosive situations. She was Rosalie Brener Grad, and was to serve as Mayor Chep Morrison's secretary throughout his entire term of office. Much later, when Moon Landrieu became mayor, Rosalie rendered invaluable service to him as well. Thus, for a span of sixteen years, she witnessed political life in New Orleans from a unique vantage point.

Another of Chep Morrison's volunteers was Edith Rosenwald Stern, who drew to her side many other women dedicated to the same ideals. Rosalie Grad, a shrewd judge of people, was thrown into constant contact with Edith and found her to be both politically astute and personally ingenious. She was particularly taken by Edith's egalitarian views.

> It was her wise and winning personality that drew her into these privileged circles; neither her wealth nor her philanthropic greatness would have been sufficient without these. She could talk with anyone without being condescending, but always stood her ground without being intimidated.

During the Morrison campaign Edith could be found at Johnny's Bar, a popular watering place for politicians and city employees, standing with one foot on the rail, eating a Poor Boy sandwich and drinking a Coke while conversing with the so-called "mullets," the political hangers-on. After the conversation, she would slide into her shiny limousine to be whisked off to her home or to preside at a formal dinner for some visiting dignitary. Edith organized the famed "Women's Broom Brigade" whose motto was "A Clean Sweep" and whose target was City Hall. She worked for and promoted any candidate or official who could help make the city a better and healthier place in which to raise families. To carry in the marches, Edith rounded up hundreds of brooms from Sears. With women to shoulder them, and posters attached to the broomsticks, Edith led the march from Canal Street to Saint Charles Avenue and on to the Jerusalem Temple. The city turned out to cheer, and Edith loved every moment of it. Supporters were moved to generous contributions, and Chep Morrison was virtually swept into office.

Edith continued to work tirelessly throughout the hiatus between the elections and the inauguration. In Rosalie's words:

> Spurred on by her passionate love for the city and her endless resources of brilliant ideas, she had a pivotal role in setting the goals of the new administration. Though the Mayor and Edith did not see eye to eye on every issue, they fostered a relationship based on mutual admiration and devotion. She was an important confidante of his, whose down-to-earth judgment he respected. He was always available to her, a reflection of the high regard in which he held her. The Mayor could be in an important conference, one for which I had been strictly instructed not to disturb him, but if I rang the buzzer to say that Edith Stern was on the phone, he always spoke to her.

Walter Samuel Smith was blind. An accident incurred playing ball when he was thirty-two and a salesman for the Gulf Refining Company had cost him his eyesight. From the limited insurance proceeds, his wife, Clementine, bought a small Ford car and began to sell clothes door-to-door, while her mother came to the tiny rented cottage on Dumaine Street to look after "Tebo," as her granddaughter Clem was called. Through the help of the Lighthouse for the Blind, an agency for the retraining of the sightless, Walter got a food and beverage concession in the Sewage and Water Board Building, while Clementine used her Ford in a job she secured with the School Board driving handicapped children to and from John Dibert School.

The bright spot in both their lives was young Clem, an outstanding student and a cheerful, loving daughter, who was now looking for a job. A casual acquaintance stopped by the counter and, during a brief chat, mentioned to Walter that he knew someone across the street in the Marble Hall Building who was looking for part-time secretarial help. Thinking that a temporary job was better than none, Clem presented herself. The Marble Hall Building, despite its grand name, was creaky with age and the small upstairs room was hardly the stuff of an employee's dreams. But the woman who interviewed her had an intuitive feeling for people and hired her on the spot.

"You understand, of course, that this is only a temporary job," said Mrs. Stern, the interviewer. As it turned out, Clem Smith served as Edith's indispensable "Girl Friday" for more than thirty years.

The stage was being set for a larger drama, one that eventually would encompass the entire nation. In his chambers at the Unites States Court House in Washington, D.C., Judge J. Skelly Wright of the United States Court of Appeals recalled those far-off, tumultuous but gratifying years in New Orleans and his acquaintance with Edith Stern. Though he knew her better in the days when bus and school desegregation were carried out in New Orleans, when Edith's support for these

causes led to her vilification by many embittered and dis-
gruntled Southerners—his description of her is accompanied
by a story that sheds light on her earlier involvement with
Voters' Registration. "She took particular interest in Voters'
Registration," he pointed out, "because she was smart enough
to perceive that that is where the most important impact can be
found."

> There was this case, decided by the Supreme Court in 1896,
> *Plessy* v. *Ferguson* [in which] many of the white people and
> some of the blacks who had speaking arrangements with
> whites actually got started in the courts in the hope of
> getting a decision from the Supreme Court holding that
> racial segregation was a violation of the constitution. . . .
> They arranged this case as strongly as they possibly could.
> They had a black man, who wasn't all that black, riding on
> a train with a dining car in it. And he sat in the dining car
> and they moved him out of it and told him he would have
> to go sit—I don't know if there was a black dining car . . . but
> they got him out of the white one. And this was a good set
> of facts to show the separation of races in interstate travel.
> This was a train that was moving up to New York and [they
> wanted to show] that the train ought not to be segregated.
> So they thought they were going to change the law in 1896.
>
> The Supreme Court decided in favor of the railroad and
> came out for segregation. When this case came down legal-
> izing, if you will, constitutionalizing, separation of the
> races, there was a great white movement to enforce segrega-
> tion more strongly than before; and, more importantly, the
> whites began to deny blacks the right to vote in the South.
> The blacks had just begun to get on the voting rolls in the
> latter half of the nineteenth century [but] this case was
> used by the whites to get the voting rights of the blacks who
> were registered taken away from them by having the laws
> repealed in various states . . . In Louisiana alone there were
> 100,000 black voters at the time of the *Plessy* v. *Ferguson* case,
> and from 1900 on there were fewer than 5,000. This makes
> the point I was trying to make earlier about Mrs. Stern. This
> is where the power is, the power is the right to vote in a
> democracy.
>
> Mrs. Stern considered it the greatest privilege.

Edith now began to probe deeper into the voter registration rolls, and what she found shocked and dismayed her. Her
investigation uncovered flagrant abuses of the system. Together
with a group of citizens determined to clean up the mess, she

set out to do the painstaking, eye-straining job of looking for "illegal" voters, finding thousands of names among the "voters" who turned out to belong to persons long since deceased. In the stifling, dingy, cramped quarters at the Marble Hall Building, the Voters' Registration League came into being.

Edith mobilized the help of her trusted friends—Lucille Blum, Olive May Labouisse, Gloria Kabacoff, Phyllis Dennery, Anne Newman, Bertha Elsas, Frances Bayon, Bland Bruns, Mathilde Dreyfous, and Gladys Reily, among others. They diligently worked over the dusty files, checking and verifying endless lists. Each of the women would bring two hard-boiled eggs in a brown paper bag and, pooling their nickels, send out for Cokes at lunchtime.

The job was monumental and needed the full-time coordination that Clem Smith was able to bring to it. She was dispatched to the Registrar's office for copies of voting lists. At first these were rather reluctantly tendered, but legislation firmly established that access to registration had to be made available. Accordingly, photostats of registrations for each ward and precinct began to flow into the files of the Marble Hall offices. Those files reposed in wine racks that Edith had hauled over from Longue Vue. Clem spent a good deal of her time in the library and post office, getting public-service maps, transferring vital data to index cards. From the Mississippi River to Lake Pontchartrain, encompassing blocks 1 through 4000, she became acquainted with every detail of the meandering streets that weave in and out of wards and precincts. Within six months, Clem had the layout of the city firmly imprinted in her mind.

Edith apparently had inherited her father's organizational genius. The way he had organized the processing of hundreds of thousands of orders at Sears served as a model in the task she faced now. Soon the makeshift offices in Marble Hall became too small for the burgeoning files, and the operation was moved to larger quarters in the Soulé Building. Here Edith conceived the idea that the service might become self-supporting through funds taken in by making lists available to politicians or others who might need such information. As soon as the word got around, the women found themselves deluged with inquiries from potential buyers. Prior to any election, business was so brisk as to necessitate the hiring of additional temporary help for the transfer of those lists on to cards and gummed labels for the convenience of interested purchasers. They often worked as late as 10 P.M., and Edith could be expected to drop in on her staff at all hours, frequently in evening clothes and accompanied by Edgar. At such times, she would not be averse to lending a hand if she thought the work warranted it. Iris Kelso, political columnist for the *Times-Picayune New Orleans States Item* recalled:

> That tiny cut-glass vase with the tiny blossoms in it on the window of a black limousine—but it still is the essence of elegance and concern for beauty everywhere to me—that little vase with its flowers was in the window of Edith Stern's limousine in the parking lot at City Hall.... She would go to her Voters' Service office, where her staff kept a vigilant eye on the voting rolls. This was in the 1950's, when good government and honest voting rolls were just gaining a foothold in City Hall. Edith would march down the hall with her secretary behind her, both of them tapping along on high heels. To me, it seemed that she was being announced by trumpet calls. Doors opened, heads popped out. SHE was here. In that setting, Edith Stern constituted a force and a warning. No funny business with those voting rolls.

And Adam Jamet, her chauffeur, remembers well the days when he used to drive a station wagon full of the household help to the polls so they could vote. That, too, was a part of Edith's concern.

When computers began to fascinate Edith, it was because of the way in which they might be pressed into service. In short order, Voters' Registration acquired an early model IBM 405 and Clem was dispatched to computer school to learn its intricacies.

Edith turned to the question of helping citizens to exercise their right to vote. Again the faithful Lucille Blum was called upon to step into the breach. Lucille's reputation for dedicated service to the school system was well established and opened doors to both public and parochial schools. Edith inquired whether Lucille could do her "a great favor." Together they called on the appropriate superintendents with a suggestion of placing model voting booths into classrooms to enable students to learn the mechanics of operating them before it came time for them to vote. The requests were granted. But Edith went a step further. When the new City Hall was being built, she made sure that space would be reserved for a Voters' Registration Office. When she discovered that most illiterate voters could read numbers, she supported the idea of giving each candidate or proposition a number on the ballot so that illiterates could vote without assistance if they so desired. The computer and the continuously updated files, were moved to the new City Hall, where Clem Smith can be found to this day in the Office of Voters' Service.

Few knew, but Mrs. Pat Rittiner remembers that at this time Edith herself aspired to political office. She had already started cleaning up the voter registration rolls when Judge Robert Kennon was elected governor in 1952. She reasoned that the best person to clean up the rolls, overseeing the removal of names of dead people, people who had moved, people who simply did not exist, and those who were recorded with erroneous addresses or misspelled names, would be the Orleans Parish Registrar of Voters, and that is what she wanted to be. The governor did not choose her, appointing instead "Uncle Mack" Dyer, a fine old gentleman with a penchant for white linen suits, who had no known record of any kind of political reform. Edith was greatly disappointed and immediately assumed that Dyer would handicap her efforts. So, with a chip on her shoulder, she called on him at his office. She was cordially received with a pleasant joke. When formalities had been attended to, she came straight to the point: "This is what I want you to do," she said and proceeded to outline some of the things needed to get the voter registration rolls in order. "Okay," he said, and, to her astonishment, did exactly what she asked. This was the first of what became almost daily meetings, always beginning with his joke and ending with her instructions. After several months, he said, very politely, "Mrs. Stern, I am running out of clean jokes."

One of the things she requested was a carbon copy of the registration form filled out by each applicant so that she could keep her duplicate records up-to-date. With her concern for detail, she instructed that the clerks in the registration offices

put the carbon copies of the new registrations on paper spikes
and that these would be removed regularly by the Voters'
Service Office. Edith went so far as to buy seventeen paper
spikes from an office supply house, one for each ward in the
parish. She picked out the biggest, fiercest-looking, and ugliest
paper spikes available. As a joke, she had them gift-wrapped,
then sent them to Uncle Mack. The spikes arrived late in the
afternoon, just as he received a telephone call from his wife
reminding him to come home early because it was their wedding anniversary and guests were expected. Uncle Mack had
forgotten and realized he had no present. So when Mrs. Stern's
gift-wrapped box arrived, and he read the card announcing it
was her "gift," he thought himself saved. He removed her card
and happily went home with the box, which was duly opened
in the presence of guests. There were the seventeen long,
pointed, steel spikes! He was not a man without resources or
imagination. "My dear," he explained, "It's the latest thing. For
place cards at the dinner table. It brings them up to eye level.
Of course, there should be some ivy or flowers twined at the
base and around the stem. But, believe me, they will look
wonderful."

Edgar was not idle. He played a prominent role in furthering the progress of Dillard University while immersing himself
in philanthropic and civic endeavors and in politics as well.
John P. Labouisse remembers an incident that took place after
the election of Sam Jones, which constituted the first defeat of
the Long political machine.

> We, together with many of our friends had worked in the
> polls for more than twenty-four hours, counting paper
> ballots. It was a tough battle and the opposition had
> resorted to the use of goon squads, plus every trick under
> the sun in order to defeat us. After it was all over and we
> had caught a few hours' sleep (going to bed thinking we had
> lost), Edgar called with the good news that we had indeed
> won. We went over to the Stern house to have a victory
> drink and I remember Edgar standing on the front porch
> stretching out his arms and saying that for the first time in
> a long while he felt he was breathing clean air again.

Another time, when Franklin Delano Roosevelt was defeated in his attempt to pack the Supreme Court, Edgar commented, "Just when you are about to give up on the American people and begin to feel they haven't got enough sense to govern themselves, a really big issue comes along and they manage to pull themselves together and do the right thing."

A humorous incident connected with the victory celebration over the Long machine bears repetition. The celebration proceeded from Longue Vue along Garden Lane to the Elsas house, where the participants downed repeated victory toasts. However, when it came time for Edgar to go home, Victor Elsas insisted on driving him. "Can't let a valuable citizen like you walk," he said. "I wouldn't dream of making you leave your home now," Edgar replied, equally firm in his resolve. And so it went for a while, gracious hospitality proffered and equally impeccable manners calling for a polite refusal. Edgar Jr. fondly remembers the incident with wry humor. Neither gentleman, he recalled, could have "hit the floor with a hat, if he had tried." Having cupped victory so thoroughly, they were apparently oblivious to the fact that they lived next door to each another!

The Stern family continued to grow. In May 1947, Edgar Jr. married Pauline Stewart, and in September, Audrey and Tom Hess presented their parents with a first grandchild, Bill. Edgar Sr. was immediately at ease as a grandfather. Edith, given to spurts of largesse when faced with a cause, seemed to revel more in her role as doting grandmother than she ever had as mother. Her children found, somewhat to their surprise, that she had bottomless patience for grandchildren. And that role grew in direct proportion to the number of grandchildren, and was extended even farther with the arrival of great-grand-children, to whom Edith ultimately became an adoring and adored legendary figure.

In fact, her devotion to causes great and small seemed boundless. When she encountered the stultifying heat of complacency and dishonesty, she could whip up a veritable tempest of action to bring about change. Once she had a firm grasp of what was at stake, she could be counted on to be a steadfast, reliable supporter. She faithfully attended a host of board meetings, and on rare occasions when some other matter took precedence over attendance, she could be counted on to read minutes of the meeting she had missed and to make constructive comments. When the State of Israel was created in 1948, she became its staunch champion for the rest of her life.

Edith also had an instinct for the moments when her presence might help to further a cause and — more importantly — used discretion in staying away at the right time. Mathilde Dreyfous recalled one such telling incident:

> The League of Women Voters was in the midst of its struggle to get a permanent registration bill passed by the Louisiana legislature. Edith quietly chartered a bus to take a load of potential League lobbyists to Baton Rouge. On our way out of New Orleans the bus stopped and a smiling Edith got on to wish us all good luck. For some reason she was out of favor, which was not unusual since her candor and her courage often made her *persona non grata* in certain quarters. "My name is mud up there, so I am not going with you today — but, good luck!" She smiled, waved, and got off the bus.

In her sponsorship of causes, Edith often searched for the larger view, the plan of action that would gain the most good, thus allowing smaller points — on which she might have insisted and prevailed with more ease — to go unresolved. In this, she emulated her father.

Julius Rosenwald customarily would travel to his far-flung destinations by Pullman car. During one of these runs, the black porter virtually rubbed his hands with glee in the knowledge that this legendary philanthropist was under his care. Expecting a royal tip from such a renowned benefactor, he rendered flawless service. Upon completion of the journey, Rosenwald politely thanked him, then pressed a gratuity into his hand. To his great dismay the tip was, to say the least, a modest one. The porter soon recovered, however, shrugged his shoulders, and delivered a telling observation: "I guess he is more for the race than for the individual!"

Pullman cars appear to have contributed a number of inci-
dents to the Rosenwald family lore. Elizabeth Varet recalls the
time her father, William Rosenwald, was traveling to Tuskegee
in the company of Henry Morgenthau, secretary of the Treasury.
The discussion got around to Lessing Rosenwald's avid interest
in etchings. Secretary Morgenthau wanted to know whether
Bill Rosenwald also was a collector of etchings. In his unassum-
ing manner, Bill responded, "Yes, but only those with your
signature on them . . . and mostly for other people."

Edgar, on the other hand, had a tendency to be more
direct and personal in his regard for causes. About that time,
he was offered a membership in the prestigious Boston Club
of New Orleans, a club that did not normally admit Jews. Edgar
inquired whether this offer meant that Monte Lemann also
would be accepted. When the committee tendered regrets on
that admission, Edgar politely declined the offer.

While Edith in her work for Voters' Service and the League
of Women Voters was helping to make New Orleans a cleaner
place politically, Edgar moved to develop the city in other ways.
In this he found a stalwart companion in his son Edgar Jr.,
whose keen interest in New Orleans equaled, if not surpassed,
his father's zeal.

The Vieux Carré, in particular, was deteriorating badly,
tending, as old sections in cities do, toward becoming a slum.
Yet the Sterns and others realized what a precious resource the
French Quarter was to the city and how essential its preserva-
tion was to the life of New Orleans and the vitality of its tourist
industry. The two Edgars, Sr. and Jr., largely were responsible
for the construction of the elegant Royal Orleans Hotel on the
same spot where the prestigious, much-acclaimed St. Louis
Hotel once stood to cater to the *crème de la crème* of society. The
style and splendor of the Royal Orleans now transports its
guests back to the magic of the *belle époque*, its unobtrusive
luxury blending modern conveniences and comforts with the
charm of the past, making it a unique experience. One expects,
rather romantically, to step out from the gleaming portals on

Royal and St. Louis Streets to find horse-drawn equipages waiting beneath magnolia trees. And it is so. The presence of the Royal Orleans gave a new boost to the Vieux Carré, making it not just a quaint historical place to visit but a place in which to stay.

By applying the same blend of reverence for tradition and enthusiasm for the modern, the Sterns not only were involved in the restoration of the French Quarter but had the foresight to select a site in the center of the old city on which to build New Orleans' first television station, WDSU-TV. By December 1948 the studio was already taking shape at 520 Royal Street, and, although no attempt was made to disguise the studio building, it deliberately took second place architecturally to its venerable neighbor, the Seignoret Mansion, built in 1819.

FIVE

Austerity Castle

LONGUE VUE was Edith's mainstay. The house and gardens were a source of constant admiration, and the staff of twenty-one ran the estate with the precision reminiscent of a well-choreographed ballet. At dawn the flurry of activity began. Gardeners were out, looking after the landscaping and starting the fountains. Emma and her helpers were in the kitchen, checking supplies and beginning breakfast. Maids were already busy with their chores; and Joh-Joh had made her forays into the garden and was in the flower room arranging bouquets to complement the bedrooms and the public rooms. Minnie, too, would be down early, scrutinizing and putting in order all the table appointments.

By 9 A.M., Edith's secretary would arrive with an air of good cheer and repair to the office, ready to sort the mail. She would look over the list of invitations and check the daily calendar. The bell would ring from the master suite, bringing Amanda Thomas upstairs to open the drapes, stopping to deposit a breakfast tray on Edith's bed.

Edith ate little in the morning, perhaps some toast or

biscuits with marmalade, which she adored, taken with her indispensable coffee. She might summon Emma to discuss a menu, then confer with Johanna and Minnie. By that time, Edgar might put in a brief appearance to inform Amanda, "I'm not up yet," which meant, "Don't make my bed." Meanwhile, Edith's maid would lay out her clothes.

Amanda, one of the old faithfuls in the household, who served for over thirty years, remembers one unusual occurrence. Being sensitive to others' feelings, Edith made it a rule never to reproach any of the servants in public. Instead it was her habit to slip a note into the pocket of a uniform, detailing her complaints. Much to Amanda's surprise and chagrin, however, she was summoned one day to the bedroom where Edith, in her secretary's presence, asked Amanda to step into the bathroom because, as she put it, she wanted to point out some spider webs that had been allowed to accumulate. Full of apprehension, Amanda followed.

There were no spider webs to be seen anywhere, and Edith posed an entirely unexpected question. She wanted to know if Amanda's house was secure and how she was coping with the mortgage payments now that her husband was ill. Edith was amazed when informed of the size of the payments and inquired how Amanda could possibly meet them. "Well, I have good sons," was her reply.

A few days later, Amanda found in the mail a note containing a check from Edith for $1,000. Once Amanda's husband was discharged from the hospital, she encountered further difficulty with the managers of the convalescent center that the doctors had recommended for him. Edith found out somehow, and a single telephone call from the Sterns' attorney settled matters expeditiously. Wages at the Stern household were not always the highest for the help, but the employees knew that they could count on help when the going got rough.

When Edith took lunch alone or with a close friend, it usually was a simple repast. She often ordered what she called a "Sternburger," a square veal patty, which she felt helped to maintain her weight. Lavish meals were reserved for guests, but even at such times Edith would indulge prudently.

A dinner party for ten or twelve was Edith and Edgar's favorite way of entertaining. Such dinners frequently were formal. Lillie Collins, who served four years as kitchen maid and later as Edith's personal maid, would greet the guests at the door wearing her evening gray uniform and perky organdy apron. She would take their wraps prior to ushering them into the upstairs drawing room where Adam stood at the English Hunt table, presiding over the hors d'oeuvres, usually caviar in egg puffs, decorated with the riced yellow of the egg, as well as other specialties of the house.

Edith and Edgar would be standing under the Waterford chandeliers, offering a warm welcome. If it was a fine evening, the huge French doors would open on a breathtaking view of the gardens with their illuminated fountains. After cocktails, the Sterns would lead their guests downstairs to the dining room. The table would be exquisitely set, perhaps utilizing a hand-embroidered tablecloth with an avian motif.

Sandra, the Sterns' granddaughter, remembered a story that Edith was particularly fond of telling. Edith preferred the bird-embroidered tablecloth over many others, but she never quite found the exact flowers to complement it. One day, while shopping at her favorite store, Woolworth, she saw some charming china birds and bought a goodly number. After the table was formally set with her bird cloth, ruby-bordered fine china, and opulent ruby glasses, Edith arranged a number of the birds around the softly-glowing candles. The effect was stunning. During dinner she watched from the corner of her eye as one of the guests picked up a china bird, surreptitiously turning it over to discover what fine porcelain maker had created this collector's item. With wry amusement, Edith noticed as the guest's face changed from nonchalant curiosity to crestfallen embarrassment when he felt her eyes upon him, after reading the label: "Woolworth, $1.69."

In the same way, Edith often imparted an impish touch to her menus. She would serve classic French food, only to surprise her guests by combining it with simple country fare. The soup might be lump crab meat, followed by chicken legs and yellow grits, with a simple dessert such as fresh raspberries, strawberries, or caramel custard. She had a reputation for remembering her guests' favorite dishes and often managed to have these on the menu, as well. Charles Stich adored the Longue Vue macaroons; not only would they be served when he and his wife, Margery, were guests but a charmingly wrapped souvenir bag of them would be offered by Minnie or Johanna at their departure. "The Big Four"—the Monte Lemanns, the Edward Benjamins, and the Kemper Williamses, with the Sterns making up the quartet—would dine together on many formal and informal occasions. Often joining them was a younger couple, the Moise Dennerys.

Moise Dennery, an attorney whose parents were also friends of the Sterns, and Moise's New York-born wife, Phyllis, became frequent visitors and traveling companions, too. Phyllis remembers Edgar's custom, no doubt a leaf borrowed from the English branch of the family, of escorting the gentlemen to the Blue Room for after dinner port and cigars. Edith would invite the women to join her in the Ladies' Reception Room where displays of rare porcelain reigned supreme and the flower arrangements had a special touch. Phyllis never ceased to be amazed that regardless of the hour, and without any overt signal, whenever the distaff side made its way back to the Library the men were always on the verge of adjourning to the Library also.

Having joined forces again, a lively conversation often ensued, lasting until late into the night. It might be on current issues, but, often as not, an arbitrary proposal was tossed out for discussion. Phyllis recalls how one night Alvin Ulrich, later head of the Aspen Institute, threw out a hypothetical, "What would happen if, let us say, the Ford Foundation would allocate $50,000,000 to be used in behalf of black children?" The possibility was given exhaustive exploration, never on the basis of mere theorizing, but with serious intent. Sometimes, reality did emerge from these discussions, to be implemented expeditiously. And for Edith, no doubt, this sort of discussion had its prototype in the ones held in the Rosenwald mansion in Chicago, a salon rarely devoted to entertainment alone.

Birthdays, Christmas, and New Year's parties were notable, since they were given over to lighter diversions. Edith held that "Christmas is for *infantry,* and New Year's for *adultery.*"

On Christmas, Longue Vue would be meticulously polished and exquisitely decorated with greenery, a profusion of specially cultivated flowers and a tall Christmas tree adorning the downstairs hall. All parties were full-dress, offering the finest foods. At Christmas, too, a party for servants and their families was held at the Playhouse, where each guest found a thoughtfully selected gift and each member of the staff received a bonus check. Household staff with a minimum of five years' service were also entitled to a gift of Sears stock intended to provide a nest egg for a rainy day. Those who withstood the temptation of turning this windfall into instant cash had ample reason to congratulate themselves on their foresight in years to come. At New Year's Eve, also, two parties were held simultaneously—one in the mansion, a gala affair for the adults; and one in the Playhouse, for the "jeunesse." When the Sterns were absent at holiday time, they happily allowed their spectacular facilities to be used by friends who held parties on behalf of worthy causes.

Considering the many occasions that the Sterns found to celebrate, Edith's Wrapping Room was often a beehive of activity. She did not simply buy gifts; rather, she kept a stock of hundreds on hand at all times.

When Edith felt the need for some rest and decided to leave Longue Vue for a while, it merely meant a change of scenery, the new location serving as a base for her worthwhile pursuits. If she rested at home, on a night when no company was coming, she often had dinner served for her and Edgar in the alcove of her beloved dining room, at the smaller table overlooking the Pan Garden. On occasions when she felt "lazy," as she termed it, she would wear a sumptuous dressing gown and indulge herself in reading a book while listening to music. If the book held her interest, she would compile a list of names of friends, relatives, and acquaintances who might enjoy reading it also. The list grew in direct ratio to her personal enjoyment. The following morning, the list and title of the book would be on the desk of her secretary, who promptly acquired copies for distribution. A printed card would accompany the book, reading, "Please accept this with my compliments and don't bother to acknowledge." Edith remembered her father doing this for his friends.

Music festivals held a great fascination for Edith and Edgar, ever since the time they had enjoyed them in Europe. Once they made a pilgrimage to the serene environment of Tanglewood, Massachusetts, and fell in love with it. The music, the rarefied atmosphere charged with all manner of intellectual pursuits, and the informal socializing carried on in the spectacular Berkshires suited them perfectly. Year after year, they settled in for the summer, and Edith always wished to stay until the blazing riot of autumn colors was at its zenith.

With her usual practical bent, Edith saw no reason why they should be dependent on indifferent food during an extended summer stay at a hotel, or put up with the difficulty of not being able to entertain properly during these months. The obvious solution was to acquire a suitable place right in or near Lenox. Unlike their normal quarters, however, this should be a simple place, compatible with casual summer living. No sooner did the idea take hold, than Edith set out in her car with Adam at the wheel and Mildred Heller seated beside her. Methodically, she combed the surrounding countryside. Eventually, she inspected a place on top of a gentle hill at 704 East Street—a small, clapboard cottage that had a glorious view of the mountains off in the distance and stood on a property dotted with ancient trees. The interior had satisfactory potential, and she already had begun mentally the process of remodeling. "I'll take it," she told the real estate agent.

"The price is $19,000, though that includes about twenty acres of wooded area," the man informed her.

"Sure, I'll take it," Edith repeated.

The agent was nonplussed by her swift decision. "We can go back to the office, ma'am, and I'll show you the papers. I can offer to help with the financing, too."

"I don't think that will be necessary," Edith said with a smile.

The agent lost no time in checking the credit references this unusual woman had given. "Can the little lady afford to make a decision involving $19,000?" he asked the bank officer by long-distance telephone. When he returned, Edith and Mildred had the distinct feeling that his high color was not entirely attributable to the warm summer afternoon.

Edith soon found the right name for her new cottage, calling it "Austerity Castle." It was filled entirely with furnishings from Sears. The outside was painted a glowing white, and Edith decided to add two more guest rooms and baths in addition to a dining room with a large bay window facing the mountains. When it was complete, she brought a staff of four or five from New Orleans. It still looked so simple from the outside that it was often a source of mild frustration for her guests. One day she invited friends from neighboring Pittsfield and watched with some amusement as their car slowed down, the occupants looking incredulously at the cottage. She saw the car hesitate, stop, then drive off. After a while, the car returned, repeating the procedure, until Edith magnanimously went outside to rescue her bemused guests. Family would converge on Lenox from New York. In particular, Adele, or "Dellie," as Edith called her, was a frequent visitor. The woods would resound with their laughter. "Let's talk about our 'exes,'" Edith would casually throw out, and in that charming, tranquil atmosphere they were able to reminisce lightheartedly over past spouses. Adele was enamored of Martha's Vineyard and tried to coax Edith to visit her there, but in vain. "There is nothing to do there but vegetate," Edith responded. Adele's rejoinder was that after a "relaxing" visit to Lenox, she always felt in need of a vacation.

Yearly, Edith and Edgar reserved two boxes at the Tanglewood Festival, allowing ample room for their friends and frequently for their staff. This was one of the fringe benefits, and Rita Jean Coleman, a maid at Longue Vue and Austerity Castle, often availed herself of those special opportunities. Edith loved the cool evening breezes, the mountains, and the animals in their natural habitat. But above all she loved the concerts, which put her within reach of all the greats of the world of music.

At Austerity Castle a station wagon was at the staff's disposal. When complaints filtered back that it had no radio for longer outings, such as to Albany, the Sterns rented a car with a radio to alleviate the situation. They also acquired another house across the road for the exclusive use of their staff. "They have to have a place to go home to at night," Edith said.

Just down the road, on the opposite side, lived Yvonne and Anthony Maturevich. Edith lost no time in inviting her neighbors for a get-acquainted chat, and the Matureviches offered to look after Austerity Castle whenever Edith and Edgar were absent. With her usual grace, Edith drew Yvonne into the Stern household. "Penny"—as Edith called Yvonne—and her husband could be counted on to help out thereafter. Frequently the children, but Philip in particular, would be quartered at the Maturevich home in order to make more room for guests. Yvonne recollected wistfully how Edith offered to finance her daughter's college education, an offer that the young woman declined, much to her parents' regret.

Shortly after the Sterns settled in, Edith had a number of "snowbirds" installed. These were small iron birds, used in harsh climates to catch drifting snow. Such objects were of immense appeal to Edith, and the quaint creatures, acquired at flea markets, reposed on the fence in front of the house. The Miller family—Pete a distinguished newspaperman, and his wife, Amy Bess, a charming, blonde-tressed, superbly educated woman—often invited the Sterns for martinis served in the shade of a particularly attractive tree, which came to be known as the Miller's Martini Tree. It was a landmark of such local repute that once a telegram arrived addressed to "Mr. Edgar Stern, Miller's Martini Tree," and it reached the addressee without delay.

To Austerity Castle, the Sterns frequently invited greats from the world of music. Edith's idiomatic French and German often was helpful when a guest of honor was not at home in the English language. Those summers did much to broaden their already far-flung friendships into a veritable "Who's Who in Music." Many a morning, they attended rehearsals, observing the subtle intricacies of a later flawless performance.

Amy Bess Miller, in the meantime, took an interest in the remnants of an abandoned Shaker Village nearby. The Shakers, a religious sect, also called the United Society of Believers, came into existence in England in 1706, claiming to have spiritual powers that caused them to tremble and sway during worship, hence the term. In 1758 Ann Lee, subsequently called Mother Ann, joined the society and took over its reins. In 1774 the

Shakers came to America, eventually establishing a number of settlements, mainly in the east. The tenets of the Shakers' religious faith did not permit them to marry or propagate, inasmuch as they felt that Christ's Second Coming was imminent. Rather, they relied, perhaps unrealistically, on making converts or taking homeless individuals into the fold. The women were called Sisters, the men Brothers – that being the relationship to which they aspired. They lived simply and peacefully, applying themselves with dedicated discipline to the work ethic. Aside from their farming accomplishments, in which they utilized only the simplest tools, they left behind a remarkable legacy of arts and crafts, certain pieces of which are much sought after by collectors. In addition, they produced a fragrant rose water for use in food such as pies as well as in bathing the sick, and the herbs they raised became justly famed. In the end, their numbers diminished and their once-beautiful farms and buildings fell into disrepair. Only three of the original one hundred fifty Shakers remained on this particular thousand-acre farm with its twenty-two dilapidated buildings. Amy Bess became the moving force of a group that sought to restore the Shaker Village to its original state – not as a museum but as a vibrant, living farm to teach future generations about the Shaker way of life.

Edith took an immediate interest in the project. Once the land was acquired, she offered to pay for the restoration of one of the buildings, her offer spurring a great deal of interest. The restoration project progressed very well, indeed, so that the Shaker Village is now a tourist attraction in the Berkshires. Among the souvenirs one may garner from a visit is the cookbook based on Shaker cuisine, authored by Amy Bess Miller. Likewise, one may wish to acquire one of the splendid woolen cloaks woven in the style of the Shaker originals. These became quite the fashion when some Boston society women wore them to a gala in their city, creating an instant market for them.

Edith loved these coats and often borrowed one from Amy Bess. This was one of Edith's idiosyncrasies. She never took a coat along on her travels, preferring instead to borrow one from her hostess. "Let's see," she would say to Amy Bess,

"I'm wearing brown today. What coat can you lend me?" Amy Bess anticipated such requests by keeping one particularly handsome coat in her closet for Edith's exclusive use. This suited Edith's taste in fashion well.

Whenever she could arrange a trip to New York, Edith would shop at Hattie Carnegie and Bergdorf Goodman. She was, however, a loyal customer of Sears fashions as well and never failed to acknowledge the origin of a particular outfit when she was complimented on it. Whenever the annual selection of the ten best-dressed women came up for discussion, Edith would comment ruefully, "Missed out again—after all, they haven't added Sears to the list of designers yet."

The Sterns and Millers were fond of taking excursions to nearby points of interest. One day, after an early Sunday concert, they set off in two cars for a picnic. They were on their way to a scenic lookout atop a magnificent mountain in Vermont. Edith had teamed up with Pete Miller, while Edgar was Amy Bess's chauffeur. The latter noticed after a while that Edgar never got out of second gear while negotiating the steep hills and said, "You're quite right to stay in second gear in such hilly country, Edgar." Edgar's disarming rejoinder was, "Oh, really, and where is third?" It was then that Amy Bess knew the reason that Edgar never bought a new car, preferring always a "demonstrator."

Mildred Heller and her sister habitually visited for two weeks each season. One year, their arrival coincided with that of Edith. On reaching Lenox, Edith learned of a flower show that was to be held the following day. Naturally, an entry was expected from such a well-known horticulturist. To Edith's dismay, however, nothing was blooming in her garden normally ablaze with color. Undaunted, she marched into the kitchen and selected an enormous country soup tureen, hastened to a meadow, and returned with an armful of Queen Anne's lace, which can be found in abundance in every ditch and meadow of Lenox. Her imaginative arrangement, utilizing bits of greenery, promptly won first prize. However, she was determined that never again would there be a dearth of blooming flowers on her grounds, and accordingly instructed her gardener to have an array of seasonal flowers, in pots, if necessary.

Another of Edith's great joys was returning to Austerity Castle in October when the autumn foliage was at its peak—deep reds and russets mingling with the evergreens against a bright blue sky. In due time, it became apparent that the construction of a new high-voltage line would mar the Sterns' favorite view of the distant mountains. Everyone expected Edith's wrath to descend upon the power company responsible for thus tampering with nature. Instead, she calmly announced that she would have more trees and bushes planted to enhance the view from their property. Nothing must impede progress.

The Stern family was growing again. Audrey Hess had a girl, Anne, in July 1949; followed by a son, Philip, in June 1950. Edgar Jr.'s family now included Sandra, born in 1949, and Eric, born in 1950. Two years later, Monte Maurice joined the ranks; and much later, in 1961, baby Lessing was born.

On August 30, 1957, Philip married Helen Burroughs Sedgwick in her father's home in New Hampshire. Bill Hess, then ten years old, recalls the gathering of the clan for the wedding. They flew from New York to Boston where a special train was chartered to convey the guests to New Hampshire. Alas, Bill's family missed the train, and a taxi was drafted into service, the longest taxi ride in the young boy's memory. Helen Sedgwick, better known as "Lennie," was a fine sculptor in addition to being a lovely blonde. She not only won Philip's heart but the hearts of her in-laws as well. Philip was happy to adopt her three children of a former marriage—Henry, Michael, and Helen. In time, they added two more children of their own: David, born in 1959; and Eve, born in 1962.

The children and grandchildren were regular visitors at Lenox. In fact, the most authentic account of the atmosphere pervading Austerity Castle can be found in a little book entitled *A Love Book for Mom,* subtitled "A Pictorial Biography of Our Stay at 704 East Street," and authored by "Stern and Stern, Inc." It is the work of Eve Stern and her mother, Lennie. It is undated, imparting to it a timeless feeling well suited to the pictures and prose of a lovely, intelligent little girl somewhere between the ages of seven and ten. Mother and daughter wrote in the introduction:

> This living tome is comprised of four chapters, or rather of four pictorial biographies of our stay at 704 East Street. The first chapter deals with food. We have made menus of the *pièces de résistance* (URP!). Each picture has a few words describing the describable, the rest is up to your imagination.

Phrases like, "We may not have done your green thumb grace," and "Ah, so be it," set the stage.

A little girl, her long hair parted in the center, neatly brushed to fall to her suntanned shoulders, which peek from a long rosebud-embroidered nightgown, sits on a sun-dappled deck, taking a tentative bite of an omelet appetizingly arranged on a breakfast tray. Another picture shows her playing tennis with her laughing mother squinting into the sun. Elsewhere, she affects a model's pose at the edge of a swimming pool, in an overexposed shot that looks like one of Monet's water-lilies canvases. A score of snapshots depict flowers in abundant profusion, a rich riot of color. A frog squatting next to a homely broom elicits the rhetorical query, "Well, if it isn't Prince Charming having fun in the sun?" The little "tome" succeeds in preserving a tender memory of a luminous, idyllic summer at Austerity Castle, grandmother's house.

SIX

Politics and Honor

THE MID-CENTURY MARK brought many changes. During the "man-less" years of the war, women had been forced to make family and business decisions as never before. The visual and performing arts had become freer, bolder. Most people had grown up under the long years of the Roosevelt administration and had difficulty adjusting to Harry Truman who now occupied the White House. He seemed to many a stopgap president, merely carrying on in the shade of his predecessor. Moreover, he seemed to avoid the limelight in the early days of his presidency, though history has gained a new perspective on the man since. Harry and Bess Truman were simply everyone's country cousins.

All the same, Truman favored the Twenty-Second Amendment to the Constitution, limiting the presidency to two four-year terms and only one term for those vice presidents who succeeded to the presidency having served more than two years already. This amendment was passed in the fall of 1951, when Truman was anxious to get out of the "great white prison," as he termed the residence on Pennsylvania Avenue.

It was a sentiment his wife concurred in eagerly. Who would take the helm?

The choice came down to Adlai or Ike. Dwight D. Eisenhower, hero of the war, was assuredly a great American, but he had thus far reserved his political leanings. Now he gave the Republican Party his nod, and "I like Ike" became the ubiquitous campaign slogan. The Democrats returned with "Gladly for Adlai," choosing Adlai Stevenson, popular governor of Illinois, grandson and namesake of Grover Cleveland's vice president.

A graduate of Princeton University, Stevenson was a devoted admirer of a Republican from Illinois, Abraham Lincoln. He was a brilliant orator, but his opponents soon found a label to attach to him—"egghead"—which not only described his receding hairline but also referred condescendingly to his weighty intellectual credentials. It was to be Ike or Adlai, and the choice was a difficult one. Many households were split over the issue. So, too, were the lines drawn at Longue Vue.

The Republican Party was of formidable strength in New Orleans. Years later, tour-bus guides would stop at a particularly magnificent antebellum mansion in the Garden District, point to it and say, "Here lived the man who made Dwight Eisenhower president." They were referring to Federal Judge John Minor Wisdom of whom it was said that he changed the face of the nation. He was the author of the court decision that mandated affirmative action in school integration. It was he who ordered the admission of James Meredith as the first black student at the University of Mississippi. He showed his mettle at an early age, graduating at the top of his law-school class. Wisdom was the judge's actual surname. Had he not been born with it, however, it would have had to be conferred upon him.

With his Harvard background, Edgar should have been a Stevenson man, but such was not the case. His deep commitment to the Republican ideology made him an Eisenhower devotee, and Edgar Jr. joined his camp. Edith, Philip, and Audrey, on the other hand, went "madly for Adlai." What fanned the flames of controversy still more was the fact that Edith was a personal friend of Adlai Stevenson.

Maxine Wachenheim also favored Stevenson. She had long been a staunch supporter of the New Orleans Symphony Orchestra (a cause that also claimed the efforts of Edgar's mother, Hanna Stern). A native of St. Louis, Maxine came to New Orleans as the bride of Albert Wachenheim. Her good-humored disposition coupled with displays of creativity soon made her a welcome addition to the smart set. Eventually, she and Edith, through their mutual devotion to music, became fast friends. Edith now found a like-minded political companion in Maxine, whose husband, Albert, was an Eisenhower supporter. Maxine described the fierce loyalties:

> By now, the campaign on both sides had reached a feverish pitch. We stood on street corners, handing out Stevenson campaign literature and buttons. My special corner was near the Krauss Company where I planted myself daily. In the meantime, Albert was supporting Ike and few words were spoken in our household during the entire campaign. Ironically, both the Republican and Democratic campaign headquarters were within a block of each other on Camp Street. The continuous spying that transpired to see what the other side was doing was simply incredible to our sensibilities. Nothing remained sacred.

The news burst like a bombshell that the battle for the presidency would come to New Orleans in the "coincidental" arrival of the two candidates. Adlai Stevenson would make the Stern home his headquarters. Two nights before the rally, Edith called Maxine in the middle of the night. They had ordered special blue silk material from Alabama that would be made into kerchiefs and flags to be waved during the rally. The color was to be known as "Adlai Blue." Edith found the packages had arrived during her absence that evening. Production had to start immediately. Maxine contacted the sculptor George Rickey, who offered to imprint the Stevenson initials. George, his wife, and Edith, plus all the volunteers they could muster, set up ironing boards in the Wachenheim home and stamped the initials on hundreds of blue silk squares.

Everything was in readiness, the house in perfect splendor, the gardens in full bloom, awaiting the guest of honor. The first meeting was to be a luncheon. During the morning, while Edith personally checked all the details, including a second look at Whim House, slated to be Adlai Stevenson's suite, a phone call came from a young senator, a Democrat, who happened to be in town. Graciously, Edith invited him to the luncheon. Hastily, Johanna was asked to set another plate. When the young senator arrived just before luncheon, Maxine remembers, he charmed everyone with his boyish good looks, his New England twang, and his easy manner. It didn't take long before he loosened his tie, opened his shirt, and showed off his deep tan and flashing white smile. Immediately, he and Adlai were drawn into a spirited discussion affording each a chance to display rapier-sharp wit and lightning-fast repartee. His name was John Kennedy. He insisted that all call him Jack.

Jack stayed for dinner. Edith implored Maxine to free herself from a prior engagement in order to spend the evening in this scintillating company. It came as a big surprise to nearly everyone when an additional guest at dinner turned out to be Ethel Merman. The three—Stevenson, Kennedy, and Merman—were longtime friends. The stars shone brightly, drawing everyone into their colorful orbit.

Stevenson stayed for several days, enjoying the consummate hospitality. On the last night of his stay, another gala dinner party was held at Longue Vue. Edith assigned her friend Rosa Freeman Keller to be Mr. Stevenson's dinner companion. Rosa, an intelligent, outspoken woman, had a reputation for espousing all sorts of unpopular causes. In 1932 her father had been given the city's highest honor, that of Rex, King of the Mardi Gras, while she was one of the foremost debutantes of the season, later to become Queen of Nereus, another krewe. In due time, she married Charles Keller. By marrying outside her faith she automatically placed herself "outside the court circle." For Rosa, being impressed with Stevenson was only one of the reasons to remember that particular evening.

> Adlai Stevenson was one of the most charming dinner companions I ever had. But I do remember that Mr. Stern was furious because his cook's house had burned down earlier, and she had indicated that it was impossible to find a place to live. He didn't believe that, so he put her in the car, summoned his chauffeur and went along himself to look for a place. That evening at dinner, he told all about this frustrating experience. He learned, he said, that she was absolutely

right. There wasn't anything—nothing—and he was furious
about that. I said, "Mr. Stern, I think maybe we can work
something out."

Such words, spoken at the Stern table seldom ended
there. The outcome was that the Sterns and the Kellers put up
money to buy land in Gentilly. They hired the man who had
developed adjacent Gentilly Woods and commissioned several
homes in a black subdivision called Pontchartrain Park. "All this
was going on," Mrs. Keller notes, "while members of the
National Urban League were meeting and reaching a decision
that they weren't going to put up with segregated housing
anymore. But the director said, "Come, let's get these houses
built and then we'll worry about desegregation!"

It was hardly the "in" thing in New Orleans at that time
to speak up in behalf of civil rights. Rosa Keller remembers the
indignities suffered at the hands of her so-called friends when
she did. Her husband received anonymous phone calls,
informing him that Rosa was "sleeping with a nigger." Many
people she had grown up with stopped associating with her.
Nothing deterred her. She spoke out on behalf of Jews, blacks,
and women. "The black guys got drafted and sent overseas to
fight; and then they came back. And now they are supposed
to sit in the rear of a street car?" she demanded. "Women, too:
when they needed them, they gave them jobs to do; and when
the men came home, they gave the jobs back to the men. That's
wrong."

Rosa spoke of the carnivals in which she had once been
reigning queen and which she could no longer attend. "The
rule is, if the husband is Jewish, the wife cannot go, though the
other way around is okay." She remembers:

I learned a lot about discrimination in health cases. I had a
call one day from Mr. Monte Lemann, who had the reputation as one of the city's finest lawyers and citizens. He asked
if he could come to see me. Mr. Lemann spoke concisely,
logically, and carefully. He came to see me, he explained, at
the request of Mr. Edgar Stern, who was President of the
Board of Directors of Dillard University. The Board had
decided to establish a Board of Management for Flint-
Goodridge Hospital which the University owned and
administered. Mr. Stern was most anxious that I serve as
chairman. I was stupefied. I explained that I knew nothing

about hospitals, etc. Mr. Lemann said that none of my reservations mattered at all. What Dillard needed at the time was a diplomat, one who could get people to work together, one whom black people trusted. . . .

Slowly, the wall of segregation was beginning to crack. In *To Kill a Mockingbird*, the Pulitzer Prize novel, the whole gamut of racial hatred is explored and exposed. Here, death intervenes in the plot before the final verdict is in. No one dared go further in those days. George Chaplin, former editor of *The New Orleans Item*, remembers when Ralph Johnson Bunche, distinguished educator and statesman, recipient of the Nobel Peace Prize in 1950, came to New Orleans to speak. No hall was "available" in the white community, at least none that would admit an integrated audience. "One is, of course," Rabbi Feibelman said, and he opened the portals of his temple.

In the end it was Ike who moved into the White House with his wife, Mamie. Perhaps it was a tribute to his successful leadership at the conclusion of the recent war. It was a time when recollections, diaries, journals, and novels concerning the war were emerging by the dozen. Herman Wouk's *Caine Mutiny*, Leon Uris' *Battle Cry*, Irwin Shaw's *The Young Lions*, James Jones' *From Here to Eternity*—all began to dissect the experience. Winston Churchill was again prime minister of England. And Mamie Eisenhower took this moment to redecorate the interior of the White House in "Mamie pink."

For all that he had personally liked Stevenson, Edgar rejoiced in the Republican victory. Edith showed that she could be a good loser, and acquiesced to the American freedom of choice. She would try again and fight again, but her loyalty and allegiance belonged in the meanwhile to the president.

She turned her attention to Edgar's coming sixty-seventh birthday. It was celebrated on January 23, with all the pomp and circumstance possible at Longue Vue. But all of this did not match the surprise celebration that awaited him the following day. A distinguished assemblage convened at International House for a black-tie dinner, headed by Governor Robert Kennon, who stood at the podium describing Edgar as:

one of America's finest men, a citizen of America and the world.... I know New Orleans is a city with a heart. It has the characteristics of a beautiful lady in its attitude toward life and that which it considers important. That is why a little thing like a birthday can occupy the time and attention of the powers-that-be.

Edith sat glowing with pleasure and pride in a black dress with a string of pearls around her neck and a white cascading corsage flowing from her shoulder. It brushed Mayor deLesseps S. Morrison, who said, "Mrs. Stern, you should know how Mamie felt last Tuesday." The governor continued, addressing Edith directly:

> She also, jointly with him and on her own initiative, has worked unceasingly in public welfare. In contrast to the many in the vineyard of life who come only to pluck the ripened fruit, it can be truly said of Edgar and Edith Stern that they have toiled in this vineyard, cultivating its soil and nurturing the roots of democracy.

Monte Lemann, seated to the left of his oldest, truest, and most trusted friend, rose to review Edgar's life. Edgar, in response, spoke of his deep emotions as he thanked his family, his friends, and his city. In closing, he uttered again the words that were the refrain of his credo: "I am eternally grateful that I was born in the United States."

In the program for the dinner, under the title "Milestones of a Busy Life," the following were listed:

1912	Orleans Parish School Board
1912-16	Charity Hospital Board
1915	President, Association of Commerce
1916-19	Director, New Orleans Public Belt Railroad
1917-18	Director, Federal Reserve Bank of Atlanta
1918-19	Captain, United States Army
1924-34	Trustee, Tuskegee University
1927-28	President, New Orleans Cotton Exchange
1928	President, Community Chest
1929	Board of Directors, United States Chamber of Commerce
1930	President, Board of Trustees, Dillard University and Flint Goodrich Hospital
1930-34	President, New Orleans Parkway Commission
1932	Trustee, Howard Tilton Memorial Library

1932-48	Trustee, Julius Rosenwald Fund
1933-44	Vice-President and Member of the Board, Bureau of Government Research
1940	Founder, Member Phi Beta Kappa Associates
1940-42	Louisiana State Welfare Board
1940	Office Production Management
1940-42	Chairman, Transportation Committee, War Production Board
1942-43	Chairman, Economic Development Commission of Louisiana
1943	Louisiana Department of Commerce and Industry
1944	Board of Administrators, Tulane University
1944	Vice-President, United Negro College Fund
1945	Founder Member, International House
1945	National Committeeman, United National Clothing Committee
1946	Chairman, Mayor's Advisory Committee
1947	Committee to Visit Graduate School of Education, Harvard University
1948	Sponsor of International Trade Mart
1950	Trustee, Public Affairs Research Council of Louisiana
1950-52	New Orleans City Charter Committee
1952	Chairman, Development Committee, United Fund

SEVEN

The Symphony

*E*DITH LOVED HER ROLE as grandmother in all respects but one. She was decidedly opposed to looking the part. So, in March of 1952, she made her first visit to Elizabeth Arden's fabled Maine Chance, in Phoenix, Arizona, staying for two weeks. She emerged slimmer and prettier after being massaged, pounded, and exercised, if not pampered. She enjoyed this experience so much that she returned over a span of more than twenty-five years, sometimes twice during a season when she felt tired and in need of rejuvenation. Somehow, though her body might be, her spirits were never in need of overhaul. Music, for one, always bolstered them.

The Sterns' deep involvement with Tanglewood fostered a widening interest that would not be seasonally confined. To this point, Edith had been committed only marginally in furthering the growth of the New Orleans Symphony, while numerous other civic and cultural endeavors laid claim to her support. Yet the Symphony always remained a cause dear to the family, since Edgar's mother had been a charter member of the orchestra after its inception in 1935.

In March 1953, the Sterns met the newly arrived general manager of the New Orleans Symphony. His name was Thomas Greene, and he had come to town at the behest of Alexander Hilsberg, who had been named music director of the New Orleans Philharmonic Orchestra the year before. Prior to that, Hilsberg was the associate conductor of the Philadelphia Orchestra, with Thomas Greene as its assistant manager. The meeting between Greene and the Sterns took place in Edgar's office in the American Bank Building. They were quick to voice their appreciation of a particular Brahms symphony that Hilsberg had conducted. Greene was pleased to say that it had been outstanding from his point of view, as well. This meeting was the prelude to a steady stream of enthusiasm and support for the orchestra. Greene later summarized this support and the Sterns, too.

> A word which is often used to bespeak the *worst* in American attitudes is discrimination. It was one of the hallmarks of Edith Stern's way of life. She and her husband possessed that special talent of feeling comfortable about agreeing that a particular project was worthy of their support while another was not. Decisions of beneficence were made "on their own." Fortunately, the Sterns had many interests and they encouraged and supported all that was good. In my twenty years as general manager of the orchestra I frequently made requests to individuals or heads of companies for favors of financial support, only to meet with the response, "We can't do that ... if we did it for the Symphony we'd have to do it for everybody." This would seem to say that the person making that reply was, in fact, helping nobody. The Sterns *could* turn down an appeal, if they were so inclined. That seldom happened ... they were more likely to make a value judgment and let the size of their gift reflect their opinion.

The Sterns' gifts were often lavish when the occasion demanded. W. B. Burkenroad, Jr., recalls that once, during an emergency when the needs of the orchestra became particularly critical, four persons helped the orchestra over the hump by giving a total of $400,000. The Sterns were among them. In addition, Edith and Edgar celebrated their own joys by giving to causes they believed in, even if there was no immediate financial crunch. On Edgar's seventieth birthday, the New Orleans Symphony, Harvard University, and Tulane University each received $70,000.

Prior to Edith's involvement, one of the most successful fund-raising ventures for the Symphony was a cooking school. The instructor was Diane Lucas, from the New York Cordon Bleu School. Diane Lucas was a veritable whiz with a frying pan, and before the admiring eyes of a food-conscious New Orleans *beau monde,* she created delicacies that delighted the eye and the palate. What was the secret of her magic? It was noted that Mrs. Lucas did all her stirring, mixing, and blending while a tall glass of orange juice reposed at her elbow. Was this the secret ingredient that turned her inspired creations into ambrosia? Orange juice? The young New Orleans matrons wondered. The answer, when it leaked out, was simpler. The apparently innocuous orange juice was laced with a generous base of potent spirits. Nevertheless, the endeavor was a success. Many a table was graced with the new, delightful dishes, and the Symphony gained a whopping $10,000.

Maxine Wachenheim prevailed on Edith to help organize a repeat of their successful culinary adventure on behalf of the Symphony. Together, they concocted an even more sensational plan. Maxine was dispatched to Paris to request that her good friend, Raymond Oliver, owner of the prestigious Grand Vefour restaurant, demonstrate his talents in French cuisine in New Orleans. So certain was Edith of Maxine's powers of persuasion that, without waiting for the news from Paris, she got Sears, Roebuck to donate all the necessary equipment. When word came of Maxine's success, chefs from all over the country descended upon New Orleans to sample the great man's masterpieces. The culmination of the week was a black-tie dinner limited to one hundred people who paid $100.00 each for the privilege of partaking of the exquisite cuisine. Toward the end of the party the equipment was offered for sale, and, finally, a Chinese raffle was held with ten grand prizes. The top prize was a pony, which had come up the elevator to join the party. Joe Jones led it victoriously from the winner's circle to his home turf, much to the delight of his cheering children. And the orchestra played on, to the tune of another $20,000 dollars in donations.

Edith figured prominently in other fund-raising ideas such as the Rolls Royce raffle in which only two hundred tickets were printed to sell for $200 each. Again, a formal banquet was held, and upon the entrance of each ticket holder a key was presented to the guest. The person whose key fit the Rolls Royce drove away in it.

On April 24, 1955, in Xavier University's auditorium, the opera *Quanga* was performed. *Quanga* was written by the distinguished black composer Dr. Clarence Cameron White. The program notes included an impressive list of his celebrated achievements in the world of music. His curriculum vitae read, in part:

> Clarence Cameron White received his early training at the Oberlin Conservatory of Music. He later spent three years in London, England, as a private student of composition with the late S. Coleridge Taylor. Recently he spent two years in Paris, France, on a Rosenwald Foundation Fellowship where he was a pupil of Raoul Laparra, the distinguished French opera composer.

The Sterns attended most musical events in New Orleans with predictable regularity and might have been present in any case, but the fact that Dr. White had a special link with the Rosenwald Foundation made their presence a certainty. The lights dimmed and the story unfolded. It was that of an ambitious Haitian emperor's struggle against the voodoo superstitions of his people. In the first act aria, a plaintive love song was performed by a spectacular young soprano. Her voice and phrasing were superb; dramatically, she knew just how to convey tenderness and pathos. Who was this beautiful child? Edith wanted to know. She consulted her notes and read the name: Annabelle Bernard.

In the past Edith had vowed that she would never sponsor a musician. "But there was this voice and this child. I just couldn't resist." She sought out Annabelle and declared on the spot that she wished to be involved in the gifted singer's future. "That night I became the protégé of Mrs. Edith Stern," Annabelle said. "We joined in high objectives and ideals. In years to come and despite the distance of miles between us, she was, next to my mother, the closest person I had."

Edith's evaluation was echoed in the newspapers the following day. "Opera Is Dominated by Soprano Bernard," cried one headline. For her part, Edith was already setting wheels in motion to ensure Annabelle the best possible training. An audition with Boris Goldovsky was arranged. Edith recalled that the piano was out of tune, but Annabelle was at her best. After that, it was a summer at Tanglewood and a scholarship from the New England Conservatory of Music.

Annabelle, when Edith met her, was just turning nineteen. She was born in Louisiana, the oldest of four children of Thomas and Clothilde Bernard. Her father was a barber, and both parents struggled in straitened circumstances, further hampered by segregation, to give their three daughters and one son the best possible education and to expose them to art. At the age of seven, in Abijah Fisk Elementary School, Annabelle's second-grade teacher was impressed by her natural talent for singing and dancing and suggested that she take piano lessons. At eight, Annabelle was performing leading roles in school musicals and taking curtain calls. At the completion of her seventh-grade work, she received the Gold Award for attaining the highest scholastic average in her class. She won a scholarship for the eighth-grade class at Gilbert Academy, a private school for exceptional black students in New Orleans. At St. Mark's Baptist Church, the music director assigned her to the adult choir in view of her special talent and competence. She was among the top ten students in her graduating class and was offered three scholarships: Fisk University in Nashville; Leland College in Baker, Louisiana; and Xavier University. Xavier had the best music department. There, Annabelle was coached by the devoted Sister Mary Elisa, chairman of the department.

Edith's support, once she committed herself, was more than monetary. Frequent letters of encouragement helped bolster the rising young star's struggle to the top. When Annabelle won $10,000 in various contests one year, Edith matched it with an equal sum, which allowed Annabelle to study abroad for a year. And Edith matched Annabelle's friendship on an equal basis, too. As Annabelle wrote,

I learned from her to like this world and to love people even more, in spite of hypocrisy and ineptitude everywhere. When I thought, as I often did, that "I can't do this—they won't let me," she would answer: "He who has confidence in himself and the ability to achieve need not set out to prove himself, for his accomplishments will speak for themselves. All barriers will be removed, and all human beings will dwell together with understanding and respect for one another."

Edith always felt that what she had given to Annabelle Bernard came back in manifold ways. She watched with pride as Annabelle soared to the very pinnacle of her profession.

The grandchildren were growing rapidly. Edgar Jr.'s family lived right down Garden Lane, and the memories of his children provide bright pictures of Edith and Longue Vue in the 1950's. Granddaughter Sandra reported:

I remember her stopping to visit on her way home from her "job" at Voters' Service. She was such a humorous, but admirable sight, coming back from a hard day's work in her chauffeur-driven limousine, carrying her "lunch pail" and beaming with satisfaction. We were allowed to enjoy her wonderful home and garden as though they were play-grounds made for small rough-housing children; play "queen" on the library steps, spread poker chips all over the library floor, run wild up and down the long hallways, jumping from priceless rug to priceless rug, pretending the spaces in between were "poison." The stairs were game, the elevator was game, the dumbwaiter was game, the spiral staircase to the wine cellar was game ... it never ended. And, of course, the house was by no means the end of our playground. The "dressing room" in the Playhouse was filled with her magnificent old gowns, hats, shoes, and make-up. We would come down the narrow, steep stairs from a dressing room, dragging a much-too-long skirt over wobbly, outsize shoes, not able to see for the enormous brim of the hat, and everyone would cringe but Mom [Edith]. The gardens were a child's paradise. Games of hide-and-seek could go on forever. Quiet times of adoles-cent confusion, or times when one just wanted to enjoy nature's beauty at something very near its height, the gardens were miraculous. Living just down the lane, my brothers and I could come and go as we pleased, always with the feeling that all this had been provided for our enjoyment and that Mom and Gramp enjoyed our being around whether they were with us, watching from a window or patio, or just hearing us from a distance.

Sandra's little brother, Monte, remembers with equal fondness the activities that Edith planned and the visits to the zoo.

> She always took a special interest in everything we did. She always supplied a child's treasure chest of toys; and when we slept over, I'll never forget the little gifts we found under our pillows. I remember, too, on the big occasions of birthdays and Christmas when I would be looking for large-sized presents on my birthday chair, she'd remind me that the best presents come in little packages.

When the Hess children came down from New York, more activities were planned. Monte remembers that when his cousins came, the days were like one progressive birthday party. "There were soap bubble machines and decorations and live music. Remember the honky tonks, anyone? There were cookouts, where the boys barbecued hamburgers for the girls...."

Once young Bill Hess declared that Whim House was his home. On a later visit, arriving in New Orleans, he found a handsome brass nameplate affixed to the Whim House door engraved solemnly, "W. D. Hess."

Among the Symphony Orchestra's annual reports, the year 1955-1956 appears under the heading "Most Noteworthy Year." The orchestra's out-of-town concerts increased to an unprecedented twenty-four, covering some 90,000 square miles in five states. As if that were not enough, the Symphony was confirmed as one of the nation's great orchestras when the U.S. Department of State singled it out for a concert tour of sixteen Latin American countries.

Thomas Greene excitedly shared the news with the Sterns, adding that, as great as the honor was to be heard in Central and South America, it was apparent that the combination of a grant from the Department of State and the concert fees would not cover the out-of-pocket expenses for the tour. "Mrs. Stern did not hesitate," he said.

> She and Mr. Stern held a dinner party in their Playhouse for a small group of Symphony friends. At the propitious moment (and Edith Stern always knew when the right moment had arrived) she announced in her best undulating voice, "Well, the Orchestra has this great opportunity to shine for itself, for us, and for all of New Orleans; and we are just going to have to give it the kind of backing that's needed. Now, Edgar and I want to pledge to help underwrite this tour and we'd like to know what each of you are willing to do." Zap! Subsequently, the pledges were made and the Orchestra went on a tour combining great adventure with well-deserved acclaim.

Edith went so far as to suggest certain sights that the members of the orchestra must see in their travels and went over Thomas Greene's makeup of the various programs.

On April 2, 1956, two planes stood in readiness at Moisant International Airport in New Orleans. On their sleek sides, emblazoned in large letters, was "New Orleans Symphony Orchestra." Under the flagship's name, *Dauntless*, the word *Allegro* had been added; its sister ship was similarly dubbed the *Scherzo*. Some ninety members of the Orchestra and almost three tons of musical instruments were on board. For a minute or two, the smiling maestro Alexander Hilsberg sat in the pilot's seat of the *Allegro*, waving good-bye to a crowd of well-wishers. Minutes later, *Allegro* and *Scherzo* added their drone to the music of the spheres, heading straight for their first stop in Havana, Cuba. On May 1, 1956, engines echoing the "bravos" and "bravissimos" garnered during the tour, the twin planes landed, bringing a triumphant Orchestra home. Doors were opened to the sound of music from a welcoming band; a crowd waved signs and balloons and bestowed accolades reserved for returning heroes as the members of the Orchestra walked the red carpet spread out to the steps of the planes.

Edith loved all the stories of the trip, but the one she cherished most was the tale of what happened at Ciudad Trujillo. There, at the tomb of Christopher Columbus, the players paid homage to the Genovese seaman. In the Orchestra's Annual Report, under the heading of *Saludos Amigos*, the following reference may be found:

On the very ground which Christopher Columbus thought to be in the vicinity of India some 460 years before, the N.O.S. Orchestra, spanning time, space and imagination, played a concert in April of 1956, adding a new dimension to the manner in which one sovereign nation can further friendship with another.

For Edgar and Edith, it was as if they had gone along. The Latin-American tour by the orchestra of their beloved city epitomized so much in which they fervently believed.

EIGHT

Night of Grief

*T*HE FIGHT AGAINST SEGREGATION was gaining ground in the mid-1950's. Martin Luther King, a man of vision and stature, emerged as a leader on the national scene. It took a march in Selma, marred by tragedy; a vigil in Washington; and the order of the president, implemented by U.S. marshals, before a small black child could be escorted to a desegregated school while an ugly mob jeered. Fortunately, many decent people, unmindful of the personal risk involved, stood up to be counted in Selma and elsewhere.

In New Orleans, Judge Skelly Wright ruled positively on the question of desegregation, despite threats on his life and the safety of his family issued by hooded hooligans of the Ku Klux Klan. William Blanc (Bill) Monroe, head of the News Department of television station WDSU, broadcast bold editorials in favor of integration, which drew fire from segregationist quarters, while lending comfort and encouragement to those fighting against the barrage of threats, insults, and physical acts of violence and intimidation. George Chaplin, editor of the *New Orleans Item*, editorialized in his uniquely effective style amid the wilderness of trenchant prejudice. Their work, and the work of those who supported them, heralded the dawn of a new era for the city.

Finally there were the Sterns, who threw their prestige, their means, and their energies behind the efforts of these gallant individuals. Edgar Jr. owned WDSU-TV, and backed Bill Monroe's bold stance to the hilt. Emulating their grandfather's example, the Stern children, seldom on the sidelines, articulately and effectively contributed to the struggle for human rights. Philip, in fact, was to become an undisputed champion in the name of equality.

The delightful book *Auntie Mame* became an instant best seller. Everyone loved the chic, rich, generous, unconventional Mame, the toast of her social set, unafraid to state her candid opinions, no matter that they ran counter to popular beliefs or trends. It seemed that the whole nation had a soft spot for her. Whom did she bring to mind? Those who knew Edith Stern made a ready identification, and Lester Kabacoff amended the label slightly to read, "Auntie Mame with a social conscience." A onetime guest at Longue Vue also caused a considerable stir in the literary world: John F. Kennedy, whose book *Profiles in Courage* won wide acclaim and garnered the coveted Pulitzer Prize.

Edith was busy sending out congratulatory notes to winners she had supported, to fighters for civil rights. She spent much time reading the minutes of board meetings for the various organizations and institutions she served. And she remained in constant contact with her children, keeping abreast of the interests of the new generation, her grandchildren.

In the summer of 1956, Edith learned that her sister Marion's daughter, Adele Rome, was taken ill in California. Marion rushed to be at her daughter's side and kept in daily contact with Edith. Edgar and Edith, for their part, invited Marion's young son, Peter, to visit with them.

By October, Edith had to go to California on a tragic mission. Marion's daughter had died, leaving behind a grief-stricken husband and three small boys. Later, back in New Orleans, Edith instinctively resorted to the one remedy that would help her cope with her own feelings, submerging herself in massive amounts of work. She was particularly outspoken in her support of civil rights.

Hate mail of the most virulent kind flooded mail boxes at Longue Vue and other homes whose owners had openly expressed their views on desegregation. Margery Stich received one such missive, attacking her viciously for her commitment to the cause of integration, full of abusive insults for her as a liberal and as a Jew. Devastated, she called Edith for counsel and solace. Edith took cognizance of Margery's distress but seemed unmoved. "Is this the first one you ever got?" she inquired. "Of course," Margery replied. "My dear, I get them every day," Edith said.

Perhaps to blot out the ugliness of the letters and phone calls, Edith devoted more time to the Garden Club. Amid the tranquil beauty of the flora and enlightening horticultural discussions, she found the perfect antidote to the racism prevailing in the streets. But was she deluding herself? Even within this circle of beauty, certain lines were drawn that demarked the vantage points from which a privileged few might view nature's indiscriminate spectacle.

At an early point in Edith's involvement with horticultural activities, she belonged to a New Orleans Garden Study Society. In time, this organization was invited to join the Garden Clubs of America. Since the latter organization did not accept Jews, Edith called a meeting of the group and offered her resignation, she being the only Jewish member. The group caucused and resolved to accept membership in the larger organization only as they were presently constituted, or not at all. Garden Clubs of America acceded.

Eleanor Roosevelt was among the many guests at Longue Vue who fully appreciated the gardens. Like Edith, she sought solace in the bosom of nature as one who witnessed the frequent cruelties of humanity. A devoted friend and admirer of Adele Levy, with whom she worked closely in the aid of underprivileged children, it was only natural that Mrs. Roosevelt should extend her friendship to Adele's sister, who shared her many concerns. Among these was support of the Democratic Party, for which Mrs. Roosevelt served as standard-bearer. However, the presence of that formidable lady in the Stern home, and her status as an honored guest, presented a dilemma for the host and his son, Edgar Jr., both ardent Republicans.

Libby Monroe, Bill's wife, remembers a party at Longue Vue in honor of Mrs. Roosevelt. Edith was brimming with pleasure and pride and betrayed just a bit of mischievous glee at Edgar's discomfiture. He was, in effect, caught between the Scylla and Charybdis of his duties as host and his loyalty to the Grand Old Party. For a time, he felt relegated to the unaccustomed role of standing in the wings in his own domain, never the style of this Southern seigneur. In the end, his gentlemanly instincts and manners prevailed. He managed to pay handsome tribute to a woman who also happened to be the widow of a man he had opposed.

On April 27, 1958, in honor of Israel's Tenth Anniversary, a concert by the Harvard University Band was held in Boston, at Boston Gardens. Senator Hubert H. Humphrey of Minnesota, and chairman of the Consultative Subcommittee on Near Eastern Affairs of the United States Senate, was in attendance among many other dignitaries. Edith was especially interested in the program. The Opera Department of the New England Conservatory of Music presented excerpts from Handel's oratorio *Esther,* and the role of that valiant, beloved queen was sung with impassioned lyricism by Annabelle Bernard.

Annabelle at twenty-three had already starred in Handel's *Messiah* with the New England Opera and won the coveted Beebe Award given by the New England Conservatory. This launched her, in June 1959, on a professional singing career in Europe. Before her departure, however, Annabelle returned once more to New Orleans to make her farewells, both personally and musically. She performed at Xavier University, her alma mater, and then gave a performance at Longue Vue for her admiring benefactor. In Europe she found her career assured, and she became the leading soprano of the Berlin Opera.

That summer, Edgar and Edith received the joyous news that Philip and Lennie had made them grandparents again — David having arrived on June 25, 1959. Perhaps it was the arrival of the new grandchild that caused Edith to miss her Garden Lane grandchildren more. Since Edgar Jr. and Polly had bought a house in Colorado, the grandchildren who used to run in and out of Longue Vue at will had been absent. Summer seemed an ideal time to visit the family; besides, the Sterns like many other American world travelers, had almost no familiarity with the American West, the "backyard" of their own country. Granddaughter Sandra had vivid memories of their stay:

> Mom and Gramp came to visit us during the summer at Aspen. There was to be a large cocktail party one day and before that it was decided that the windows needed washing. (There were more windows than walls; and some were as high as twenty-five feet.) Apparently, there was no one available for the task outside of the immediate family, so Mom and I decided "it would be fun" and volunteered. It took the entire day, plus what must have been hundreds of bottles of glass-cleaner and countless yards of paper towels in addition to the entire life of a squeegee to produce the most streaked, striped, smudged windows ever viewed at a cocktail party, but we did it!

It was August 1959. The train bearing Edgar and Edith was speeding through Bryce Canyon, Utah. There is a kind of magic in riding a train through a summer night, enhanced here by the majestic silhouettes of the rock configurations. As Edith told Amy Miller later, she went into Edgar's compartment to kiss him goodnight. Moved by the splendor of the night, and perhaps by the stirrings of memories of their wedding train so many years before, she said, "Edgar, you are such a handsome devil."

A short while later, Edgar suffered a massive heart attack and died. Edith summoned the conductor, who offered to stop the train. Edith decided that such a gesture would be futile. She refused to broach the news to the children at such an hour and with so many miles separating them. Accordingly, she thanked the conductor and advised him that she would be all right. She held her own vigil with Edgar and somehow managed to get through the night.

It was a selfless act, one that demanded the utmost of her moral fiber and fortitude. She may also have sought this last night alone with Edgar, perhaps to relive the journey of their lives while his physical presence was still before her, perhaps to gird herself for the desolation to come. Through the night, still together, they sped toward a dawn that would find Edith alone—alone in a way she had not known since the day she met Edgar. Later, Edith spoke to family and some friends about the less personal aspects of that tragic night. She told Margery Stich that for parts of hours she read Leon Uris' book *Exodus*. One is struck by the thought of the chapter headings of that book. It is the fifty-seventh Psalm of David that begins the next to last chapter:

> *Awake in Glory*
> Be merciful unto me, O God, be merciful unto me, for
> my soul trusteth in thee; yea, in the shadow of thy wings
> will I make my refuge, until these calamities are over.

And the quotation ends, "Awake up, my glory ... I will rouse the dawn...."

In the morning light the new realities became all too clear, and Edith attended to them with meticulous care: arrangements, formalities, phone calls, telegrams. Finally, the wings of Longue Vue embraced her. She came home, with only the memories of Edgar.

The last rites were held on August 28, 1959. Rabbi Julian B. Feibelman of Temple Sinai officiated. He opened the service by intoning the lines of a sonnet.

> Let none of you weep for me,
> Especially you with whom I've smiled.
> Nor bow down your head in utter grief....
> Say that I lived, enjoying each mortal breath.

It was not a lengthy sermon, for the Rabbi had given careful consideration to the setting. Longue Vue itself was a sermon, he seemed to say.

Night of Grief 209

Nothing human was alien to him. Yet he was a simple man, and an humble one. He said to me at one time, "I can never thank God sufficiently for all the blessings that are ours." When this beautiful home, which he deeply loved, was dedicated, and after blessing was besought upon it, he asked to say a word to us gathered at the threshold. He petitioned God to be gracious to his beloved one, his children and himself, that they might worthily live and always share their blessings. Then he thanked God and asked Divine favor upon the work of all their hands, and to let them dwell in this house in peace. He said "Amen" and then he fixed with his own hand the little silver ornament of home to the doorpost, the one his father and mother had given to him and his bride in their former home.

On another occasion he said to me: "Life is a steward-ship." He was reflecting the lines of our Sabbath Prayer, read in Temple Sinai, to which he was so good and always responsive, "Our deeds should speak Thy praise; our will-ingness to share Thy blessings with others should testify to our gratitude. For we are but stewards of whatever we possess." This faith he professed and this faith he lived. It was the faith taught to him and exemplified in the lives of a distinguished father and an honored mother.... Then came the rare and perfect love brought to him by his wife.... Of his beloved he could say, "Many daughters have done valiantly, but thou excellest them all." Togetherness has been their labor, their studious planning, and their great accomplishment. Because there is no gift without the giver this bond has been unique, devotedly encompassed not only by shared interest but also with personal partici-pation.... His final joy was the reunion, in this week, with children and children's children, and as if a providential Father wished to fill again his cup of life giving joy before it was taken from his lips. From them he rode away, happy and confident that life is good, but that the simple and joyous devotion of family surpass all.

Many who attended the service may have had their own memories of it, but Bill Monroe articulated his feelings with the greatest precision. Monroe had been news director at WDSU-TV in New Orleans, working closely with Edgar Stern, Jr., and coming into contact with the elder Sterns in those years. Later, of course, he left New Orleans and eventually became a familiar guest of millions of television viewers who welcomed him into their homes on Sundays on the NBC *Meet the Press* telecasts. He observed:

There were not numerous, strong centers of liberal and enlightened thinking about racial and political matters in New Orleans. The Sterns and Monte Lemann gave you a feeling, as far as most of us were concerned—we didn't know them well—as people who were. We could occasionally see their influence. When we visited the Stern home at some major party, Dr. Dent was often there. There were very few homes in New Orleans where there were blacks present. It was an all-white society with the exception of very few homes where a mix took place, and there were social interrelationships between blacks and whites and it was very significant that Dr. Dent was there and there was social interaction.

I had an odd feeling—I went to Mr. Stern's funeral service and had a feeling of some kind of triumph—that this had been a life that had been well lived and meant a great deal. There was some happiness, probably not a good word—but a sense of realization of achievement. I have seldom gotten at funerals something like this feeling.

Rabbi Feibelman put it in perspective: "Death is only a horizon; and the horizon is nothing, save the limit of our sight."

Still in the throes of initial shock and grief, at a time when others might have sought rest, Edith wrote,

My dearest friends:

In this moment of solitude, my thoughts are of you who have shown a selfless devotion I have never seen equaled.

Everything I see, everything I touch, brings me your message of devotion. I know half of it is for me and half for our beloved one. Of all the tributes that have been paid to him, none is greater than your solicitude for me and mine —no, for us and ours. My heart is overflowing with gratitude that I have not the strength to tell each of you, individually, at this time; so you will share this as we have all shared so many things during these years—joys and sorrows, but mostly the joyous. Do know that no detail has escaped my notice and each of these touch me deeply.

Some of us are going to services at the Temple tonight at 8:00. I need not tell you that any one of you who would like to join us is warmly welcomed.

Your grateful,
Edith Stern

Less than three weeks after Edgar's death, on September 13, his closest friend, Monte Lemann, died. Of him, Justice Felix Frankfurter said, "From a rare occasion a tired cliché can gain fresh vitality. And so, one unashamedly dares to say that Monte Lemann was an ornament of his profession – for that he was." New Orleans had lost two of its giants, but the work they had initiated and the seeds of the ideas they had germinated would see a full harvest in time to come.

Mayor deLesseps Morrison, Edgar, Edith, and Monte Lemann at an award presentation for Edgar.

Edgar and Edith Stern at the New Orle... Philharmonic Symphony. Mrs. Hilsburg, ... of the conducter, is seated beside them.

Sixty-seven descendants of the Julius Rosenwald family gathered in Chicago in 1983 for the fiftieth ...versary celebration of the Museum of Science and Industry.

NINE

People Give
to People

EDITH WAS SIXTY-FOUR YEARS OLD when Edgar died. In a fairly short time, she overcame the numbing shock and her pragmatic side asserted itself. She seemed to function with total efficiency, and as she resumed her activities she allowed little time for her personal grief. Calling a meeting of the household staff, she informed them that their positions were secure. They would be with her, she said, as long as the money would last, which, by the look of it, would be for quite a while.

During this period of transition, she found the next generation a source of support—not only her own children, but as her grief was compounded by the loss of the beloved Monte Lemann, by his children as well. She could rely on Monte's two sons, Thomas and Stephen, for legal counsel and advice, such as their father had always supplied. She tended to lean heavily on Thomas. Difficult as it must have been to labor in the shadow of his illustrious father, Tommy (as he was generally known) soon cast a giant shadow of his own.

A great deal of Edith's energy was now directed toward Dillard University, where Edgar had given so much of his time, thoughts, and philanthropy. City politics absorbed most of the remaining hours, and she was in constant contact with the mayor's office, tendering her special brand of advice.

She had attended the National Democratic Convention, held in Los Angeles in 1959, where her path again crossed John F. Kennedy's, and she had stayed to see him get the presidential nod. Even then, she only mused *when*, not *if*, he would win the election, she would no longer call him Jack, as he had requested, but "Mr. President." Rosalie Brener Grad, the mayor's indispensable secretary, sat in Edith's box at the convention, viewing Edith's fervor and the pleasure she derived from this highly charged atmosphere.

Edith had mentioned to Rosalie earlier that the West Coast trip would afford an opportunity to view Zsa Zsa Gabor's house. This came about by courtesy of the mayor of New Orleans, who prevailed upon his friend Zsa Zsa to extend an invitation. The visit proved to be a highlight of the trip. Edith seemed almost as excited by her visit to the Gabor home as by Kennedy's nomination.

Integration was the most talked-of issue within Edith's circle, though it was pointedly ignored in many another elegant residence. Edith was deeply enmeshed in this cause in all its ramifications. More voices were being raised in public, however, among them that of Father Thomas H. Clancy. A close friendship grew out of their mutual involvement, and the priest came to admire Edith for her civic concerns and her courage.

Father Clancy originally came to New Orleans as a faculty member of Loyola University. He already had a long list of impressive credentials. His writings were vast, and he contributed to the *New Catholic Encyclopedia* and the *Dictionnaire d'Histoire et de Géographie Ecclésiastique*. He was deeply impressed when he heard that the state legislature had cut off funds earmarked for teachers in desegregated public schools, and rumor had it that Edith Stern was putting up money to meet these payrolls. Edith was likewise impressed when she met this intelligent, articulate Jesuit priest who later served as chairman of the Department of Political Science at Loyola and then became the Superior of the New Orleans Province, a Society of Jesus that covers ten states in the South and Southwest. Father Clancy still recalls that the Stern Fund endowed the first few years of the Institute of Politics, a seminar devoted to preparing citizens to go into politics, that had its seat at Loyola.

Edith's involvement in politics highlighted for her certain inherent weaknesses in democracy. Her father had set the direction, and Edgar had continued working in it, and now she found herself steering a course that aimed to achieve greater equity for blacks in education. She was convinced that if blacks were equipped to compete for job opportunities they would gain a better life-style and reach higher levels of society. In her work for Voters' Registration, and for eliminating corruption in City Hall, she felt she was helping to restore the original concept of democracy. At least one key to equality lay in the ballot box.

The election of John Kennedy to the presidency provided her with other opportunities. President Kennedy appointed her to the National Cultural Center Advisory Committee on the Arts. She was full of ideas but was forced to pause for more immediate personal concerns.

Adele was not well, despite her habit of making light of her illness in their daily telephone conversations. On March 12, 1960, less than seven months after Edgar's passing, Adele died. Edith once again was plunged into grief and despair. At the memorial service, the tall, stately Eleanor Roosevelt touched the hearts of the mourners when she paid her tribute. She spoke movingly, not as a public figure but as a grieving friend.

> I meet here today with those who really cared deeply about Adele Levy.... They knew, I think, everyone of us here knows that the qualities she had are qualities we need in the world today and we should strive to have them.
> She had courage. She would stand for lost causes. All her life she worked for those who were less fortunate than she was.... But she had also great sweetness. Someone told me today that in speaking of her or in writing of her someone had said she had a listening heart. I think that is a very wonderful description because to really understand you must listen and Adele Levy, I think, really understood....

"A listening heart." The phrase was telling for Edith, and she derived a measure of comfort from it, knowing that within her remained much of Adele that would be hers always, that no passage of time could ever obliterate. Later, Edith wrote to Marion: "There is *no* hour of the day without the reassuring contacts my thoughts of you evoke. Like a soft obligato, Adele is hovering over both of us. I love you dearly."

More and more, Edith relied on her family and friends. Lillian Feibelman, Mildred Heller, and Phyllis Dennery, among others, rallied around her. Each shared some part of her activities — music, politics, the arts. That summer she accompanied the Dennerys on a trip to France, concentrating this visit on the milieu in which impressionism had been spawned.

Phyllis was working on a project for which she sought Edith's help. Having concluded her impassioned plea, Edith was unmoved. "I wouldn't touch this one with a ten-foot pole," she offered. Undaunted, Phyllis went home, got hold of a pole eleven feet long, decorated it with colorful flowers, among them some of Edith's favorites, and — figuratively — hurled the lance into her "adversary's" court by means of a local messenger. Predictably, Edith picked up the challenge, and the project was launched.

In 1962 Edith became the target of personal attack in a hotly contested mayoral race that took a rather nasty turn. The rivals were Adrian Duplantier and Victor H. Schiro. Edith backed the former. In some of Schiro's campaign literature, Duplantier was depicted as dangling puppet-like from a woman's hand. The lady's wrist was adorned with a flashy bracelet, an innuendo that left little doubt of the wearer's identity. Edith bore the insult, considering it beneath her to reply.

She was resigned, likewise, to the fact that the incoming mail at Longue Vue would bring its share of vitriolic messages from segregationist groups, many threatening violence. She shared some of these with her grandson Monte, apparently wishing him to be aware of the price one paid for one's convictions.

Schiro won the election, much to Edith's chagrin, and the bitterness she felt on this occasion was evidenced by her remark to Monte's sister Sandra: "If the man you vote for loses, then you know you've voted for the right man." She worked toward the next election, of course.

Time and again, Edith voiced her concern about the future of responsible leadership. It was therefore balm on her wounds when the Jewish community of New Orleans felt the need to immortalize the two men who had brought so much luster to their city. Thus, in 1962, the Lemann-Stern Young Leadership Group was formed. Its aim was to groom young men and women for Jewish leadership roles. Membership was by invitation only and continues to be highly coveted. It has attracted a cadre of young people of the highest caliber, who have lived up to the noble aspirations envisaged for it.

On a lighter note, Edgar Jr.'s son Monte formed a "Politics Club" as a fifth grader. "Mom became chief organizer of our meetings and a stimulating discussion leader," he noted. And he suspects to this day that it was she who asked Representative Hale Boggs to write a congratulatory letter to the club's founder. No doubt Edith reminded the congressman that one never knows on whose support a politician may need to rely in the future.

Bill Hess, Edith's firstborn beloved grandson, visited often and stayed as long as he could. Edith so loved the role of grandmother that she was wont to say, "Babies are such wonderful inventions." At the same time, one of Edith's most attractive traits was her ability to see the spouses of her children as more than mere appendages, as complete human beings. She had always been fond of Lennie, Phil's wife, admiring her sculpture and her maternal competence in equal measures. The birth of their daughter Eve, in 1962, brought another measure of happiness and contentment.

She also showed a special fondness for Tom Hess, Audrey's husband, despite the fact that she and Audrey were not as close as Edith might have wished. Perhaps their similarities of character, their respective drives and ambitions, made a relaxed mother-daughter relationship difficult. Yet Edith took enormous pride in Audrey's accomplishments, which, in certain areas, surpassed her own.

In New York's sophisticated literary and artistic circles, where Tom was held in high esteem as editor of *Art News*, Audrey carved out a position of eminence in her own right. A sense of obligation brought her to the kind of work that her beloved Aunt Adele had initiated and that had been carried on by Aunt Marion in tandem with Audrey's sister-in-law Betty Wolff. It was the Citizens' Committee for Children. Audrey's other interests ranged from support of such national political figures as Stevenson and later Kennedy to the full gamut of the performing arts—from opera to ballet to the New York Philharmonic. And her sense of social justice was evidenced by her staunch support of such causes as prison reform. Meanwhile, her parties earned her renown for originality, chic, and a flair for bringing together an assemblage of guests that represented the ultimate in sophistication.

Unfortunately, Audrey's health began to fail, aggravated, it appears, by her constant strenuous dieting, in search of a perfection perhaps beyond her reach. Edith voiced her concern. The two headstrong women—proud, driving, competent—inevitably clashed when Edith attempted to tender advice and Audrey refused to listen.

When her political foe occupied City Hall, Edith drew ever closer to the arts. In the course of these pursuits, her friendship with Margery Stich blossomed. Edith's shrewd assessment of people alerted her that here was a woman of great competence. Tall, attractive, distinguished, and exuding *savoir faire*, Margery seemed to be just the kind of co-worker Edith loved.

Margery remembers well the eventful telephone call. Edith said, "People tell me that you have a talent for getting a job done—that you stick to it, and you follow through. Also, I understand that you have a lot of public-relations savvy and I need someone to help me with a helluva job right this moment. So, can you have lunch with me tomorrow?"

They lunched in the dining room, beside the bay window overlooking the Pan Garden. Edith explained the situation. She had been appointed to the presidency of a fledgling organization called the Cultural Attractions Fund. It was a miniature United Way, dedicated to raising funds for all cultural organizations in New Orleans through one annual campaign. Margery succumbed to Edith's offer and took a position as head of the publicity campaign. She called on the foremost critics of the performing arts and other leading columnists of the day to write on the topic "What does CAF mean to me?" The response was overwhelmingly positive, exceeding all expectations. Edith and Margery celebrated their successful collaboration at a Valentine's Day party. It was a gala occasion. All the other guests were men.

Margery's admiration for Edith grew with each passing year. When in need of advice, she could always rely on the elder woman's wisdom. She was fascinated by the imaginative uses to which Edith put her philanthropy. Like Julius Rosenwald, Edith was a firm proponent of the "matching funds" theory of giving, and she went on to refine the process. Her dollars usually went toward obtaining more funding from others but were geared also to enlisting maximum involvement of individuals. Most philanthropists believed that maximum participation depended on complete understanding of a cause. Yet Edith was often heard to say, "People give to people, not causes."

TEN

Edith at Seventy

W HILE SHOPPING IN WOOLWORTH'S, Edith came across some lovely shoes. They were as comfortable as slippers, and the price was only $4.88 a pair. She bought a few pairs and was so enthralled with them that she returned to purchase pairs in every available color. Typically, she did not stop at that, but called the manufacturer and praised him for his product, suggesting that perhaps she could help him by investing in his company or bringing his company to the attention of the buyer at Sears. The man thanked her profusely and indicated that, for the time, he had as much business as he could handle. In fact, he said, his last year's earnings were somewhere near one million dollars.

Edith often laughed at herself since she had thought the manufacturer was struggling to make ends meet. From that point on, however, the manufacturer made special matching pairs of his shoes for Edith from cloth swatches that she forwarded to him. These "custom" shoes ran the gamut of fabrics and patterns, from beachwear to formal attire.

On another occasion, Margery Stich mentioned to Edith that her mother was frustrated at not being able to obtain a special type of fine hairnet for her gray coiffure. In short order, Edith triumphantly produced a number of these from Woolworth's, sufficient to last for the rest of the lady's life.

Her other gift to Margery's mother, Hilda "Skipper" Katz, was more substantial as well as more practical and original. On Hilda's ninetieth birthday, workmen appeared at the Stich home, where she was a frequent visitor, with instructions to install a wrought-iron railing that would facilitate mounting the steps leading to the front door.

Following Edgar's death, Edith's many friends vied for the privilege and pleasure of entertaining her. Among the many parties devised for her diversion, one was planned by Maxine Wachenheim, who invited about thirty people to take part in an unusual evening. Knowing Edith's penchant for the new, the innovative, and the revolutionary, Maxine invited a group of young men who happened to be visiting from England and who produced music with a remarkable new beat, in sharp contrast to their prim Edwardian garb. Edith was charmed by the polite youths, who needed little prompting to present their own brand of syncopation in the cradle of Dixieland jazz. All the guests agreed that no ensemble before had produced more infectious music than this foursome—Paul, John, George, and Ringo—The Beatles.

Much of Edith's philanthropic work at that time was carried on through the family foundation, the Stern Fund. Helen Hill Miller had been employed on a part-time basis to administer the fund, but Edith felt that a full-time director was needed. Combing the foundation world, she found a much respected young man named David Hunter, who was working at the Ford Foundation in the areas of youth problems and urban affairs. Although Hunter enjoyed the work he was doing at what he called "the behemoth of the foundation world," Edith's offer of the chance to manage "a small, active foundation" was irresistible.

Edith came to rely on his ideas, his keen understanding of issues, and his scrupulous honesty. She was in constant contact with Hunter in his office in New York; whenever necessary, he would spend some time in New Orleans. Edith always entreated him to bring his charming wife, Barbara, arguing that it was not good for a marriage if partners were frequently separated. Thus the Hunters often stayed at Whim House.

Once, Barbara, David, and Edith took a picnic lunch on the steps of New Orleans' City Hall. A delicious meal, prepared by Emma, included all the accoutrements of silver and fine nappery. They must have presented an unusual spectacle for the bustling crowd of citizens passing by on their way to and from offices.

The foundation went through a series of name shortenings, beginning as the Edgar B. Stern Family Fund, then changing to the Stern Family Fund, and, finally, to the Stern Fund. In its formative years, its board included a number of nonfamily members. As the family grew, this was changed also, so that the board comprised family members only, with the exception of the Fund's attorney. At the time of that change, Edith saw to it that each of her grandchildren, upon reaching the age of eighteen, would be invited to join the board as full voting members. This was her way of ensuring that they would learn as much as possible about the structure of philanthropy. It revealed, too, her respect for young people and their capabilities. As David Hunter pointed out,

> She never talked down to them and often indicated how much it meant to her to see them participating in the work of the Fund. She always felt that but for that opportunity, she would have missed important aspects of this maturing generation's characteristics, personality, and intelligence.

Edith frequently alluded to Julius Rosenwald's philanthropy by quoting his axiom, "It's harder to give away a dollar wisely than it is to earn it."

From the start, David Hunter realized that the Stern Fund had a "liberal" cast to it—as the Rosenwald fund had also—especially in its concern for the disadvantaged, in the main, for blacks. Yet it had an overarching aim, as well. In his words:

The term "black" was considered opprobrious then. The struggle then was to get the word "Negro" capitalized. Although the direct objects of its philanthropy have changed with changing times, it has, from the beginning, been concerned with fostering democracy, helping to improve the life of people in the lower reaches of our society, and particularly in the early days, the support for the arts.

Board meetings were held two or three times a year and lasted for two days. Among those in attendance was Marilynn M. Klein, the foundation administrator, who worked hard in preparation for each meeting.

We sent to the Board notebooks filled with lots of material to read ahead of time about organizations being considered for funding. In addition to the written information, the Stern Fund invited to the meeting representatives from each of these groups. Mrs. Stern encouraged this practice and felt it added a human dimension to the written proposal. By the time she entered the board room, she had read assiduously everything in her notebook and in her usual, very organized fashion, had made copious notes, including comments and questions about each project.

At the beginning of each meeting day, she would sit down at the large table; take enough needlepoint out of her suitcase to last the better part of a month. So immersed did she appear in the world of flame stitch, gobelin, mosaic, and herringbone, that occasionally one might have thought she was oblivious to the discussion at hand. Hardly the case! In the middle of a heated discussion, she would stop, look up, and with a pertinent and relevant comment, would bring everything into the proper perspective.

The board meetings and the activities of the Fund took in a wide range of subjects, David Hunter recalled, including: civil rights, civil liberties, community organizations, environmental and energy-related questions, government openness and accountability, abuse of power, maldistribution of wealth and power, maintenance of peace, etc.

In judging potential projects, the board considered the possible impacts of a project on the broad issue of social justice, whether or not the project could hope to raise funds elsewhere to supplement what the Stern Fund might provide, the quality of the leaders seeking funding, their timing, their strategy, and how innovative they were in their approach.

A plan was proposed to build an elevated highway along the French Quarter. Edith, together with other concerned citizens, objected strenuously to it. She desired to protect and preserve the beauty and unique quality of this famous and historic section. The Fund eventually disbursed some $100,000 in the course of the fight against the elevated structure.

Other issues raised in the course of discussing potential projects were the My Lai massacre during the Vietnam War and Ralph Nader's inquiries into the trustworthiness of manufacturers' claims. Once Gloria Steinem was invited to a board meeting to express her stance on women's liberation. Ms. Steinem's presence was sufficient to bring to the meeting a granddaughter of Edith's who had heretofore shunned the gatherings. The granddaughter came attired in the rather loose mode of the day and used language that her grandmother probably abhorred, but Edith did not flinch.

At one of the meetings, a highly explosive issue came to light: corporate responsibility. Edgar Jr., the consummate business executive, felt this area was not subject to decisions by a philanthropic organization, that the issues involved were essentially of a managerial nature, to be solved internally within the corporate structure. His convictions on the matter were so firm that he indicated his impending resignation should the majority of the board decide to enter this arena. Edith held the decisive vote. She asked David Hunter to review once again the purposes and aims of the Fund. This done, she deliberated for but a moment, then cast her "aye" vote in favor of consideration, and against Edgar Jr. Edgar lived up to his promise and resigned. No doubt, Edith's decision was taken with a full consideration of this possibility. And it might be argued that her vote was counter to the best interests of her "class." But, even if so, it was in adherence to what she considered right. To the credit of all concerned, the disagreement stayed with the conference room and did not cause a rift of any kind within the family.

Philip's son David, Edith's youngest grandson, became president of the Stern Fund. He embarked on a career as an attorney because, in his own words:

I want to pursue a "public interest" law career. It is the
unfair treatment of people without means, to fight for their
rights, that inspired me to want to become a lawyer. The
origin of those values comes directly from the Stern/
Rosenwald family. I am very proud that their contribution
to our nation is reaching our generation. . . .

And he concluded, "The values connected with my
family inspire me to reach for the stars."

Edith's grandson Monte once came into direct conflict
with her.

When I was at college, studying economics, we had our
only fight and it was a big one. I disagreed with the direction of the Stern Fund, as it turned from the liberal causes
of the sixties to the more Leftist cause of promoting social-
ism. I was uncompromising on the matter and resigned
after a particular grant was approved. Some months later,
I received the most loving, respectful letter from her that is
my most cherished memory of her. A strong-willed, proud
and powerful woman in her seventies, sending a deferen-
tial letter to her defiant, even intolerant, teenage grandson.
She continued to be a supportive confidante and protective
of my search for my own destiny.

Edith was not one to adhere to social or moral standards
once they became passé. This was as true in her activities
within the Fund as in her private life. Monte, if he expected an
almost Victorian stance from his grandmother, was taken by
surprise on another occasion.

I was at her home during vacation when she personally
served a bottle of champagne and four glasses on a silver
tray. Then she left the room, closing the doors behind her,
leaving me, my best friend, and our dates to our privacy.

How many young men, even now, can tell such tales
about their grandmothers?

Edith continued to receive good news about Annabelle
Bernard from abroad. Whenever she was in Europe, Edith tried
to arrange a flight to Berlin to see her protégée. Annabelle
meanwhile had chalked up some amazing firsts. She was the
first black person to sing the title role of *Madama Butterfly* in
German, before an audience at the Stuttgart Opera. She also

made brilliant appearances at the Heidelberg Opera and other prominent German opera houses. She gave a command performance before Prince Louis Ferdinand of Prussia at his ancestral home, the Hohenzollern Palace in Bamberg, where she received rave reviews. Edith treasured a photograph taken at the Prince's palace showing a radiant Annabelle, gowned in splendid satin and long white gloves. In light of Edith's German experiences in the 1930's, thoughts of the incongruity and irony of such an event must have crossed her mind, even as deep pride and satisfaction filled her heart.

In 1965, when Edith was turning seventy, the biblical threescore and ten and the first big birthday she would not share with Edgar, her family and friends decided on a nonstop celebration that would stretch across time and distance. Perhaps this was meant to fill the void that Edgar's passing had left, or perhaps it was in consideration of a dawning awareness of the fragility of life itself. Some of the giants of contemporary history succumbed in that year: Winston Churchill, Bernard Baruch, Adlai Stevenson, Felix Frankfurter, T. S. Eliot, Albert Schweitzer, and Martin Buber. Edith had known most of them personally, and some of them were her friends. What was wanted for Edith, with her concurrence, was a celebration of life. This required several months of touring, "from Ritz to Ritz," as she termed it.

At a farewell party in New Orleans, the Stiches and the Roy Schwarzes honored her with a dinner in the Stich home. The two couples pooled their considerable talent and imagination, and the result was a lovely, original party that poked good-natured fun at "The Store." The central theme of the skits was "The Affairs of Edith." Outside the entrance stood a life-size cardboard figure of the Beefeater Gin man in red uniform — to reflect Edith's favorite evening beverage. Clara Schwarz, a co-hostess, carried in a bird cage complete with bird, along with other items mentioned in the popular commercial lyric *Sears Has Everything*. The other co-hostess, Margery Stich, wore a huge hat featuring a fountain in its center and grass and flowers on its brim and carrying the title *Longue Vue Gardens*. Charles Stich was in graduation attire and carrying a sign indicating that he was the first white graduate of Dillard. Dessert was a chocolate treasure chest filled with assorted pastries, each one iced with the logo of some organization in which Edith had an interest. Edith roared with enjoyment and approval and was touched to tears when a song floated into the room, the magnificent voice instantly recognizable: Annabelle Bernard, serenading her benefactor with a special birthday melody. The co-hostesses had the foresight to arrange for the recording. As the journey was about to commence, Edith instructed her staff to rest up well, because, upon her return, there would be parties on top of parties.

The first stage of the trip was a stay in Spain. Edith had asked her good friend Lillian Cohn to be her travel companion. Their arrival in Madrid posed something of a mystery for Edith who discovered her hotel suite lavishly filled with flowers. Much as she adored them, this sort of abundance made her feel, she said, as if she were attending her own funeral. True, she had made many acquaintances in Spain, and some of her South American friends had alerted governors of provinces or mayors of the larger cities to Edith's coming. Beyond that, it puzzled her that there were floral arrangements from countless members of an aristocracy she had yet to encounter.

Lillian Cohn unraveled the mystery. A Spanish society woman with whom Lillian was acquainted had mentioned within her circles that Lillian, in the company of a Sears heiress, planned to be in Madrid. This rumor unleashed a race by eligible males, titled or otherwise, all of whom were vying for the privilege of meeting Edith. Edith declared that she had never had so much fun in her life.

After touring Spain, they spent a week in Paris. When it was time to move on, they parted ways. Lillian departed for the United States, loath as she was to leave her friend. The last leg of the journey took Edith to Israel where Margo Miller, daughter of her Lenox friends, was her companion. She was delighted to be accompanied by this intelligent young woman with whom she could share the excitement of the trip, the sights of this ancient/new country, and the eccentricities of the characters they met. Teddy Kollek, the mayor of Jerusalem, personally arranged their itinerary and provided a driver by the name of Katz, whom Edith promptly dubbed "Katzele." In Israel, drivers often are excellent guides, informed on everything from the Bible to modern history and from food to archaeology, and seemingly have an inexhaustible supply of anecdotes for every sight. Katzele was no exception. Thanks to him, Edith entered, as she said, her "age of anecdotage." Katzele knew everything: places, history, the famous, the notorious; on their drives through Tel-Aviv, Haifa, Beersheba, and Jerusalem, he would regale his eager listeners with endless tales.

Edith and Margo were received by government officials and notables, among them Lord and Lady Samuel. Edith kept a few bottles of vodka and gin in her room. A drink, and a little rest, and she was ready always to push on. Remembering her earlier trip to this land, she could not help but marvel at all that had been accomplished since. These achievements surpassed even her highest expectations. Agriculture, in particular, interested her. She was awed by the reclamation of the desert and the draining of the swamps, which had turned arid or mosquito-infested stretches into rich farmlands. She loved Caesarea's antiquities, but also the new amenities there, including a golf course. She attended a harp competition held in the Roman-built amphitheater of Caesarea, finding the acoustics to be equal to those in the best concert halls of the world.

In Jerusalem, she decided against a visit to Yad Vashem, the memorial for the six million victims of the Holocaust. But she visited the forests planted by the Jewish pioneers, and the idea of planting trees in this once-barren land appealed to her immensely. (Later, back home, she would send tree certificates in lieu of Christmas greeting cards.) She developed a special affection for Katzele and went so far as to lend him money for the purchase of a home. Yet even in this case, she was careful to check the reliability of her recipient and—as applicable—the potential for repayment of the loan. In Katzele she found the requisite integrity; nor was she disappointed. Margo observed that, when it came time for farewells, Edith left most of her clothing for Katzele's wife—not only those pieces bearing the Sears label but French designer dresses as well.

Edith returned to Longue Vue full of vigor and bursting with new ideas. True to her word, she proceeded to launch a series of parties.

A call had already gone out to New York to secure the services of Rudy Stanish, *chef extraordinaire*, in whose capable hands Edith placed her most brilliant functions on a regular basis. Stanish first came to Edgar and Edith's attention in 1953, when he concocted outstanding dishes for the investment firm of Goldman, Sachs with which Edgar enjoyed a close association. The Sterns had just taken an apartment on Beekman Place in New York City and enthusiastically engaged Rudy to display his virtuosity for their guests. The entire clan was smitten with his talents, and he was subsequently engaged by Adele Levy, Marion Ascoli, and Audrey Hess for similar parties. Thereafter, Rudy became a familiar, though sporadic, employee, creating exquisite banquet tables for the entire family. Among the Stern relations, he dubbed Audrey his guiding light. She was acquainted with all the intricacies that the preparation of fine food entailed, and he found working with her a special delight.

Rudy came to consider his engagements in New Orleans part business and part pleasure. Edith, always cognizant of the human side of a relationship, never treated the matter as strictly business. After the job was done, there was always time for leisurely pursuits. Rudy Stanish usually moved into Philip's room, provided there were few house guests; otherwise a room would be reserved for him at a pleasant hotel in the French Quarter. Unfailingly, a typed program would be waiting for him, outlining the entire function, containing explicit suggestions and special wishes, prepared by Edith. Most frequently, she was content to leave the menu entirely to Rudy's discretion. She would, however, take pleasure in going over the planned dishes with him.

Sometimes everything would be all set up and then suddenly, for some seemingly inexplicable reason, word would be passed down that Mrs. Stern requested a change.

The help would be vexed, eyes would roll heavenward, but her changes, Rudy admitted, were invariably for the best.

One dinner, especially, stands out as the *non plus ultra*. It was given in honor of Valéry Giscard d'Estaing, the president of France. The preparations for this banquet were not without a certain drama and suspense. In the middle of the great day, word was flashed from the fruit market to the chef that the strawberries intended as dessert—*Fraises Cardinale* to be exact—had been hijacked. What kind of sinister plot could possibly be behind this? Direction came from on high: Hijack them back from the hijackers! How the contacts were made is still not clear, but the diplomatic tightrope was somehow successfully traversed (the culprits, who might not have been aware of the political implications of their deed, were no doubt aware of the high perishability of their treasure). The strawberries arrived by van to Longue Vue just in time. The meal progressed without a hitch.

Praise from Edith would usually be accompanied by a gift, Rudy recalled, and she would arrange for a few days of rest after a function, with pleasant activities to round them out. For Rudy, this might mean a brunch at Brennan's, followed by a sightseeing tour, a concert, or a visit to the museum. "You were royally entertained after your duties were done," Rudy said. "Usually Minnie and Johanna would accompany me: Emma invariably declined the invitation, saying, 'I've seen it already.'"

Edith's granddaughter Sandra described her grandmother's relationships with the servants in another light:

> She was not overly generous in her payment of salaries to her staff, yet they were never heard to complain on this account. In fact, she relied on them heavily, her own housekeeping skills being nearly non-existent. Once, during a trial move away from Longue Vue, Edith retained only a basic complement of the servants. Her conclusion at the end of the experiment was that she never closed a drawer, rarely picked up anything she put down, didn't know how to get ice cubes out of a tray—in short, was perfectly helpless without her retinue.
>
> It was one of the great ironies of Edith's life. The blacks, whose cause she championed, without whom her house would have been a shambles, fared poorly at times in her service. It was, perhaps, attributable to a lack of

understanding as to what their tasks entailed, what their lives were really like. She knew of their plight intellectually, responding generously through her general philanthropic endeavors, but could not bring this down to a personal level. In that connection, generosity and empathy were sometimes missing. She never went shopping at a market, never prepared a meal from scratch, and may have failed to comprehend the value of hours and overtime, though she would pay when members of her staff agreed to work on their days off.

However, Sandra added, "All the same, most of her staff stayed on for twenty, thirty, and, in one instance, even fifty years."

Her secretary, Vilma, once tabulated that the combined length of service of Edith's most devoted staff members came to four hundred years. It may well be that some of them considered their status elevated through some of the "fringe benefits" that were readily available—the luncheons at first-rate restaurants, the concerts, and the host of other entertainments. While this might not have sufficed to command loyalty in every household, it did in Edith's. One thing is known: All who entered Longue Vue as guests sensed a very special brand of all-encompassing hospitality that concerned itself with their total well-being, and the staff contributed to that feeling in great measure.

When Jack Benny was performing in New Orleans, he also put in an appearance at Longue Vue which included some entertaining on his part. A lavish party was given in his honor. Roy Schwarz happened to be in the room that Edith referred to as the "Porch" and was just about to turn into the Art Room when Jack Benny and Mary Livingston entered. Roy was in the shadows, and the Bennys thought themselves alone. Jack said, "This is the most beautiful house I have ever seen." Mary did not disagree.

About this time, Edith added numerous pieces to her Creamware collection. "You can't open a cupboard without it spilling out," she commented—such was the abundance of it. This particular earthenware, so cherished by Edith, evolved in England in the eighteenth century. It was the first non-porous, hygienic tableware that the middle class could afford. Its sturdy, yet graceful, no-nonsense beauty derived appeal from the origin of the special clay that imparted durability and form, allowing it to be molded into pieces of high appeal. Latticed and pressed, fluted and simple—endless variations all held their innate, strong, unique charm. Could Edith see something of her personality reflected in them?

The year of Edith's seventieth birthday closed on a note of personal fulfillment. No recognition she had received in her long and active public life gave her more pleasure than her selection as the recipient of the *Times Picayune* Loving Cup, an honor that had once been accorded to Edgar.

Ceremonies were held at Metairie Park Country Day School, itself a product of Edith's activities. Photographs of the occasion reveal her as an almost-tall woman in shimmering black satin, her upswept coiffure imparting a look of elegance. Her mien is uncharacteristically serious, almost somber. Perhaps the moment reminded her too vividly of Edgar when he had received the Loving Cup some thirty-five years before.

The editor of the *Times Picayune* and *State's Item* recited her praise. "For almost forty years," began George W. Healy, Jr., "Mr. and Mrs. Stern labored together in many fields to improve the lot of all their fellow men. . . ." He went on to laud the quality of independent thought they had displayed. Edith replied simply, graciously, "So much love, heartfelt warmth, and sincere appreciation of friendship have already been poured forth from this handsome trophy that 'Verily, my cup runneth over.'" Edith and Edgar were the only couple to have been singly awarded this Loving Cup, which represented the highest service rendered to the city of New Orleans. Just how much it meant to her did not become fully clear until after her death. In the meantime, the two Loving Cups reposed in the drawing room on the George Washington mantel, flanking the portrait of Edith's grandmother.

ELEVEN

Art, Justice, and UJA

I N GENERAL, PAINTINGS held no overwhelming allure for Edith. Tom Hess often kidded her that she would go to any lengths in order to avoid hanging art on her walls. To an extent, she had to admit, that was true. She and Ellen Shipman, for instance, had gone to considerable trouble to peel off the Chinese screens in Ellen's New York home to transfer them to the walls of her dining room. Longue Vue's upstairs hall was papered in a charming mural block-printed in 1823 by Félix Sauvinet—a delightful view of the city of Lyon, France. Against this were the Kandinsky in the Blue Room and the painting of Edith's grandmother over the mantel.

But something inside Edith was changing shape. After Edgar's death, she was heard to say, "Gardens are lonely places; one should not enter them alone." Instead, she now preferred to contemplate them from her windows.

Edith began to take an intense interest in the Delgado Museum, serving on its Board of Trustees. Her sister Adele had made an unusual gesture by willing her priceless art collection to a number of smaller museums, thereby making her treasures the stars of whatever collection they enhanced. Edith considered how New Orleans' museum of art might be improved, how it might be made a unique showplace.

The story of how the famed Cuzco paintings, now known as the Stern-Davis Collection, became the property of the Delgado Museum is worthy of elaboration. It exemplifies the thinking, the approach, and the implementation of Edith's passion for sharing. As with many of the causes that Edith espoused, it was her interest and relationship with individuals —in this case Arthur Q. Davis, the distinguished New Orleans architect—that was crucial.

On returning from a stint in the Navy in 1945, Arthur Davis wished to attend Harvard's prestigious School of Design for the purpose of studying under the legendary Walter Gropius of *Bauhaus* fame. Though his credentials for entrance were impeccable, he was nonetheless aware that Gropius had restricted the size of his class to twelve students. The chances of being admitted, he calculated, were extremely marginal.

In desperation, he decided to call on Edgar Stern, an old school friend of his mother's. (His mother fondly recalled that, in those early days, Edgar had what amounted to a crush on her.) Arriving at Longue Vue, he found that Edgar had gone off on a duck hunt. Crestfallen, he poured out his plight to Edith. In her usual concerned manner, she assured him that she would convey his problem to Edgar. Edith was as good as her word, and Arthur Davis was among the twelve lucky students in Gropius' class that fall.

Years later, Arthur Davis had established his practice in New Orleans, becoming a good friend of Edgar Jr. The latter desired a swimming pool for his home on Garden Lane, and entrusted the task to Davis. The result was a pool of exciting pattern—free-form, "organic" in shape, a large body of water beginning near the house and winding through a narrow neck and a grove of trees into a small widened end dubbed "meditation pond." Before construction commenced, the boundaries of the ground to be excavated were demarcated by lengths of ordinary garden hose, showing the projected shape and size. Davis had just put this display in place when Edith arrived on the scene. Intrigued, she engaged the architect in conversation regarding the relationship of the pool to the grounds and landscaping.

During the discussion, Davis noticed Edith kicking the hose, without disturbing the form, gradually expanding the pool until it reached nearly twice its envisioned size. "She was entirely correct," Davis observed, "since there was no reason to skimp, either ... aesthetic or financial.... It is a delightful pool and, thanks to Edith, a grandiose one, as well."

On another, far grander occasion, Arthur Davis once more encountered Edith's creative urges. His firm was designing the Royal Orleans Hotel. There had been a succession of attempts over ten years to erect a hotel where the venerable St. Louis Hotel once stood. Several architects had proved unequal to the task already. It was an undertaking of special importance, and it became a personal challenge for Davis to succeed. He recalled:

> At the far end of the site, on St. Louis Street near Chartres Street, there was a portion [consisting] of granite arches of the original St. Louis Hotel. Enter Edith Stern. She dragged me out to the site on a very cold December morning while we were still working on the concept for the new hotel. Pointing to the arches, she said, "Wouldn't it be wonderful if we could in some way incorporate a small part of the original hotel in the new design? ... It was a dramatic suggestion, and I decided that we must find a way.... They are now a part of the facade of the Royal Orleans Hotel on the Chartres Street elevation. She was that kind of a person. Her suggestions were not only practical, but exciting and intriguing.

Arthur Davis considered the purchase of the Cuzco paintings "my most important and dramatic adventure with Edith Stern...." The adventure began at one of Edith's parties, when the Peruvian ambassador, Celsor Pastore, was among the guests. As Davis unfolded the story:

> My wife was able to learn from [Pastore] that he had an extensive collection of Cuzco paintings from the Colonial period, currently stored in a warehouse in Washington,

D.C. She also learned that he was of a mind to sell his collection since he had fallen out of grace in Peru and did not intend to return to that country as long as the present government was in power.

I had seen one or two of the Cuzco school in the Brooklyn Museum, which also has a fine collection. Edith Stern's son-in-law, Tom Hess, an important art critic and editor in New York City, came to visit the Sterns and — knowing of Edith's strong interest in the New Orleans Museum of Art — ventured the suggestion that the Delgado Museum should have a definite direction in its acquisition program, such as the "Arts of the Americas."

This concept was adopted while Edith served on the Board of Trustees of the Museum.... On my wife's suggestion, I decided to approach Edith Stern in order to find a way of obtaining this great Peruvian collection.... I was somewhat reticent about approaching her on this subject since she had just given a new auditorium wing to the Museum and I did not know how she would feel about additional financial commitments.

I could have saved myself the anguish because she agreed we should jointly attempt to purchase Ambassador Pastore's collection with the intent at some future date to present [the paintings] to the Museum. Ambassador Pastore agreed to let us see the paintings and, although they were stored in racks, it was pretty obvious that they were magnificent examples of the Cuzco school. Some of them were large, as much as 14' tall by 6' wide, but there were some smaller gems as well.... We were able to purchase twenty-six paintings and one larger-than-life sized statue of St. George slaying the dragon. This piece needed extensive restoration, which was done at the National Gallery in Washington....

Edith and I bought all of the paintings and the St. George, sharing equally in all costs, plus restorations.... [It was] by far the largest single art purchase I had ever made in my life, but certainly worth whatever agony was involved in matching dollars with Mrs. Stern.

Shortly after we purchased the paintings and had them restored (about half of them needed extensive restoration), Edith suggested that we have an exhibition and we joined forces with the Brooklyn Museum, which redesigned its entire main floor to accommodate our joint collection. Our display of Cuzco paintings received rave reviews from the New York Times, as well as from quite a few national art publications....

At the end of the exhibition, the New Orleans Museum of Art housed the paintings and had them on display. They were still our property, on loan to the Museum, and I was prepared to give the paintings to the Museum, but Edith had other ideas. She said she would like to give the paintings on the assumption that after a proper appraisal had been made, the Museum would match our contribution dollar for dollar, and by this method raise considerable funds. Finally, the collection became the property of the Museum and once again Edith was quite correct; since the people of the Delgado had a stake in the purchase they are much prouder of the acquisition than had it been an outright gift.

In any event, without Edith's support, without her concept and vision to exhibit at the Brooklyn Museum, followed by bringing the paintings home, this adventure could never have been a success. Through Edith's guidance and imaginative conceptualizing, the entire Cuzco experience was not only a pleasant and exciting one, but also a great contribution to the Museum as well.

She was able to touch so many through her generosity. Her example will be an inspiration to all civic leaders interested in the betterment of our community.

Edith, for her part, did not consider her work finished. Accompanied by David and Barbara Hunter, she embarked on a six-week tour to museums, artists, and dealers in Columbia, Ecuador, Peru, and Brazil. Barbara Hunter noticed that nothing seemed to faze Edith. On one leg of the journey, one of the airplane's engines failed, but after a short scare and a safe landing, they continued undaunted.

Though accustomed to the finest service the world had to offer, Edith could still bring herself to eat in places of the "greasy spoon" variety, downing such simple and sometimes dubious fare with nary a complaint. Traveling light, Edith had taken only two pantsuits along, and not having time to seek out help, she performed the unaccustomed chore of washing them herself. Barbara remembers Edith being amazed at the quantity of water that the fabric could absorb.

The trip, which further cemented the friendship between Edith and the Hunters, was a great success from all points of view. In one sweep, a vast "buying spree," they managed to acquire a goodly number of valuable and worthwhile paintings, in addition to some extremely unusual furniture. The collection of the Delgado Museum, New Orleans' Museum of Art, grew by leaps and bounds, becoming what Edith had determined it should become, a treasure trove of Latin American art.

In March 1967, a national news item sent shock waves through New Orleans. Muriel Bultman Frances, returning from a museum board meeting, received an agitated call from her husband, who happened to be in New York. He had just heard, on national news broadcasts, that Clay Shaw had been placed under arrest by the New Orleans district attorney, Jim Garrison. Shaw was alleged to have taken part in a plot to assassinate President John F. Kennedy some four years earlier.

Muriel Frances had lived away from New Orleans for many years, returning in 1964 to take over the family business. In New York, she had been a theatrical agent and had also represented a few successful enterprises such as the International Trade Mart, of which Edward Durell Stone had been the architect. It was through her association with Stone that she first met Clay Shaw, then the managing director of the International Trade Mart.

A highly perceptive, sensitive, and frequently amusing man, Shaw was something of a loner. He was a preservationist and, from time to time, invariably with good taste, bought and restored properties in the *Vieux Carré*. His best-known work was the restoration of what is known as the Spanish Stables, which he converted into charming apartments with alluring courtyards that did much to enhance the beauty and authenticity of the French Quarter. The hideous accusation that he was involved in a crime of such nature and proportion seemed totally out of character to those who knew him.

Iris Kelso, the respected local political reporter on WDSU-TV, obtained Muriel's consent to be interviewed on the air. Asked whether she believed that Clay was guilty, she retorted, "Absolutely not! A leopard doesn't change its spots. Clay has always been a builder and preservationist. He could never become a destroyer."

Edith Stern also had had some peripheral encounters with Shaw; hardly surprising, inasmuch as the Sterns themselves were interested in the restoration of the French Quarter. From the time of his arrest, Edith became a devoted friend to this now controversial figure.

Even when he was free on bail, Shaw was a recluse. It took time and effort to coax him out of his shock and devastation. He did not wish to inflict his presence on friends and acquaintances, feeling he would be an embarrassment to them. Edith, however, was tireless in his support; it was the sort of *cause célèbre* that brought out the best in her. She gave small dinners for Shaw, planned outings with him, and insisted that he escort her to public places. Well known to have been an ardent Kennedy supporter, Edith's stand in Shaw's defense did not go unnoticed.

Clay Shaw forfeited all his material possessions in his defense. Everything went: his real estate, his life's savings, all of it. As might be expected, Edith contributed handsomely to a fund set up by Shaw's friends to help meet the all-devouring trial costs. After a prolonged, nerve-shattering ordeal, Clay Shaw was acquitted. His friends set up a day-long celebration, but Edith went one step further. According to Margery Stich, "She set up a real estate arrangement whereby she engaged Clay to restore some small houses she owned (and, perhaps, specifically purchased for this purpose) which were located in Clay's beloved French Quarter." Edith professed to Clay, in words Margery remembered:

> I own this darn old property, and I wish, for God's sake, to get out of this mess. With neither Edgar Jr. nor Philip being here any longer to advise me, I really need your help on this one. So let's you and I do something productive and profitable about it. . . .

Shaw complied readily. The first restoration was also to become Shaw's last home, it turned out, but he proceeded to restore the rest of the properties. Despite his enthusiasm and acumen for this work, his heart was no longer in it. The bizarre accusation, the two years of suspended animation consumed by the trial notwithstanding his acquittal, had broken his spirit and undermined his health. Not long after, he died.

Edith called a meeting in her home to discuss a fitting memorial for this gentle and valiant man. The result was a handsome brass plaque, which today graces the entrance to the Spanish Stables at 724 Governor Nicholls Street. The inscription commends Clay Shaw for initiating an important twentieth century effort to restore and preserve the best of the French Quarter buildings. Engraved on it is a map noting the locations of the dozen or more structures that Shaw had redeemed. The design of the plaque is by Lin Emery; most of Clay's friends had the privilege of making a token contribution, while Edith paid the lion's share. She was a formidable friend, ally, and champion in a cause that cried out for simple justice.

Another cause, far across the seas, attracted Edith's attention in 1967. War broke out in June that year in the Middle East. Again, Edith spared no effort, this time to help a country she deeply loved, Israel. Her interest in that land took shape during her eye-opening visit with Edgar in 1937. After World War II, when a gigantic fund-raising campaign was launched as a consequence of the tragedies of the Holocaust, the Rosenwald family, minus Lessing, assumed a dominant role in the formation and implementation of the United Jewish Appeal. Adele headed the Women's Division, and Bill was a leading spokesman for the organization. In her own way, Edith, too, took part.

In those days, women, with few exceptions, gave only small token gifts. As could be expected, Edith was the first to host a Women's Division Donor Luncheon of the New Orleans Jewish Welfare Fund. In the 1946-1947 campaign, it required the unheard-of minimum gift of $100 to attend the luncheon. Slated initially to be held at Longue Vue, the affair had to be moved to the Patio Royal, a fashionable restaurant in the French Quarter, owing to overwhelming response. Edith spoke and the women were genuinely moved. More pledges were made, and the meeting was successful beyond all expectations.

Among the women who became deeply involved in the cause from the very beginning and whose stalwart support, tireless work, tact, and intelligence laid the foundation for awareness in the community was Mrs. Sara (Saul) Stone. Sara Stone's fair assessment affords a unique insight into Edith's perspective on matters Jewish. Edith was in no way a religiously observant Jew and was sometimes criticized by those who felt her involvement should have been more profound.

> There were tremendous demands on her for her money, her time, her name, the use of her house. She could not possibly meet every request, but she knew when it was important to make an appearance, lend her name, or— reluctant as she was to do so—speak when she thought it counted. She never turned us down. We used her house, ate her food. She never said no, and we asked often. When one considers the fact that she liked the new, the innovative, the exciting, the path-finding, she was steadfast in her support of Israel. Aside from her large gift to the campaign, she always made a generous gift to the Women's Division. She was a strong supporter of the State of Israel and she never wavered in that support. Her financial contribution was considerable, but she gave much more than that.

When the occasion demanded it, she could rise to great heights. Frank Friedler, former chairman of the Welfare Fund, remembers with great clarity the evening after the Yom Kippur War broke out in 1973. In the company of Alan Bories, head of the drive, he went to Edith's house.

> Alan and I got there, I would imagine, about 5:30 in the evening. She had just finished talking to her brother Bill ...who had made a very substantial gift ... a million dollars, an additional million dollars to the Welfare Fund; and Mrs. Stern was well prepared for our visit. She was anxious to give, but [wanted] to try by her gift to involve other people. We told her ... that rather than have a matching gift effort ... if she stepped forward with a very substantial gift [it] would attract a great number of people to raising their sights.... I believe that Mrs. Stern's gift that year was well over a half million dollars.

Following this visit, Edith requested a meeting of the Lifesaver Division of the Women's Division. At the meeting, she spoke about a visit by two young men. According to Edith, they asked her to double her gift of the previous year. Her reply was that she would, if they would. One answered that he would have to go to the bank and borrow the money, and the other said that he would have to sell stock in order to do that. Her answer: "What do you think I do—pick it off a tree?"

When Frank Friedler and Alan Bories left, they visited one of Edith's neighbors on Garden Lane. They told the story of what Edith had done and what they had agreed to do. Though the husband was extremely ill, when his wife heard the story she went directly to his room and relayed it to him. He also doubled his already substantial gift. The story spread and many more gifts were doubled.

In the Women's Division, minimum donors' affairs were abandoned at one point in the 1950's. Many who had responded warmly to the plight of the victims of the European slaughter found it more difficult to respond to the establishment of a Jewish state. To some, its existence even posed a threat. A few, among them Edith, tried hard to change that outlook, but their efforts remained, for the most part, futile.

Margot Garon's gentle powers of persuasion managed to revive a more active interest in Israel's plight. In 1967, just before the outbreak of the Six-Day War in Israel, she prevailed upon Edith to speak to the women. Simultaneously, there would also be an exhibit of Israeli art, the first exhibit of its kind in New Orleans. Edith composed a poem which she recited, paraphrasing Poe's "The Raven." Her parody was entitled, "Quoth the Schnorrer [alms-collector], 'Evermore,'" and it brought the house down. Margot asked for a copy of the poem, but Edith demurred. "No, my dear, I just prefer to keep it." Having served its purpose, it was relegated to the void.

When the Six-Day War was over, with Israel triumphant, a noticeable change of attitude occurred in many quarters. Some of the most reluctant Jews, theretofore Israel's severest critics, betrayed a stirring of pride, feeling themselves personally involved in that electrifying moment in Jewish history when most of the world's nations applauded the State of Israel.

TWELVE

*Public Life
and Private*

T HE FIRST MONTH OF 1968 brought Edith pleasure and
recognition. *Life* magazine published an article on January 26,
entitled "The Grandes Dames Who Grace America." Fewer
than a dozen women were chosen, Edith was among them.
A formidable array on ten glossy full-color pages, they represented the zenith of American society, and the article opened
by stating:

> For more than 200 years we Americans have boasted that
> our country has no aristocracy. And so we are at a loss to
> describe the kind of ladies portrayed on the next ten pages,
> who are the exception that prove the no-aristocracy rule. We
> usually flee to the French and call them *grandes dames,*
> which can be pronounced, if one is of a mind, in somewhat
> depreciatory italics and not precisely defined. Here then are
> some of America's more illustrious *grandes dames,* each of
> whom was born before the turn of the century. They and
> their sisters, who underwrite symphony orchestras, lend

their prestige to social action, succor opera companies and set styles in living, are the republic's closest approach to an aristocracy—an aristocracy of taste. . . . But this aristocracy is not hereditary. The quality these American *grandes dames* have in common is not birth but flair—a view of life and the vitality to pursue it with passion, whether it be centered around music or civil rights or simply the beautiful—and a bearing that is as commanding as it is splendid.

It was a careful selection—peppered with names like Astor, Belmont, and Peabody—and the ladies were chosen not for their names, or even their millions, but rather for their achievements.

Mary Elizabeth Parkman Peabody, mother of Massachusetts's former governor Endicott Peabody, a Boston Brahmin, went to jail in Saint Augustine, Florida, in 1964 as a "witness" to her unshakable belief in civil rights. Eleanor Robson, once an accomplished stage star in England, had married August Belmont. During World War I, she was a tireless worker for the American Red Cross and remained so for a quarter of a century. When the Depression threatened to destroy the Metropolitan Opera, she started the Opera Guild to "democratize opera" and to raise funds. Mrs. Christopher Temple Emmet, ninety-four years old when her picture was taken, sat on a Victorian sofa swathed in white. A grandniece of William B. Astor, she made her debut at her aunt's legendary ball held for the original Four Hundred in 1892. At twenty she was presented to Queen Victoria, curtsying correctly, but when confronted with the Prince of Wales, the future Edward VII, she merely bowed, explaining that "he was a disreputable public figure."

Georgiana Farr (Mrs. Harper) Sibley gave over her one-hundred-year-old house in Rochester, New York, as neutral territory where both factions could meet during the city's race riots in 1964. In honor of her eightieth birthday, Jewish, Catholic, and black leaders joined Protestants to pay tribute to a great lady's contributions in behalf of interfaith and civil-rights causes. The lady declared, "The hottest seats in hell are reserved for those who remain neutral in a crisis."

Mrs. Nicholas Longworth, the irrepressible Alice Roosevelt, also made the list. Her father had readily admitted that he could not govern Alice and the country simultaneously. Music and civil rights were her causes.

These were the same causes that brought Edith Stern to the list. Both ladies were known for their wit and headstrong, iconoclastic behavior. For the occasion, Edith struck a dignified pose, sitting in the Drawing Room at Longue Vue, preparing *café brûlot*. Behind her, in soft focus, hangs the picture of her grandmother.

Edith felt herself drawn to modern art—certainly a departure for someone her age. It might have been particularly surprising in that she had access to the finest of the old masters and the impressionists. But for Edith the new and avant-garde held special allure. She did not delude herself about her basic lack of art education. Instead, she exercised her curiosity by finding herself an adviser. She turned to Lillian Florsheim, sister of the first Mrs. Lemann. Lillian was already considered a first-rate artist, excelling in painting, expressive in sculpture. Her ultramodern works in Plexiglas are prized in some of the most prestigious modern collections of the world. Together, the two women cast off to explore the world of modern art in Paris.

Lillian set Edith free to choose to her heart's content, rendering succinct judgments on each selection. The ultimate verdict was that Edith was not beyond hope; in fact, she appeared to have innate good taste. When it came to picking a *nouvelle vague,* for example, she unerringly focused on Max Ernst. In the meanwhile, Lillian and Edith made the rounds of Paris galleries, meeting artists, making forays into the French countryside, taking time out to dine at restaurants like the Grand Vefour, one of Edith's favorites. Rushing from the Riviera to a hair appointment in Paris, they might stop to enjoy a leisurely picnic lunch in places where Renoir and Manet had sought inspiration. Pressed for time, they would fly in a private plane to attend art exhibits, the copilot serving Bloody Marys, the food tasting invariably mediocre. Edith finally insisted that on-board meals should be ordered in advance from Maxim's.

Lillian Florsheim introduced Edith to Victor Vasarely, and Edith was instantly smitten by both the artist and his work. Vasarely's memories of Edith are equally warm, and he remembers fondly a visit to Longue Vue. Many years later, from his studio in Annet-sur-Marne, he wrote:

> In this marvelous mansion everything was perfect; from the service to the entertainment. Thanks to her, I was invited to a great reception given by the City of New Orleans, at which occasion I was accorded the distinction of "Honorary Citizen of New Orleans.". . . I will never forget the classical concert, given in our honor, by black university students, an event of which Edith Stern's great humanitarian initiatives were a part. There was a *"grande dame."*

It was always difficult to find an appropriate birthday present for Edith. It had to be original and, if possible, unusual. Not that she would be ungrateful in accepting any present, but family and friends wanted, in particular, to please her. Her granddaughter Sandra agonized over a present for Edith's approaching birthday.

> I was living at Berkeley at the time and wanted to give her something special for her birthday. She was endlessly curious about people, their customs, habits, different ways of life. So I decided to make her a "Hippie Kit." It contained the Berkeley street people's newspaper, the *Berkeley Barb*; some beads; a few sticks of incense; a very elaborate brass and bead roach clip (used for holding the butt of a marijuana cigarette, a "joint"); some cigarette papers; and two joints. She was so pleased; thought my gift very special. I was quite surprised that it made such a hit. Quickly though I realized I had created a problem. She obviously didn't understand that possession of two marijuana cigarettes was *not* something to brag about in the Louisiana of '67 or '68. Quite innocently, she would show them to so many people that, for safety's sake, I went over to her house and one afternoon when she was napping removed the contraband and replaced it with two hand-rolled *real* cigarettes. I left no longer worried about finding my grandmother behind bars one day!

In the summer of that year Edith was at her retreat in Lenox. Amy Bess Miller remembers that, for the first time in all the years she had known Edith, she noticed a change. During performances at Tanglewood, Edith would hold scores, following every note with rapt attention. During that season, however, Amy Bess noticed that often the pages would lie in Edith's lap. She would turn to introspection, listening to waves of familiar music evoking other scenes. Amy Bess once wore a soft woolen, navy-blue wrap against the crisp chill of the mountain air. Edith laid her hand on it and said, "It feels like Edgar's jacket."

In the fall, Edith spoke of selling Austerity Castle. Before closing up the house, she made the customary rounds, stopping by the Matureviches down the road to bid them farewell and leave specific instructions pertaining to the care of the property. She broached the subject of her intentions. Mrs. Maturevich mentioned to Edith the meadow across the street from Austerity Castle.

> I said, "Mrs. Stern, should you want to sell it, may we have the first option to buy it? Unless, of course, the price is too prohibitive." She looked at me and said, "My dear, I have a much better idea; I'll give it to you. It is of no use to me: I bought it as insurance against would-be noisy neighbors."

If she seemed distant in Lenox, it was business as usual back home. The following year, New Orleans was gearing up for another mayoral election, and Edith's favorite for the number one spot was Moon Landrieu. Moon had an impressive list of credentials. A native of New Orleans, he graduated from Loyola University in 1954 with degrees in business administration and law. He served in the Louisiana Legislature from 1960 to 1966, then as councilman-at-large for the City of New Orleans from 1966 to 1970. Hailing from a blue-collar family, he understood the needs of the people better than most. He was an All-American athlete with movie-idol good looks, an easy manner coupled with persuasive logic. To top it off, the image of the ideal family man was bolstered by his lovely wife, Verna, and their nine children. In short, Moon Landrieu had all the attributes to make him an ideal public figure. To an insider like Edith, there was something more: absolute integrity.

Edith threw herself into the campaigning, and victory, when it came, was sweet. Moon Landrieu was the first liberal to be elected mayor of New Orleans and the first mayor to bring blacks into full participation in the city government. He wasted no time in appointing Rosalie Brener Grad to serve in the same capacity in which she had distinguished herself for Chep Morrison, that of secretary. But, beyond that, he trusted her as his indispensable aide and adviser. Edith was out of the city when the victory celebration was held in the ballroom of the Jung Hotel, filled to overflowing with Moon's supporters. In his speech, Landrieu paid homage to Edith, lamenting her absence, since, as he said, "I wanted to publicly embrace her."

Edith once more had entrée to City Hall, and the mayor made frequent use of her counsel. When he disagreed, he did not hesitate to tell Edith. Once, when the discussion centered on how to raise more funds for the city, Edith came up with what she thought was a brilliant idea. "Mardi Gras costs the city an awful lot of money," she said. The mayor agreed. "Why not, then, put a tax on it?" Perhaps, behind her suggestion was the fact that the festival's policies of religious elitism still rankled. Landrieu took a wistful look at his friend, older than he by thirty-five years and more practiced in worldly wisdom by far, and finally said, "Do you think my Mama raised a crazy kid?" They both burst out laughing; the matter was closed.

Landrieu had his finger on the pulse of the city. He showed a profound understanding of what ailed so many other communities. Small wonder then that he became president of the United States Conference of Mayors and a member of the Board of the National League of Cities and the National Urban Coalition. In 1976 and 1977, the *U.S. News and World Report* named him the "second most influential mayor in America." Considering the multitude of people he encountered in all strata during his long years of public service, it is interesting and rewarding to note that he singled out Edith as among the warmest and most reliable. He chose to honor her in a way that he felt she would most appreciate by renaming the Municipal Tennis Club, the "Edgar B. Stern Memorial Tennis Club." Edith regarded it a most fitting honor for Edgar; she no doubt understood it to be an honor for her as well. Looking back, Mayor Landrieu stated simply, "She was not hard, she was not harsh; she was so much like Sears, Roebuck—no frills."

Always the private Edith contrasted with the public persona. Though she was generally without pretense, her self-esteem could occasionally border on vanity. During the last decade of her life, Edith frequented Mary Jane Daret's hairdressing salon twice a week for a shampoo and set. On Tuesdays there would be a scalp-oil massage, which Edith loved, followed by a comb-out on Fridays. Mary Jane knew that Edith admired the "classy" style, a little on the flashy side. In the beginning, Edith would hold a hand mirror up close and practically tell Mary Jane where to put each hair. When her hair began to show gray, she had it colored every three to four weeks. The color had to be subtle—Edith wanted no hint of gold or red.

A natural curiosity about the life-styles of people around her once led Edith to inquire concerning the preparation of Italian food. Mary Jane said she had an excellent recipe for stuffed artichokes. Would Mrs. Stern come to her home for an Italian dinner? Edith accepted with alacrity, enjoying Mary Jane's cooking immensely. She prompted the Darets to bring out their photo album and show pictures of their travels, betraying great personal interest and telling them that she admired their values. They spoke of parenthood, and Edith pronounced that whenever the Darets would be ready to have a child, she was sure they would be excellent parents.

Once, Mary Jane inquired why Edith was so enamored of slacks. Edith hiked her pants up to her knees. "Look at these bony, skinny legs of mine; how should I wear dresses with those?"

THIRTEEN

A Woman

WHEN A GROUP OF LEADERS of the New Orleans Section of the National Council of Jewish Women met in 1971 to discuss a slate of candidates for the Hannah Solomon Award, agreement was unanimous on who unquestionably met all the criteria. The award derives its name from the woman who was instrumental in bringing about and shaping the concept of the Council of Jewish Women, an organization that strives to maintain the highest principles of human dignity, attained through education, compassion, and service.

The Council was born at almost the same time as Edith, and also in Chicago. It was 1893, the year of the Columbus Exposition. This world's fair was held in Chicago to celebrate the 400th anniversary of the discovery of the New World. But the lofty spirit and the excitement of the preparations could not conceal the terrible state of depression the country was in. Five hundred banks had failed; millions of people were unemployed. Waves of immigrants, fleeing Europe with practically nothing, were swelling the population, landing in teeming slums as bad as, or worse, than those they had left behind. The use of child labor was widespread; disease was rampant in the slums. In addition, most of the newcomers were unable to speak English, which left them easy prey for confidence men.

President Grover Cleveland had voiced his opinion, shared by most of his contemporaries, that "woman's best and safest club is in her home." Hannah G. Solomon did not concur. Observing the dismal conditions in which a large segment of the population lived, she had strong views on the role women could play to bring about necessary changes. Hers were among the first tentative steps toward an American feminist movement.

In 1893 the Chicago Women's Club was to host a reception for participants in the so-called "Women's Congresses." Mrs. Solomon, one of the first two Jewish members of the women's club (the other being her sister, Mrs. Henry Frank), was assigned the task of organizing the participation of American Jewish women. She had strong convictions that their participation should come as members of a "Parliament of Religion," which was going to be a prominent feature of the Congress. To that end, she threw all the energy of her resourceful mind into the planning of an outstanding event, proudly presenting details of her program laboriously conceived over several months to a committee of Jewish men, offering to coordinate it with their plans. Her plan called for Henrietta Szold to address this Parliament on "What Has Judaism Done for Women," followed by Josephine Lazarus (sister of Emma Lazarus) on "The Outlook for Judaism." She was not prepared for the outcome of the meeting. The men politely rejected her program, offering the women an "ornamental" role as hostesses.

Mrs. Solomon was a mere four and a half feet tall, but she could, under certain circumstances, rise to imperious height. Never more so than when she requested that "the fact of our presence at this meeting might be expunged from the records." The rest is history. Within a few years, the ranks of her organization swelled to thousands of women across the United States and Canada. Miss Sadie American, the national corresponding secretary, wrote in a report to the Board of Directors on May 22, 1895: "We do not claim to have done much; only to have awakened to the realization of what we must begin to do. We must bestir ourselves and stir others." In the same week these words were written, Edith Rosenwald was born.

In Edith's first year of life, the delegates at the Congress of the National Council adopted a three-word motto: "Faith, Hope and Humanity." Julius Rosenwald's motto had been "Investment in Humanity," but Edith carried this still further in her work. Seventy-six years later—years devoted to implementing Hannah Solomon's guidelines and to interpreting and bringing to fruition her own visions—Edith was presented with this highest award that the Council of Jewish Women could bestow.

The presentation was made by a young woman who had come from a life of privilege, much like Edith, and understood the need for a better future for all people. Her name was Jane Kessler Buchsbaum. In a well-modulated voice, she articulated what many felt:

> You may wonder why I was afforded the honor of presenting this award to Edith Rosenwald Stern, instead of a famous personality or old friend of long standing. I believe that I am the spokesman for my generation, the young, involved Council women who are participating in an unparalleled experience of excitement and challenge. As the seventies unfold, we are privileged to see the work of other generations of the concerned come to fruition. Civil rights is a reality. Israel is strong. Women, more than ever before, are leading their communities to greatness. The cultural life of our city in particular is awakening. Concurrently, while the urban plight is being pushed back with a start toward decent housing, job opportunities, and education, a new awareness of the importance of culture in our community is occurring. For truly, the human spirit is pulsing with life which requires nurturing just as the most basic needs must be fulfilled. What good would it do to save our cities for our children if we did not also work towards challenging their creativity and stimulating their imagination about the beauty of life?
>
> There is a woman among us, one of the concerned who broke many a path for my generation. Even before it was fashionable to work for the issues which mean so much to the Council of Jewish Women today, Edith Stern recognized the needs and dedicated herself to the principles of human dignity, human welfare and commitment to positive

change. Her uniqueness, however, lay in knowing that beyond the basic necessities, which she was able to help provide, those other needs of the human spirit must not be overlooked. Perhaps I have not been privileged to know her as a personal friend, but I and my peers have had something even finer: we are direct recipients of the atmosphere of change in this community which she did so much to create. The guidelines of the Hannah Solomon Award specifically charged us to select a woman through whose civic efforts some progress has been made in meeting the urban crisis, especially as it affects the well-being of our children. Someone who realizes the importance of change in saving our cities for our children. Mrs. Stern is this woman, and because my generation is already reaping the rewards of her unique concerns, it is fitting that I, as spokesman, have the privilege of making our highest award to her.

The award itself was a magnificent sculpture of a woman's head—delicate, yet strong, intelligent and warm—arrested in youth, looking toward the future. Edith held the award tenderly as she made her acceptance speech. She chose to recite a hilarious poem from *How to Be Hip and Over Thirty* by Judith Viorst. Needless to say, this delighted all. Edith had that uncanny ability of finding the *mot juste*—she knew how to draw on the unexpected, the charming, the funny.

Vilma Schnexnayder joined Edith's staff about that time to serve as her secretary. In many ways she was a younger image of her employer: bright, tough, and wise. Though they held one another in esteem, they would clash at times. Edith could be imperious; Vilma, proud and principled. They both found the on-again, off-again pyrotechnics stimulating.

I had worked for many professional men prior to my coming to Longue Vue, but none taught me what Mrs. Stern did. There are no men who could phrase a letter the way this non-collegiate could phrase it.... I once told her teasingly that she should have been Chairman of the Board of some conglomerate and she just looked at me, smiled, and said, "But I don't know if I would have any Board to work with.".... She was a paradox, as so many gifted people are.... I poked fun and was sometimes cynical at "great

occasions" like Christmas, when presents were distributed
to staff and their families and everything was, oh, so sweet.
A chorus of voices could be heard chanting in unison:
"Two, four, six, eight ... Who do we appreciate? The
Sterns!" *Ad nauseam,* I thought, but now every day I try to
put into practice the things I learned from her. She was one-
of-a-kind, self-disciplined and unique.

Somehow the entire household was aware of this. Minnie
would hover over Edith in total devotion, submerging her own
personality "for the good of the house." Johanna, effervescent,
pretty, brunette, and chubby, did likewise, but in a more lighthearted fashion. Lillie Collins, Edith's personal maid, worked
with a special grace, avoiding any semblance of Edith's dis-
pleasure. Adam, the indispensable factotum, could never say
"no" to her.

On the other hand, Isaac Delandro, the chauffeur, who
stood six-feet-three in his stockings and weighed more than 250
pounds, often looked down at his diminutive 98-pound
mistress and spoke out. Unlike his biblical namesake, he was
not one to be sacrificed on any altar, even that of class distinction. It was generally Isaac who was summoned to fetch
take-out portions of Popeye's Fried Chicken from a local
fast-food restaurant. "Lord, Miz Stern," he would say, folding
his arms across his ample chest, "with Emma bein' the best
cook in any kitchen, why d'ya want them ol' chicken bones?"
Edith responded in the same frothy banter. She was friendly
and approachable, but never intimate.

In the letters she dictated to Vilma, she managed always
to strike the right chord. It is perhaps unfortunate that few
letters survive in her own hand—that decisive, large, elegant
script invariably penned in green ink. Mrs. Louis Frierson did
keep one such letter, which she received the day after the
Symphony Opus Ball at which Edith had been honored and
presented with a lapel pin depicting a lyre. It is a glimpse into
Edith's gracious, warm tone—a tone that was controlled and
never allowed to become gushy.

> My dear, dear Ruthie,
>
> I am not surprised your phone doesn't answer. I hope
> you are having a secluded Sunday and a much deserved
> rest. I cannot let one more hour pass without telling you I

am still in orbit and refuse to touch earth. Why can't we coin a superlative for "thank you"? That is so inadequate for all I have in my heart. From the champagne party at Jimmy's to the adorable little nosegay, each and every detail was carried out with love and efficiency. Could one ask for more? Everyone says they had a marvelous time. The decor was stunning, the food superb, and you, my guardian angel, overwhelmed me. Long will I remember returning to my seat of honor, a veritable prima donna with my sheath of red roses on my arm, your words of tribute echoing in my mind, Queen for a night. The lapis creation shall be worn with Pride and Joy—but over and above all else, is the warmth and affection you injected into each of the many thoughts that made the whole episode a memorable occasion.

Thank you! Thank you! Thank you!

From a grateful
Edith Stern

As she began to worry more about Audrey's health, Edith took solace once again in music and nature. Her friends contributed to keeping her busy much of the time.

When Lucille Blum, a much-honored patron of the arts, organized the Louisiana Council for Music and the Performing Arts, Edith invited the entire Board of Directors and their spouses, a group numbering one hundred people, to visit the gardens at Longue Vue and partake of dinner.

The Garden Club was equally delighted with Edith's luncheon at a time when everything was in full bloom. Several hundred ladies were served in a garden bower setting, provided with box luncheons that consisted of Louisiana delicacies packaged in a charming, beribboned box which included a small bottle of champagne. Seeing how much pleasure the women derived from the gardens, Edith shared with Lucille the thought of opening them for public viewing. Lucille thought that the visitors' pleasures might be enhanced still more by instrumental music, ballet, and choral singing, all of this to take place on Sunday afternoons. Edith found the idea gratifying and immediately commenced by securing the necessary performers. It was thus that she and her friends often sat upstairs on a Sunday entranced by the double pleasures of a performance on the portico and the public on the lawns.

When Aaron Copland came to New Orleans at Lucille's invitation, the two ladies arranged a splendid supper party for him. Another time, when a large company of Lucille's friends arrived from Dallas to view the King Tut exhibit on display at the Delgado Art Museum, Edith rose to the occasion by entertaining them royally.

Edith was scheduled to be out of town when Mrs. Lily Guest, accompanied by Mrs. Hugh D. Auchincloss, would come into New Orleans from Washington, D. C. Being aware of Janet Auchincloss's great interest in gardens, and possibly recalling remarks the lady had made when standing in for her daughter, Jacqueline Kennedy, when Mrs. Lyndon Johnson named the famed White House garden in Mrs. Kennedy's honor, Edith suggested that Lucille bring her guests to Longue Vue for tea. The gardens were spruced up to perfection, and Johanna held the house and staff in readiness. Later Edith was immensely pleased to hear how much the visit had been enjoyed by the whole group and particularly delighted that Mrs. Auchincloss had singled out Emma Brown by complimenting her on her biscuits.

When Edith and Lucille went to Washington, it was not merely to visit friends and view art treasures. Rather, they made this special trip to obtain funds for the establishment of a repertory theater in New Orleans. Lucille had learned that such theater projects were to be funded for a period of three years in three sections of the country. Funding in the amount of $500,000 per year was to come from the National Endowment for the Arts and the U. S. Office of Education. When Roger Stevens, chairman of the National Endowment for the Arts, came to New Orleans, along with his committee, Edith entertained them. Then she and Lucille and Dolly Jordan Stubbs (now Mrs. John Dean Kyle) flew to Washington to "close the deal" for New Orleans. After many months, and with the help of others, they succeeded in obtaining $1,500,000 for the project, and the New Orleans Repertory Theater became a reality.

Lucille wanted to do something special for Edith.

It was spring—one of those glorious springs that are pleasantly cool, yet not too cool, a season when suddenly everything is in bloom. Edith had heard that the tulips at

Dutch Gardens in Tensas Parish were a riot of color. She asked me to show her the gardens since Tensas was my original home base, but she wanted to do practically the impossible by making the five-hundred-mile trip by automobile in one day. I borrowed a two-motor airplane and early one morning three of us—Edith, Lindy (Mrs. Hale) Boggs, and I were off and flying. What a delightful day it was! Ed McDonald, a life-long friend and the owner of Dutch Gardens took us on the "grand tour" in an open mini-train that ran on miles of tracks throughout the gardens. Thousands upon thousands of tulips of every variety and color blanketed acres and acres of the flat, fertile farm lands. Full-sized windmills, imported from Holland, seemed to give an authenticity to the Dutch gardens. Edith was ecstatic! She wanted to see everything and go everywhere! There was no stopping her. She conferred with Ed about the practicality of opening gardens to the public and about the benefits of such attractions to the state. We tasted various cheeses imported from Holland and fitted wooden shoes that were quickly inscribed with our names. We visited the Museum of Antique Music Boxes and Edith danced to those delightful old tunes. We had a ball!

They ate a full four-course meal at luncheon, and Edith, who usually ate sparingly, found her appetite sparked by the surroundings. She delighted the chef by saying, "Never had a more delicious meal at Antoine's." They visited a Museum of Antique Farm Implements, in which city-born and bred Edith delighted.

Edith was touched when she learned that a local Tensas school had been named Rosenwald in honor of her father and in recognition of his known interest in the education of blacks. The three then went, at Edith's behest, to visit Lucille's father's plantation, Linwood, nearby. Edith was intrigued to find a state marker where the plantation met the Mississippi River telling of how the explorer Sieur de La Salle stopped there on his first trip from Montreal down the river by canoe to be greeted by the friendly Tensas Indians, who invited him to spend three days in their villages. A tour of the property revealed the old "Manager's House" built before the Civil War and the cabins where once slaves lived when the plantation was under prior ownership and which had later housed tenant farmers. At Lucille's home Edith met Ernest Pearl, Lucille's houseman, who had "decked the halls."

As he showed them the house he made sure they learned that he was born on Linwood in the "first cabin." He said it was such a happy place to live that more families wanted to live there than there were cabins, so sometimes two families would live together in one cabin. He told them that there was always "singing and guitar-playing—and church-going on Sunday." . . . Edith was fascinated and urged him to tell her more. He very proudly told about his great-grandmother who had been a slave on Linwood Plantation. She and four successive generations of her family lived there. Ernest drew himself up to his full six feet two inches and with great dignity proclaimed his great-grandmother was "a *woman*— she could pick as much cotton as any man on the place." This was a revelation to a person who had never known this phase of southern plantation life.

By now the sun was setting and our visit had come to a close. It had been a full day, but Edith gave no evidence of being tired. As our plane landed in New Orleans, she said, "Now, let's go back to Dutch Gardens next spring—and then let's go to Baton Rouge to see the collection of plantation cabins and memorabilia recently assembled there." Lindy and I exchanged glances. We realized that Edith had added yet another interest to her already numerous ones. . . . Many changes have come about with the passage of time. The Dutch Gardens are no more; and in the place of tulips there is cotton. Ed McDonald has gone to his reward, and so has Ernest. The cabins of Linwood have succumbed to the ravages of weather and age. . . . Time takes its toll.

FOURTEEN

Family Joy and Sorrow

*L*INDY BOGGS assumed the seat left vacant in the United States Congress when her husband, Hale, was lost in a twin-engine plane accident over Alaska in 1973. Sitting in her office in the massive Rayburn Building in Washington, D.C., Congresswoman Boggs recalled her close association with Edith Stern.

> Personal, social, and political recollections melt into one picture in our association ... We became friends around 1938 ... in the aftermath of a great scandal in Louisiana when a number of top officials went to jail. At that time it was difficult to vote and have the vote honestly counted. My husband and a group of concerned citizens formed a political organization we called "People's League." The Sterns were our mentors, our social conscience, and our financial backers ... They were involved in everything that was for the common good, were *avant garde* in their approach, yet conservative in the very best meaning of the word. They conserved and preserved the natural beauties of the world.

They wanted to share not only what they possessed but what they had learned with as many people as they could reach. They encouraged the young and one felt honored to be included in their political and intellectual salons.

Unraveling memories of Edith in the role of mother, Congresswoman Boggs marveled at how Edith had managed to prevent her children from turning into obnoxious, rich brats, given the temptations that such wealth inevitably brings with it. She had discussed this with Edith and congratulated her on her achievement. Edith wondered whether she might not have overdone things on that score, citing as an example how one day Audrey came to her complaining of a painful elbow. "It hurts, it hurts a lot," Audrey told her mother. "How much do you suppose it hurts?" Edith inquired. Audrey was unable to gauge precisely. "Does it hurt a quarter's worth?" Edith asked. "Oh, no—not that much, Mommy," replied the overwhelmed Audrey. "The poor child," Edith said to Lindy, "she had a broken elbow."

They once spoke of Edgar's irresistible charm and hand-some good looks. It was no secret that he could make many a woman's heart skip a beat. Lindy asked, "How on earth did you ever manage to catch that man, Edith?" And Edith, who could well afford to jest, rejoined, "Oh, but I was sooo rich!" Both women broke into laughter.

The very special partnership of Edgar and Edith was often a subject of discussion. Commenting on it, another friend, journalist Pat Rittiner, struck upon the very explanation that Edith herself would probably have offered.

> Although Mrs. Stern was unbelievably rich, that appar-ently never bothered her husband who was rich himself by New Orleans standards. He was definitely not intimidated by her money. They acted like two persons who had pooled their resources, so there was no "his" and "hers," but only "ours." She arrived in New Orleans, red-headed, Jewish, enormously wealthy; a Yankee from Chicago, full of energy and married to a rich, handsome, charming man who had been the town's most eligible bachelor and one who had the sense and character not to be overwhelmed by his wife's great fortune.

Mrs. Rittiner added that when Edith was old and ill, a friend wrote, "I would not want to live in the kind of city New

Orleans would have become, had you not made it your home."
Such an investiture of "native" status upon Edith came matter-
of-factly. "But after all," Pat Rittiner concluded, "she was always
Mrs. Edgar B. Stern."

Through her travels and telephone calls, Edith kept up
with her widespread family. And a member of the third generation arrived at Longue Vue, her daughter Audrey's son, Bill
Hess. Even as a small boy, Bill had often promised that he
would some day live in New Orleans with his grandparents.
What began as a childhood fantasy became a reality some
thirteen years after Edgar's death.

Bill had completed his education, first at the American
School in Lugano, Switzerland, then at New York University.
He had a burning desire to enter the field of television and came
to work for his uncle, Edgar Jr., taking up residence in the
Whim House. Edith enjoyed his presence immensely.
Whenever he was available, he would escort her to various and
sundry functions, as he did on one memorable night in May
when they went together to hear the Symphony.

During the concert intermission, Edith was surrounded
by friends; and Bill, too, found several of his contemporaries.
In the group was a tall, elegant, dark-haired girl who immediately caught his attention. Her name, he learned, was Susan
Okun. Susan held season tickets to the Symphony, and before
the evening ended, Bill contrived to be her escort for the next
performance. Proudly, he introduced her to Edith.

Bill and Susan found many other common interests
beside the Symphony and were soon spending much time
together. Susan hailed from New York City, was in the midst
of obtaining a divorce, and had a little boy named Darren. Bill
spoke of his blue-eyed Susan often to Edith; and Edith was
anxious to get to know her better.

About a month after their first encounter, Susan was
giving a dinner party for a few young couples and extended an
invitation to Edith. On the menu that evening was matzoh ball

soup. Edith, the ultimate gourmet, accustomed to the finest of French cuisines, succumbed without a fight. Not to the soup alone, but to Susan and her charms.

The couple spoke of marriage as early as August, and when Susan's divorce was finalized, they took their vows in New York. It was November 24th, Thanksgiving time, and there was much to be grateful for as the family stood in the Library of the St. Regis Hotel to witness the nuptials.

Susan and Bill purchased a home not far from Longue Vue. Susan would regularly take lunch with Edith, sharing the "Sternburgers" served up on crust-free bread. In the course of those waist-conscious rendezvous, Edith grew very fond of Susan and came to consider Darren her great-grandchild, showering him with her special affection. When Susan's grand-mother, Leah Ury, came to visit, Edith and Leah became good friends, and in Edith's parlance, "grandmothers-in-law."

On Darren's sixth birthday, Edith was not expected at the party since she had been ill. But, as the festivities got under way, she appeared, a tiny, slim presence. Behind her, larger than life, stood Isaac carrying a huge beribboned go-cart which instantly became Darren's favorite plaything.

Edith was proud to show off her handsome couple at many of her parties. One Christmas Eve, Edith planned a celebration the idea for which was provided by Tom Hess. Naturally, Susan and Bill were invited to join the party. They found an enormous bus, festooned with ornaments, waiting in readiness at 6:00 P.M. Guests of all ages were invited to board, each receiving a beautifully gift-wrapped box containing every imaginable delicacy to munch on. The destination was top secret.

The bus made its way to a site along the Mississippi River bank in St. Charles Parish. There, in a custom time-honored by people living along or near the river, mounds of wood some fifty to sixty feet high stood along the riverwalk. Workmen began assembling these immediately after Thanksgiving and the pyres grew for weeks, some standing alone, others grouped in clusters of four or five, all the way from New Orleans to Baton Rouge. Now, on Christmas Eve, the bonfires were lit, illumi-nating the river banks for miles and miles. It was a moving scene, the flames reflected in the dark waters, the sparks floating upward like a million fireflies, till all that remained were the embers. Slowly Edith's guests boarded the bus and were taken back to Longue Vue, a warm and welcome sanctuary where such an enchanted journey might be completed in the proper style.

Edith was happy to have Susan and Bill so close at hand and pleased that Tom Hess had been able to join in the unique Christmas Eve party he had helped plan. They were all relieved as reports of Audrey's state of health continued to be encouraging. Audrey showed some signs of improvement, in fact, though she was still plagued by a rheumatic heart and excessive loss of weight.

Tom Hess served as Senior Editor of *Art News* up to 1972. From the editorial pages of that publication he championed the school of Abstract Expressionism from the 1950's onward. When he left it was to do free-lance work for *New York Magazine* and *Vogue*. Tom early on recognized the genius of Jackson Pollack, at a time when many others in the world of art were still speaking of Pollack's "dribbles and scribbles." And among his many contributions to American art history were his discoveries of Willem deKooning and Barnett Newman. In early 1978 he joined the staff of the Metropolitan Museum.

Watergate aroused Edith's ire. Nothing bothered her more than corruption in government; and she was angered to find it in the highest places. When Richard Nixon resigned on August 9, 1974, Edith took the occasion to quote Edgar who, in a similar context, had stretched out his arms, saying, "I feel I am breathing clean air again." Despite the fact that the administration remained Republican, Edith viewed Gerald Ford, Nixon's successor, as a decent sort; and, above all, this is what she required of those in public service.

Watergate was still fresh on her mind during the lonely weekend of August 24th and 25th. Bill and Susan were away on a brief holiday in Florida, and Edith was looking forward to their return.

It was about ten o'clock, Sunday evening, still oppressively hot and humid in the way only New Orleans can be, when Susan and Bill entered their home, rushing to answer the persistent ringing of the telephone. "It's Mom," Susan called to Bill who was still hauling in the luggage. Edith wanted to know if it was all right for her to come over. "Why, Mom, we just walked in and it's so late . . ." Susan began.

"I want to talk to you . . . I must talk to Bill . . ."

"She sounds terribly upset," Bill said to Susan. Then they both remembered that the previous day marked the fifteenth anniversary of Edgar's death. Perhaps that was the reason — but it seemed so unlike their Mom. Before they could speculate much farther, Edith was at the door. They were both startled by her appearance. She was leaning on a cane and looked very ill, years older. Before they could express concern, she shocked them with the news she had been bearing alone for the last several hours: Audrey had died. They were stunned. In a way, it was totally unexpected. Just when it had seemed that Audrey was doing better . . .

Heretofore, at times of crisis, Edith was always a tower of strength. Somehow, she knew how to cope, how to marshal her grief and work with it. Yet it is a cruel reversal for a parent to bury a child. Nature makes little allowance for such an interruption of its ordinary flow. Like a river forced to change course, the surface waters appear calm after the initial turbulence, but the riverbed is altered forever. So, to all appearances, Edith remained calm, her resignation and control astonishing those around her. But she was never to be the same person again.

She drew on her close ties with her sister Marion who had also lost a daughter. The common pain strengthened their bond even more. Bill, too, showed his mettle, by helping his grandmother to cope with the depths of her loss. And nature intervened. Susan was two months pregnant when Audrey died; and, by spring, the time of renewal, Susan gave birth to a little girl. They named her Audrey. She was one of the three great-granddaughters born in that season, all within the span of a few short weeks. The other two were Carol, daughter of Eric — Edgar Jr.'s son — and his wife, Joan; and Lauren, child of Edgar Jr.'s oldest daughter, Sandra.

That April Edith posed for a photo that gave her such pleasure she had it reproduced for the benefit of all her friends. It showed a smiling Edith with a baby in each arm. The caption read,

Right arm—Audrey Hess, 5 weeks; by Susan and Bill Hess.
Left arm—Carol Stern, age 7 weeks; by Joan and Eric Stern
Center—me—4152 weeks. Taken April 6, 1975.

Edith Rosenwald Stern.

FIFTEEN

The Magician of Garden Lane

THE WORK OF THE Council of Jewish Women always had Edith's deepest respect. "Those wonderful Council girls," she would say, or, in passing, make reference to "those wonderful women who contribute so much to the life of our city and all they do overseas." Though she termed herself a mere "sideline booster," her boost was so powerful that it lifted many a project of the Council to unprecedented heights, thus elevating the New Orleans chapter to well-deserved national prominence.

The organization not only stood for the things Edith fervently approved of, but Council's innovative ideas matched her own in creative approaches to problems. It was natural for her to lend her support, often as a direct participant.

When the idea of an "Angel Ball" was first broached, many feared that it would bring to mind an association with the Mardi Gras Ball, which might prove fatal to the project. Edith, however, liked the idea so well that she consented to serve as honorary chairman of the first such affair. It proved eminently successful and remained so in time to come. The theme of an Angel Ball several years later was the *Bal de Tête* and the attendees contrived to wear some amazing headgear. Edith left an unforgettable impression on one young matron, *enceinte*, who remembers the evening clearly.

> I was most concerned about what to wear and squeezed into a full-skirted formal, and with it wore a black, wide-brimmed straw hat, decorated with fresh orchids from my father-in-law's famed greenhouse. Feeling better, but still somewhat anxious about my appearance, my husband and I set off for the ball. Imagine my surprise when I saw Mrs. Stern in a lovely ballgown, her hair tightly wound around multi-colored, plastic curlers. I introduced myself, adding a thought about her wonderful aplomb. She chuckled, "Honey, when you are as old as I am, you are entitled to be eccentric."

That same woman, Eddy Rosen, today wears a different though equally impressive hat as president of the Council of Jewish Women. In 1975 the New Orleans Section of Council adopted a heartwarming idea for its participation in the Annual National Support Campaign. National Council President Esther E. Landa wrote: "The National Council is extremely proud that the New Orleans Section is undertaking the sponsorship of the first of our Research Institute's educational projects, HIPPY, in the town of Or Yehuda." Quoting Golda Meir, Mrs. Landa went on to say, "Hunger is a relatively easy problem to solve. But there is a hunger that is far more painful than the mere physical lack of food; that is the hunger for learning. This hunger brought about the gap between those who know and those who don't know. It is in our hands to fill this gap." HIPPY is the acronym for Home Intervention Program for Preschool Youngsters.

Though thousands of miles separated the women of New Orleans from the culturally deprived settlement of Or Yehuda, and the sophistication of the New Orleans Jewish community from the Moroccan and Yemenite Jews of Or Yehuda, they nevertheless found a common meeting ground in their appreciation of the most basic Jewish yearning, that of a better life for one's children through education.

All who were deeply involved in that project refer with gratitude to Edith Stern for her willingness to provide the major grant. Edith had said, "I feel so strongly about it that I am matching dollar for dollar up to $5,000, the contributions that are made. I urge you to make my gift good to the last penny." Thus the women of Council were able to say to their sister members, "Your fifty-dollar gift is really a one-hundred-dollar contribution." When the campaign went over the top, Edith came back with, "For every dollar over $10,000, I might come up with twenty-five cents. I don't know yet what the terms will be, but I'll come up with and sign a second agreement."

The game was fun, but not for its own sake. There was the satisfaction that these efforts resulted in the betterment and enrichment of deprived children's lives. To further raise the ante, Edith turned to her friend Sunny (Mrs. P. Roussel) Norman, a noted collector and internationally recognized patron of the arts. As expected, her friend responded generously, not only with money, but with an idea. It was her suggestion that in the following year Council should develop a family plan, a pooling of funds from mothers, daughters, sisters, and sisters-in-law. The idea was enthusiastically implemented and worked very well.

It was not the only time that Sunny and Edith had "matched." One time, when the Audubon Zoo was raising funds for animals, Sunny received a call from Edith. After some initial chitchat, Edith came to the point: "Sunny, how would you like to be the back half of a giraffe?" Sunny had little doubt as to who was slated to be the front half.

Edith's eightieth birthday was approaching. She suspected that, in a family known for making a great deal out of birthdays, this one in particular would be a stellar event. She herself had organized so many. Much as she loved center stage, however, Edith perceived that she had changed. She no longer wished to be feted. But how was she to circumvent the inevitable? To this task she set her considerable originality and wit. She hit upon a notion that her outspoken family and friends termed insane, or strange, to say the least. But the young crowd cheered. She declared that she wanted to celebrate her eightieth birthday in a real Magic Kingdom, the one in the recently opened Disney World. What's more, she insisted that *she* would take charge of all the arrangements and planning, from beginning to end.

Having turned the spotlight away from herself in this ingenious manner, she brought all her old zest to the details. Vilma found herself loaded with work again, as the old executive fire burned bright. Upon encountering certain frustrations with the arrangements available in Orlando, Edith did not hesitate to go to the top of the organization to state her grievances. She was amused to learn, later, that heads nearly rolled within the Disney empire on her account.

The logistics of the event were nothing short of staggering, and Edith wished nothing short of perfection. During her frequent trips to major cities, a routine of flawless arrangements had always been worked out to tick off with military precision. No matter whether she flew in the family plane or by commercial airline, her favorite driver and limousine would unfailingly be standing by to meet her. Hairdresser appointments with favorite operators were booked far in advance. Special tables awaited her arrival in favorite restaurants where waiters would hover unobtrusively to render instantaneous service. Long years of practice had honed the art of preparing such a complex itinerary to an almost effortless, everyday occurrence.

By contrast, Disney World did not operate this way, and Edith was unknown as far as the people in the rank and file of the Disney operation were concerned. To add to this, Edith was making special requests for specific suites; and the logistics of housing the retinue of twenty-five plus, ranging in age from two months to eighty years, were formidable. First-class airline tickets were sent to all the celebrants, and each baby was to be accompanied by a nursemaid whose expenses were also fully underwritten.

Susan Hess's housekeeper was invited to accompany Darren, this in addition to the services of a nursemaid for the baby. Since the housekeeper had difficulty in leaving her own young daughter, her child, too, was invited to come to the

Magic Kingdom. The whole affair was run with much the same technical proficiency as a high-level military operation. Despite this, Marion Ascoli decided that she would have nothing to do with "that madness."

Her pique notwithstanding, on the big day Marion appeared, not by magic but propelled by love and devotion, to help Edith and her brood cut the giant birthday cake. In this they were assisted by none other than Mickey Mouse, who joined the celebration. Each participant, upon arrival, was handed a Polaroid camera with which to document the visit and an envelope with a generous amount of money, sufficient to cover even the most extravagant forays in the many "lands." There were four fun-filled days and enchanted nights. At night, Cinderella's castle was lit by countless floodlights, while fireworks illumined the skies over Orlando and Mary Poppins flew with her umbrella from the castle's turrets to the bedrooms of her sleeping charges. Like Peter Pan, Edith gave evidence of being forever young.

At the last dinner, Edith distributed gifts, in keeping with her custom. To each of the girls she gave a piece of her own jewelry. Polly received a beautiful amethyst necklace; Bill's sister Helen came into possession of some wonderful old corals; Susan, however, received a pin that she did not consider particularly attractive. The shape, she noted, was lovely enough, and there appeared to be some large fake stones set among the stylized ivy leaves. Susan put it in a box with her costume jewelry, and in years to come it served as a favorite ornament for children's dress-up. Bill once found it in the sandbox abandoned by the children. He noticed its fine lines and told Susan to have it commercially cleaned by a jeweler. Susan did. After years of neglect, the diamonds were restored to their original luster making a dazzling impression in the fine sterling setting. It was an extremely valuable piece.

As for Edith herself, once the clamor and excitement of the event had subsided, she reverted to form. She felt compelled to undo any possible consequences of her unhappy encounter with the representative of the Disney organization whom she had considered so inadequate at first. She had Vilma dispatch two letters, one to the woman in question and another to her superior. In them, she expressed her total satisfaction with the ultimate accommodations provided and included the offer of an all-expense paid vacation at Longue Vue for the lady who had so displeased her initially. The offer was gratefully accepted, and, by all accounts, the lady had a lovely stay.

Edith's arrangements for grandson David in the dating department, though equally well meant, were less successful. David appeared for a visit, bringing a friend along.

> Mom would always make sure that we had fun while we visited there. . . . she set up two blind dates for us. We were sixteen and at that age you cannot imagine dating someone two years younger. Those were the ages of the girls she picked. To make matters more awkward, she had Isaac, the chauffeur, drive us around in her limousine and wait for us until we were finished with our dinner. We felt apprehensive with the girls and were aghast at the thought that someone was waiting outside to take us to our next destination. For a sixteen-year-old, that was a little too much.

On another occasion, a guest of David's, unfamiliar with the finger-bowl ritual, drank the contents and pronounced the concoction "simply delicious."

Visiting with his grandmother in those years, David felt a distance between them that he could not totally bridge. No doubt it had to do with a certain awe inspired by the imperious figure this eighty-year-old cast. It would not have surprised him to discover that she possessed magical powers.

> In fact, she seemed to perform a type of magic at every meal. Whenever she wanted Joh-Joh or Minnie, they would appear in genie-like fashion, as if summoned by magic. We were puzzled how they could read her mind whenever she needed them, and decided to subject the dining room to close scrutiny, checking her chair and the table for any secret buttons. But we never found anything. And she relished our obvious bewilderment. We would carefully watch her hands during the meal to catch on to what she did just before the two came into the room. It was only much later that we found out about the secret button that was hidden under the carpet near her chair.

When Vera Stern, wife of violinist Isaac Stern, came to New Orleans to speak on behalf of the America-Israel Cultural Foundation, of which her husband was chairman, it was quite natural that she should stay at Longue Vue. Edith was in total accord with the aims of this group, which endeavors to provide promising young Israeli and American artists with the means to develop their talents and further their careers. She had done the same kind of thing herself, after all. Vera came, however, not only as an eloquent spokeswoman for the Foundation and the wife of a man who became a legend in his own time, but there were recent bonds of friendship with Edith, cemented by the memory of a time of tragedy they had shared. Considering their deep involvement in the world of music, it was inevitable their paths should cross; sharing the same name merely added to the affinity they felt, despite their failure to trace a common ancestry. Their shared grief came in a most unlikely setting.

Early in September 1972, the *SS Renaissance*, a gleaming, splendid cruise ship, flying the French flag, embarked on a two-week Mediterranean cruise. On her polished decks, as in the exquisitely appointed staterooms, the musical muse reigned. On board to entertain the passengers were a veritable "Who's Who" of the world of music, among them Isaac Stern accompanied by Vera. Present to elucidate the stellar performances in his succinct, inimitable style was the redoubtable musicologist Dr. Karl Haas. A total of two hundred and fifty passengers were aboard. The weather was exceptionally balmy; blue skies met an azure sea as the bow of the white ship cut through the waters toward Gibraltar. The news, when it came, began as whispers, then spread in waves of stunned disbelief. In Munich, at the Olympic Games, Arab terrorists had killed two Israeli athletes and were holding nine others hostage. When, after a long, agonizing vigil, it became known that all nine of the hostages had been murdered, Isaac and Vera Stern asked the captain's permission to assemble at the theater for a memorial service.

Every passenger was present, as were many crew members. Vera spoke simply, movingly; few words were needed to convey what was in everyone's mind and heart. All had been

united by the universal language of music and now were forged
by yet another bond – of loss and of grief.

As a guest at Longue Vue, Vera was treated to that very
special brand of hospitality for which Edith and the house were
famous. Added to it was a level of warmth reserved for those
whom Edith particularly cherished. Back in New York, Vera
was hard pressed to think of something to send her gracious
hostess, even as a token. But Vera, like Edith, could be creative
and astute. She found an enormous box containing no fewer
than fifty felt-tipped markers, providing all the colors of the
rainbow and then some. When Vera received a thank-you note,
she had to remind herself momentarily of the nature of the gift.
No box of emeralds, rubies, or sapphires could have triggered
more profuse thanks than the receipt of these colored pens put
to immediate use by their recipient.

Late in November – a month still redolent in Washington
with displays of fading fall glory – Edith gazed on the Kennedy
Center, studying the grace of its columns, the massive strength
of the building itself, the ethereal shimmer of crystal against the
solid weight of marble. For her, it evoked the image of the man
for whom it was named. His strength and grace, as she
remembered him – the young man with the deep tan and
flashing white smile, loosening his tie and settling down in her
dining room. Entering, she was handed a program for the
performance of Mozart's *Cosi Fan Tutte*. It was a standing-room-
only house. The management, besieged by would-be patrons,
had made additional viewing possible via closed-circuit tele-
visions in the lobby.

Fiordiligi's lilting opening, *"Ah guarda, sorella ..."* floated
across the footlights and the audience was hushed as Annabelle
Bernard, clad in rococo costume and white wig, stood on stage
a vision from another time and place. It was Annabelle's
American debut as a member of the touring Berlin Opera
Company. At the conclusion, there was complete silence
followed by one of the most tumultuous standing ovations
ever witnessed in that magnificent hall.

Edith sponsored a reception following the performance. Among a host of admirers and friends were, first and foremost, family members. Annabelle's mother, Clothilde, was justifiably proud but sad that her husband, who was ill, could not share in their daughter's triumph. In addition, there were Annabelle's oldest brother, Alfred, a band teacher and conductor and an executive in a large life-insurance company; her sister, Joan Bernard Armstrong, juvenile court judge for Orleans Parish; and her youngest sister, Florence Bernard Jacobs, chief of the Training and Development Branch of the Internal Revenue Service. Annabelle could feel, indeed, that her family, Edith included, were gathered.

The reviews after the concert were as thrilling as the performance itself. "... a singing actress of international star quality ..." "Her success in Berlin represents a great loss to American opera, and it is hardly comforting that the loss is self-inflicted." " ... she sang like an angel. Why she hasn't sung here before is mind-boggling."

Edith collected the reviews and sent copies to Annabelle's mother, concerned lest they might escape her notice. Clipped to them were notes imploring, "Please do not bother to acknowledge." In a letter to Mrs. Bernard, Edith wrote, "I've had so many cards from Annabelle. She cuts them out and makes them herself, and they are just as if she were walking into my room. In addition, she must have written a florist here, because some beautiful roses came and the card read: 'With love, from Annabelle!'"

It was the kind of glory—direct and reflected—that was the breath of life for Edith. It brought her enthusiasm and vigor to the fore as little else had since the death of her daughter. To be sure, Edith was suffering from a circulatory problem and had to have surgery on her legs. Her vision had undeniably deteriorated, but this was more easily corrected. But there was a change in her mental state as well. She began to be haunted, it seemed, by fears of not finishing her life's work. She wanted to see her projects implemented to perfection. Among them was Longue Vue itself—an extension of Edgar and Edith's dreams.

SIXTEEN

The Case of Longue Vue

O N APRIL 19, 1977, the *New Orleans Times-Picayune* carried an article under the heading, "Mrs. Stern Wins Estate Battle." Those unfamiliar with the issue, which had raged for nearly four years, might have mistakenly assumed that this referred to a court decision amounting to a personal gain for Edith. What was at stake was something quite other. "Mrs. Stern, in the courtroom on Monday, commented, 'Did you ever know it was so hard to give some money away?'"

The controversy revolved around a magnificent gift Edith wanted to bestow on the people of the city of New Orleans. It was her home, her showplace, her Longue Vue. The earliest mention in the press about the Longue Vue litigation appeared in the *Vieux Carré Courier* as early as November 1972, under the headline, "The Battle of Garden Lane." The notice read:

Art and politics collided before a special meeting of the City Planning Commission recently, the minutes of which finally have been published. Mrs. Edith Stern, the city's wealthiest person, and its only philanthropist of national note, is attempting to give the city her estate, Longue Vue, as a branch of the New Orleans Museum of Art, specializing in the decorative arts. The city has devised a special addition to the zoning ordinance to accommodate her bequest. Mrs. Stern has previously given the city some of its most important paintings and sculpture, a recital hall/ auditorium during NOMA's recent expansion, and the gardens of her estate, Longue Vue Gardens, where ballet performances and public tours are conducted regularly. The crunch of all this comes from her neighbors on Garden Lane, the private road in Metairie, lined with the Stern and other estates. Attorney Harry McCall, representing the neighbors, claims that Mrs. Stern's husband signed a restrictive covenant to keep the property residential. Mrs. J. Frederick Muller, Jr., president of the NOMA board, says that the proposed museum branch would be fully endowed, so as not to cause a financial burden to the city, and that the emerging NOMA complex would therefore be "among the foremost major museums in the southern United States."

In July 1973 the same paper reported, in part:

Mrs. Stern's defense will probably be based on the claim that when she started operating the gardens publicly, she notified all the other Garden Lane residents, and none of them objected—so they were, in fact, saying the 1931 contract was no longer in effect.

The casualties of the long litigation were some highly treasured friends. John P. Labouisse recalled years later:

Our relationship with Edith sadly ended on a somewhat sour note, as we joined with the rest of the people in Garden Lane in opposing making the Lane the principal entrance to the Museum after she dedicated the house. The matter finally wound up in court before settlement was reached and Edith could never understand why we were in opposition. The relationship was always somewhat cool after that, but we will never forget our warm and pleasant associations with the Sterns.

In the agreement finally reached, Garden Lane was respected as a private road. Edith, the city, or the museum would have to construct another road to the estate parking lot within two years.

With the litigation settled, Edith provided for a $5,000,000 endowment, of which $1,000,000 would be used for the conversion of Longue Vue to Longue Vue Museum, $2,000,000 for the sustenance of the new museum, and the remaining $2,000,000 for the continued maintenance of the gardens. As John Labouisse said, Edith could not comprehend the opposition to the project. It was foreign to her way of thinking that she was willing to make a great sacrifice while others were not willing to make a lesser one. Still, it takes a special type of strength and vision to put in jeopardy the friendships cultivated over a lifetime. Perhaps Edith realized that long after the battle would be over, after she and her neighbors would be gone, Longue Vue would remain in all its beauty and perfection for future generations to enjoy. She was never one for compromising her principles to expediency.

In September 1976, Bill Hess was going to be twenty-nine years old, and within two days of his birthday Susan would turn thirty-one. Edith combined these two milestones and, striking a balance, gave them a joint thirtieth birthday party. This time it was a square dance. Jim and Grace Ward, head gardener and wife, belonged to a square-dance group, and the entire group was pressed into service. A band was hired, augmented by a jug band complete with washboards and home-made instruments fashioned of gourds, pots and pans, saws and the like. The normally sedate air of Garden Lane was split by the sprightly hoedown and the rhythmic sounds of "do-si-dos." The dancing took place on the parking lot beside the tennis courts, decorated to suit the occasion. Some sixty friends of Susan and Bill paired up with members of the Ward group, twirled and met and curtsied in nicely executed squares. The theme of the party was "30 Square," Edith's brainchild, for, she said, she heartily endorsed the idea of "squareness" after thirty! Susan twirled in a red-tiered square dance dress, her dark hair flying about a face flushed with pleasure, while two-year-old daughter, Audrey, somehow got hold of her great-grandmother's cane, the latter trying in vain to retrieve it from the midst of the twirling melee.

A few weeks after the party, Edith, accompanied by Phyllis Dennery, flew to Washington. Shortly after their arrival, an unusually striking flower arrangement was brought up to their suite. Edith read the attached card, while Phyllis studied the arrangement of wild orchids. "What do you think of those pansies?" asked Edith. Phyllis was aghast. Had her friend's eyesight so deteriorated? Hardly—after all, she had just read the card. Then, her mind? Delicately, Phyllis offered, "Ede, those are orchids, you know, not pansies." After a moment's silence came Edith's deadpan retort. "I was speaking of the *donors*, not the flowers!"

Norma Freiberg told how one night when Edith was having dinner at the Freiberg residence, she recounted an experience she had as a young woman while visiting the home of the Baron de Rothschild in Paris. She said that her first mistake was to take a taxi rather than to hire a limousine and chauffeur; thus she might have avoided the disdainful gaze of the doorman. Then, at dinner, in the midst of this Continental elegance and ambiance, she picked up her intricately folded *serviette* only to find crackers flying out in all directions, which earned her the scorn of the footman. It was clear from her remark and from her reminiscence that Edith in her youth was an original American, but in old age was an American original.

Despite her progressively failing health, she was capable of displaying some of the old spunk. The difference was that it took her longer each morning to "ease into the day." Once the gears were engaged, though, she could still accomplish more than most people half her age. Going through the vast accumulations of possessions occupied a great deal of her time now. Before she left Longue Vue, Edith was determined to find a place for all these things, one that would be uniquely suited to the interests of the new owner. It was a formidable task, but she approached it as she had all her projects in the past—squarely—determined to see the matter through.

SEVENTEEN

A Truly Great Lady

*I*N 1978 EDITH'S eighty-third birthday coincided with Israel's thirtieth year of statehood, both to be celebrated in the month of May. The Jewish Federation wished to honor them both. It was well known that Edith had been personally responsible for the donation of thousands of trees for planting in Israel's soil. Each time she purchased a tree certificate from the Jewish National Fund in honor or in memory of someone, another tree was planted in Israel. And Theodore Heller once swore that every time a ball from the adjacent golf course landed in her garden, Edith planted a tree in Israel. She had become something of a legend for sending thank-you notes and acknowledgments of Christmas greetings in the form of tree certificates for Israel.

Thomas Greene, after retiring from the New Orleans Symphony, accepted a fund-raising position with another institution. Volunteers from that group approached Edith Stern for a contribution and failed. Greene decided to try himself. He reported, "I did not get a contribution either, but a week or so after her refusal, I received a lovely personal note from Mrs. Stern informing me that she had arranged to have a tree planted in my honor in Israel."

Theodore Heller hit upon the notion, and everyone approved at once. The Federation would not plant trees in Israel in Edith's honor; entire forests were already thriving there on her account. They would reverse the process. Chaim Herzog, Israel's ambassador to the United Nations, along with his wife and two children, were invited to New Orleans. This man, who had distinguished himself in the British Army during the Normandy landings, for which he was awarded knighthood, and who later became president of the State of Israel, now performed a strange ritual. Turning over a spade of earth at Longue Vue, he represented his country as the State of Israel planted a tree in New Orleans in honor of Edith Stern.

Edith, in dark slacks and a colorful blouse, escorted by Bill Hess, looked very frail but smiled brightly. She leaned on her cane to read the bronze plaque at the base of the cypress tree:

> *Chamaecyparis.* Grown in the State of Israel and planted in Longue Vue Gardens on May 21, 1978 on the occasion of Israel's 30th Anniversary, in honor of Mrs. Edgar B. Stern for her life-long commitment to the New Orleans community and to Israel.

Theodore Heller concluded the ceremony with a fitting passage from Isaiah.

> For ye shall go out with joy and be led forth with peace; the mountains and the hills shall break forth before you into singing, and all the trees of the fields shall clap their hands. Instead of the Thorn shall come up the Cypress, and instead of the Briar shall come up the Myrtle; and it shall be to the Lord for a memorial for an everlasting sign that shall not be cut off.

That evening the Jewish community held a joyous celebration at the Hyatt Regency Hotel. The theme was, "For Everything There Is a Season and This Is the *Time of Celebration.*" The Federation committee that had planned the dual celebration turned the evening into a rousing success. Mrs. William (Nat) Leon presented her poignantly beautiful "To Israel With

Love" and "To Mrs. Stern With Love." Millie Gitter dedicated the evening, "To you, Edith—*Mazel Tov* on your eighty-third birthday. May you live, as it is written in the Torah, as Moses, to 120 years of age, with your eyes undimmed and your vigor unabated."

A scant eight weeks later, Edith could no longer marshal the wish to live to such an age. She wrote to her young friend, Marilyn Barnett, thanking her for a letter of sympathy.

> Bless you, Marilyn dear. Every word came right from your heart and brought me love, sympathy and understanding, for which I am deeply grateful. This one hurt—Tom has been such a factor in my life. I loved him dearly and I don't relish a future without him.

Tom Hess's death came like a thunderbolt from a cloudless July sky. He was at the pinnacle of his profession. He had just become consultative chairman of twentieth century art at the Metropolitan Museum. On that summer day, as he was sitting at his desk, he suffered a massive heart attack and died. He was just fifty-eight years old. It was a cruel blow for Edith. She was more frail than ever, could hardly eat. Only at Johanna's persistent coaxing did she down a specially extracted vegetable juice prepared by Minnie. But it seemed that she accepted it more in acquiescence than from a desire to recover her strength. Deep concern surrounded her; near and far, her loved ones worried.

Then, that fall, to the joy and astonishment of all, Edith rallied and announced that she would give a party, a gala affair in honor of Moon Landrieu, who was about to leave office, having served the prescribed two consecutive terms. The festivities were set for the evening of Moon's last day in office, and the party was jointly sponsored by Edith and Margery Stich. One hundred and twenty-five people were invited— family, friends, people who had been closely associated with the mayor's administration. "It was a bittersweet evening. An era was ending for most of us who were there," Iris Kelso, the political reporter, remembered. "But it was very gay. The house was filled with people, with flowers and laughter."

Iris had written and produced a marvelous video short for this moment, consisting of cleverly edited film clips that had the mayor saying and doing things that appeared to be stupendous gaffes.

Margery had also concocted a brilliant jest. When the guests arrived, each was supplied with a facial mask on a stick. The face was that of Nat Kiefer, Moon's arch rival and political opponent—the face that Moon would least like to see. When the guest of honor arrived with Verna, his wife, the look of astonishment on his face reflected a myriad of mixed emotions as over a hundred Nat Kiefers rose to greet him.

Also present were all nine of the Landrieu children. By prior arrangement, they had composed a moving tribute to their dad, the mayor. The youngsters were perched on the stairs leading to the balcony of the Playhouse as Mitch, the eldest son, delivered the eloquent message. It was an ode to a father who had had to spend many more hours away from home than most but who had gained his children's respect and under-standing nonetheless.

And there was more. Phil Johnson, television journalist and editorialist, produced a special video editorial for the evening. A pianist-composer was on hand to play and lead a "sing-along," written as an affectionate spoof of the guest of honor. Edith spoke, bridging the entertainment and the dinner. Margery recalled:

> As usual, she was simple and to the point. She knew, as did we, how much Moon Landrieu would be missed by the city. The buffet dinner was a marvelous sight to behold. We named every dish after a member of Moon's staff, the usu-ally unsung heroes, a menu that was exclusively in French.

That evening, which could easily have been a sad one for Moon Landrieu, turned into one endowed with fun and camaraderie, easing the transition for him from the end of one era to the start of another. And it was one of Edith's finest hours.

Edith understood well that when time is up and the play is done, the exit is far more important than the opening lines. Much more loomed in the wings that night than Moon's departure from public office. Though few were privy to the fact, this was Edith's last night at Longue Vue. According to plan, her beloved Longue Vue would become a Museum of the Decorative Arts. It was a night of leave-taking, painful and permeated by nostalgia.

Edith was sitting in the center of all the gaiety when she told Iris Kelso. "We're going out with a bang," she said, smiling. "This house has always been fun, and that's the way I want to end it." To Iris the news was like a bombshell exploding silently in the midst of the din and noise. "No tears for Edith Stern," she said. "She was a woman who regarded changes in her life as adventures."

Late that night the house fell silent. The headlamp beams of the last car had swept across the imposing approach on Garden Lane, and the lights dimmed all over the expanse of the mansion until they finally went out in Edith's bedroom, the room she had shared with Edgar, the one with the lilies-of-the-valley. Thanks to her, there had been friends behind the masks of Moon's rival, but was she masking her own fear behind the laughter and love of her friends? She wanted to go out with a bang and a blaze of lights, that strong, gallant woman. But when the music faded and the lights no longer burned, one rather thinks she did not go out without tears.

As she had always left explicit instructions before leaving home, Edith had not planned to leave Longue Vue without exhaustive guidelines. She did not want the house to be simply a place where people would come to gape at what someone with lots of money had built. In an interview with Pamela Pierrepont Bardot, curator of decorative arts at the New Orleans Museum of Art, on July 3, 1977, Edith cited an example of what she meant.

> We bought all these old clock cases—cases without the works—we just electrified them; but they make awfully decorative things, I think, and they are fun. Anything like this—other people can do also.... I'd even like some exhibits now and again of artificial flowers with real garden greens mixed in. Because the average fellow cannot have all fresh flowers and greens.

Miss Bardot inquired whether she was talking about a teaching unit. Edith replied, "Not pupils so much and not for research, but influencing people." Miss Bardot interpreted that to mean, "Most people have an idea of what they want in their lives, but they aren't sure how to do it or where to begin; so they come here and see this as an example." Edith made another suggestion:

> I think the dining room table should be set up from time to time with my linens, china and silver; sometimes with flowers; sometimes with something else. It might be of great interest to people.

Despite her willingness to make a $5,000,000 bequest, Edith harbored certain apprehensions, shared by the Museum staff, about whether the noble experiment would work. Both she and the Museum board recognized some of the difficulties that might arise from a venture like this. Edith said, "Let's live in sin for a while and then if it works, we'll get married." By mutual agreement, the Museum would run Longue Vue on a trial basis. Accordingly, a curator was assigned to the estate for a period of time. Unfortunately, "living in sin" did not work out and the "marriage" was never consummated.

Edith had learned from experience that at times even the best of intentions are not necessarily crowned by success. Once Edgar Jr., Audrey, and Philip gave to the Museum, in Edith's honor, a work of art created by the renowned Washington artist Rockne Krebs. It was entitled *Rite of Passage* and consisted of a prism through which a single beam of laser light was refracted into six beams, each of differing hue. Through a system of individual mirrors, strategically placed, the beams created a cat's-cradle effect. The work was to stand outside the Museum, to be lit at night. But, to be seen effectively, it would have been necessary for the street lights around the Museum to be turned off, creating a security hazard. The project was abandoned.

The agonizing decision of leaving Longue Vue made, Edith chose to settle at the Pontchartrain Hotel. Acclaimed as an aristocrat among the world's hotels, it enjoyed the reputation of combining understated elegance with flawless service and unsurpassed cuisine, earning it a top rating in the *Guide Juilliard de Paris*. The Pontchartrain was built originally as an eighty-unit apartment hotel on St. Charles Avenue near the famed Garden District, and its red canopy bespeaks an inviting warm elegance. Five gas standards line the sidewalk in front of the entrance, evoking Paris. Indeed, they are exact replicas of those that grace Place Vendôme. The stately Georgian gate was imported from London. The atmosphere is imbued with a sense of family pride, and a quiet feeling permeates its rooms. Founded and owned by E. Lysle Aschaffenburg, who established its high standards, it has since passed on to his son Albert and his daughter, Mrs. Donald Waterman, who made gradual improvements in the ancestral manor. Chef Louis Evans, of international reputation, reigns over the kitchen, while "Tuts" Washington, a veritable Pontchartrain institution, entertains at the piano in the Bayou Bar. It is said that people make reservations for Tulane graduation week at the Pontchartrain when their offspring enter college.

Walking through an unobtrusive lobby, its vaulted ceiling and faded, pink-toned oriental rugs subdued, Edith would ascend to the fifth floor by a small elevator. Rooms 503, 504, and 505 were now "home." The suite consisted of a living room, dining area, a card room, two unprepossessing bedrooms, two baths, and a kitchen. Few objects betrayed the grandeur of her former environment. However, she decided to furnish her bedroom with pieces from Longue Vue's Lilies of the Valley Room, a former guest room that would now serve as the museum office.

Mindful of space limitations, Edith took only odds and ends— some from the attic, others from the Playhouse. She did relocate a treasured small George I walnut secretary desk, which had belonged to her mother, and a watercolor map of Europe that traced the meanderings of the "Sentimental Journey" of 1936 and 1937. She also brought a fine old music box in a walnut case and a card table that had stood in her favorite place, the Blue Room. The top of this table represented a handsome needlepoint rendition of the layout of the entire Longue Vue estate. In keeping with the simpler life she seemed bent on, she chose the dining-room furniture that had been at Austerity Castle. She did not neglect to bring along a child's rocker for visiting great-grandchildren and a portion of her beloved creamware, augmented by a modern five-piece sterling coffee/ tea set. Most of her exquisitely hand-embroidered linens of heirloom quality had been given away to family, friends, and their children. What was left, she turned over to the New Orleans Section of the National Council of Jewish Women, with the proceeds of the sale going for Annual National Support funds. Even those pieces netted the Council several thousand dollars.

Edith maintained that she was perfectly happy in her new abode. All the same, her health continued to fail steadily, and her activities were further curtailed. Her circulatory problem worsened, confining her to a wheelchair a great deal of the time. Iris Kelso remembers seeing her once when Iris was taking visiting relatives to see the splendor of the new Museum.

> As we stood in the hallway with a tour group at the end of our visit, Edith arrived in a wheelchair, accompanied by Phyllis and Moise Dennery and a friend of theirs who was to see Longue Vue for the first time. It was obvious that she had become an invalid.

It occurred to Iris how Edith must feel in these autumnal years, returning to this home where every corner echoed a memory of a full and, for the most part, happy life with her family. Now strangers ranged through it.

> When I spoke to her, it was as if she heard my thoughts. "It's wonderful to see people enjoying it," she said, smiling as gaily as on the night of a party. Edith was a lesson in living one's life victoriously. . . . it was her personal qualities which made her a lasting influence, not only for those who were close to her, but those who saw her from afar.

Seeing her new home, Sunny Norman suggested that Edith have murals painted on her window shades to depict some of the exquisite views she had been used to. Edith categorically refused. Perhaps her cocoon was closing and she relied on vistas within. No longer did she look for apparent beauty, for none of it matched the memories she bore.

Valiantly, she tried to maintain a semblance of her once tight regime. She arranged to have her nails and hair done regularly in her own suite by Mary Jane, but sometimes failed to recognize her. Amanda came to prepare delicacies that she had enjoyed over the years, but she could hardly swallow. Her weight, never robust in recent years, slipped and went precariously below seventy pounds.

She had long been plagued by circulatory problems, coupled with respiratory difficulties aggravated by years of smoking. Perhaps worst of all, an interior ear affliction—a reaction to an antibiotic administered following surgery many years before on the circulatory system of one leg—upset her equilibrium. It left Edith with permanent vertigo and a rolling walk ameliorated by a cane. Yet when Vilma reported for work in the mornings, Edith would attempt as before to dictate letters, often proving herself as nimble as ever in turning a phrase.

One thing was certain: Edith lacked a true desire to see her life prolonged. She remarked once that she was bored with trying to die. Her children gathered round on her eighty-fifth birthday and were confronted by this undeniable evidence of her shocking deterioration. Soon after this landmark was passed, the doctors thought the family had better come back again. Edith was sinking rapidly.

With the family gathered around her, Edith's spirits were buoyed as in the olden days, in the "must-not-let-them-down" determination. She rallied sufficiently, and the family dispersed once more.

One of her few pleasures in those last weeks of her life were the daily visits by Bill and Susan, and frequent visits by faithful friends or loyal servants. Edith was well acquainted with Arthur Wing Pinero's saying, "The future is only the past, entered through another gate."

On Wednesday, September 10, 1980, Susan and Bill visited her. They found her weary, dozing off intermittently. At 11 o'clock that same evening, Eloise, her trusted nurse, called the family, apprising them that Edith's condition was worsening.

When Bill and Susan arrived, they found, despite the lateness of the hour, that Vilma and Isaac were present. Edith appeared to be sleeping peacefully. By 3 A.M., Bill and Susan decided to go home to be with their small children. Vilma and Isaac stayed on with Eloise to keep a vigil through the night.

In recapturing the events of those hours, Vilma, never given to melodrama, said in precise and measured tones:

> I feel privileged and honored to have been in that room at 5:30 A.M., just before dawn. It was as if a tall, majestic, beautifully burning candle were on the verge of going out. One final flicker and its flame was no more.

The news of her death traveled rapidly. Sandra, Edgar Jr.'s daughter, summed up many feelings of that moment with her own.

> Of course, it had been expected for months, but somehow I was still unprepared. She was the most powerful person I had ever known and probably will ever know. I expected her to be in control of everything and to be there, always, for me; interested in my life, open to all my feelings, and endlessly enamored of my children. I used to joke that she would never die: she wouldn't allow it. After her death, I realized that I hadn't really been joking — I believed it. Actually, in many ways, I still do. I think she welcomed her death, worked for it in her last days. I also believe that she has moved on to another path, another life, that somewhere she's still moving and shaking the world around her.

Most of her friends still experience the dynamics of her presence, feeling it long after the power of her physical being is no longer there to secure it. There were parting gifts, as well, as one might expect from the family that had been raised at Longue Vue. Sunny Norman was moved to tears when a package arrived one day containing Edith's magnificent leopard cape, one that Sunny had always admired. It came on a satin hanger, replete with bow and note, saying "Mother would never have understood if you would not have gotten it." Lucille Blum received a lovely porcelain plate with a note, "Our family thought that you would like to have this memento which we send with our affection and best wishes." Both notes had been signed by Edgar Jr.

Lucille also remembered a poignant memorial to Edith when the Louisiana Council for Music and the Performing Arts arranged a commemorative ceremony in which all Edith's friends participated. It was held in the Spanish Garden at Longue Vue. Susan Straley returned to New Orleans to sing on this occasion, and the Dillard University Choir chanted the hymns remembered as being Edith's favorites. Bill Hess spoke movingly of his grandmother's love of people, her life of dedication. Father McInnes, Rabbi Murray Blackman, and the Reverend David Mason offered prayers. The garden was never more beautiful than this.

> It was a bright day, but suddenly a cloud covered the sun, and a soft breeze stirred the air, gently touching our cheeks and then quickly disappearing. The sun shone again. We were convinced that our beloved friend was present at the ceremony, and that her spirit hovering over us, had given us her final blessing.

Edith's nine-year-old great-granddaughter Erica, Sandra's daughter, remembered best how Edith "was always in a good mood ... She got me a little tricycle and used to play games with me a lot. Like mousie, mousie, mousie! She would make her fingers look like feet walking across the table. Then they went up and tickled me until I turned red. I will always remember her forever." There were many who did not think of Edith as "always in a good mood." There were those who thought of her as tough, resolute, determined, even fierce. They knew her, but did not know her. There were others who found only her softness, kindness, and caring; others who encountered her only from a distance and so thought her aloof, proud, perhaps even haughty. They knew her, but did not know her. There were those who knew her for what she did — for the gift of a college education, a scholarship, a grant; for a tree in Israel, a school or two in New Orleans. Tens of thousands more were unaware of the identity of the benefactor who provided the opportunity of a better life for them. They never knew her, but perhaps knew her best.

George Bernard Shaw wrote: "The reasonable man adapts himself to the world; the unreasonable one persists in trying to adapt the world to himself. Therefore, all progress depends

on the unreasonable man." Had he known Edith, he might
have amended his pronoun. And would it not have been the
same for Albert Einstein, if he had Edith in mind when he
said, "There is one thing we know: that man is here for the
sake of other men."

The funeral was held at Longue Vue. Her youngest child,
Philip, spoke for the family at the funeral service.

> I do not speak for myself alone today. What follows are, to
> a great extent the *collective* memories of Edith Stern's
> immediate family.
>
> As sad as this moment is, it is not inappropriate to
> think of it more as a moment of thanksgiving than one of
> mourning.... There is a Jewish belief that to die as Mother
> did, on Rosh Hashanah—at the dawn of a new year—is a
> *mitzvah*—a blessing. That is particularly evident in her
> case.... if any among us could doubt that Mother has an
> afterlife, we have but to look around us here at the aesthetic
> perfection she and Dad created here at Longue Vue—and
> to reflect upon the joy it brings and will continue to bring,
> to the thousands who visit here and revel in the beauty of
> this blessed spot. What an afterlife!
>
> Or consider the millions who have thrilled to the
> voice of Marion Anderson, an unknown and unheralded
> talent whom mother...invited to her home, to give her gifts
> a wider audience. That simply wasn't done, in those days
> in New Orleans. But Edith Stern did it.
>
> She lives on, too, in the person and the voice of ...
> Annabelle Bernard.... What joy she took in Annabelle's
> achievements! Annabelle was just one of many protegés—
> adopted children in a sense—about whom she used to put
> on what she called her "mama face."
>
> Her afterlife finds expression, too, in her children,
> grandchildren and her great-grandchildren. *Lest* anyone
> doubt the impact she had on them, listen to ... her grand-
> children.
>
> Mother lives on, too, of course through her philan-
> thropy, in which she carried on the precedent set by her
> father before her—not so much in *what* she gave as in *how*
> she gave it.... It was far more than Mother's money that
> breathed life and spirit into the Voters' Registration League,
> one of the great joys of her life.

In that personal dedication she was joined by Dad, and nothing gave her more pride than that she and Dad were both recipients of the *Times-Picayune* Loving Cup.

Together, they were careful to sow the seeds of their philanthropic wisdom in their descendants . . . by putting them on the Board of the Stern Family Fund.

Mother lives on, too, in the many ways she touched and added joy and beauty—through the museum, the symphony and countless other institutions—to this city she adopted as her own. My, how she did love New Orleans. . . . I'm sure many of you who dined here share my memories of this Yankee invader presiding with flair and panache over a Café Brûlot bowl.

I need not remind most of you here that Mother was not—to put it mildly—a person to be thwarted when she set her mind to something. . . . There was a standing family joke that if an airline had the audacity to tell her there were no seats on the flight she wanted, she would first call the company president and tell him not to be ridiculous—and if that didn't work, she'd take steps to buy the whole damned airline!

But that stubbornness. . .also served her community well. When she found, for example, that New Orleans did not have a nursery school to her liking, she applied her torrential energies to founding a new one.

When she observed casually, a few months ago, that when she and Dad moved to Metairie none of the streets there were paved, her sister Marion exclaimed, "Good God, Edith, don't tell me you did *that* too!"

No matter how powerful the adversary, Edith Stern was a person to be reckoned with. She was once engaged in a legal controversy with the United States government and when my brother saw the papers in the case designated "Edith R. Stern versus the United States of America," he said, "Hell, that's not an even contest. The United States of America doesn't stand a chance!" And you know what? It didn't. Edith Stern won the case. Little wonder she earned the nickname, "RAU"—"Right As Usual."

Her family, reminiscing last night, remarked that there was a certain magical quality about Mother. . .she could be exasperating; and there are many here today who suffered through her more difficult moments. And yet there is probably not one among those same people who would not have laid down their lives, almost literally, to bring her aid and comfort when she asked for it—and sometimes when she didn't. . . . Words cannot adequately describe the loyalty and patience with which those in her employ served her over those years.... Nor can words adequately convey the gratitude her family feels for the devotion showered upon her through those many years—and, especially, during those final, trying months.

Mother was blessed, too, by the devotion of her brothers and sisters. It has been said that the Rosenwald sisters could not really be considered singly, but only as a threesome, and Mother was the beneficiary of their selfless love, especially that of her beloved Marion. Surely this lady was rich in more than money.

I suppose that her magic attraction lay in large part in her spirit of fun and adventure. How could you help but be drawn to a person who would take up underwater diving at age 60, celebrate her 75th birthday in Venice, and her 80th at Disney World!

So there is much for which to give thanksgiving today:

—that Edith Stern lived.

—that she brought joy and beauty into the lives of so many.

—and most of all, we can all give thanksgiving that we had the pleasure and privilege of saying "we knew Edith Stern. We knew a truly great lady."

The interment was private. Edith was laid to rest at the side of her beloved Edgar and next to Audrey and her husband Tom Hess. The headstone marking the spot is simple, almost austere. Beyond names, it bears just dates of birth and death. No flowers are planted on their graves—only grass, nature's basic garb. There is one slight frill though, curious and fitting. The headstone is flanked by replicas of the two loving cups given to Edgar and Edith. They were intended to honor them individually—for their individual efforts, though they were the only couple in the city's history thus honored. But by their wishes, the replicas are now the only adornments that mark their final resting place. Nearby stands a tree, not very tall, but from its trunk sprout many branches. It is a favorite nesting place for birds; their song fills many a warm New Orleans night.

Epilogue

*E*ARLY IN THE SUMMER OF 1983, sixty-seven descendants of the Julius Rosenwald family posed in front of the impressive columns of the Museum of Science and Industry in Chicago. A corresponding newspaper headline drew attention to the special occasion, "Museum's Golden Hour." Julius Rosenwald had created this world-famous museum because of his sensitivity to his own son's excitement when Bill had visited the *Deutsches Museum* on holiday in Munich. In the spirit of sharing so typical of this philanthropist, Julius Rosenwald had been determined to provide for the children of Chicago and the public at large a center similar to the one that so fascinated his young son.

Unfortunately, the boy who had inspired the creation of that marvel, a man now of eighty years, was unable to attend the ceremony because of a foot injury. He nevertheless drew vicarious pleasure from the fact that his children and grandchildren starred as guests of honor at a black-tie dinner given for four hundred civic and business leaders in salute to the vision and generosity of the Museum's founder and his descendants. An enormous birthday cake was cut by the oldest and youngest of the Rosenwald kin present. The oldest was the still stunning, gray-haired patrician, Mrs. Lessing Rosenwald, garbed in an elegant gown of flowing chiffon. The youngest was Elizabeth Ascoli, age eight, daughter of Peter, the youngest son of Marion Rosenwald Ascoli. She was a vivacious, fair-haired girl, attired in bright candy-striped dress.

Bill and Susan Hess had come from New Orleans, the last of Edgar and Edith's descendants still residing in that city. There they continue to uphold the family's proud tradition.

Look around. This is the city in which it began. This is where horse-drawn wagons delivered the goods ordered from Sears, Roebuck and Company catalogues. This is the city that witnessed the meteoric rise of Julius Rosenwald's career and his ensuing commitment to philanthropy. This is the city where Booker T. Washington broke the shackles of race prejudice as guest of honor at a banquet given for him by Julius Rosenwald. This is the city in which Edith was born. It is not the first city of the nation; it even refers to itself as "Second City." But it was the crossroads of the railways that linked East to West and North to South. It was the middle ground of America, the proving ground, the testing ground, the ground zero of the nation. Today the twin spires of the Sears building tower over it like a lighthouse with two beacons pointing heavenward.

It is not the Chicago of the turn of the century any longer. It has come far, not as measured chronologically but in terms of progress. Now, Harold Washington, mayor of Chicago is black. So is Ernest "Dutch" Morial in the city of New Orleans. Surely, the Rosenwalds and the Sterns were a part of the kind of progress that they stand for today for their own people, and for all people.

The goods listed in Sears catalogues are no longer delivered by horse-drawn wagons. They speed through the night on enormous trucks and in the holds of jumbo jets, routed to their destinations by electronic wonders that form the nerve center of the Sears Tower that soars one hundred and three stories into the sky.

From afar, the Tower, the tallest structure in the world, dominates the skyline of this well-muscled city, conveying the

image of a scroll of knowledge. It is a monument to persever-
ance, at once a tribute to the past and a lodestar for future
generations in quest of the American Dream. Its founder's faith
was realized beyond the limits of even his vast vision. As
always, the view from the top affords the panorama of a greatly
expanded horizon. But today, due to the energies and toils of
Julius and Edith, of their friends and families, and of the
millions they inspired whether knowingly or unknowingly, the
chance to glimpse that view is offered equally to all.